A Publication of the National Institute for the Psychotherapies

SHORT-TERM APPROACHES TO PSYCHOTHERAPY

VOLUME III IN THE SERIES
NEW DIRECTIONS IN PSYCHOTHERAPY

Series Editor
PAUL OLSEN, Ph.D.

EDITED BY

HENRY GRAYSON, Ph.D.

Executive Director
National Institute for the Psychotherapies, New York

HUMAN SCIENCES PRESS
72 Fifth Avenue   3 Henrietta Street
NEW YORK, NY 10011 ● LONDON, WC2E 8LU

Library of Congress Catalog Number 78-27605

ISBN: 0-87705-345-6

Copyright © 1979 by Human Sciences Press
72 Fifth Avenue, New York, New York 10011

Printed in the United States of America
9 987654321

Library of Congress Cataloging in Publication Data

Main entry under title:

Short-term approaches to psychotherapy.
   (New directions in psychotherapy; v. 3)
   Bibliography: p.
   Includes index.
   1. Psychotherapy.   I. Grayson, Henry, 1935–
II. Series. [DNLM: 1. Psychotherapy, Brief.
W1 NE374FE v. 3 / WM420.3 S559]
RC480.S4   616.8'914   78-27605
ISBN 0-87705-345-6

CONTENTS

3

Introduction

There is increasing concern with the question of how to shorten the long process of psychotherapy. Classical psychoanalysis has often required 5 to 15 years of 3 to 6 sessions per week. Such therapy, however, is restricted to only a very small portion of the population. Even once a week therapy for 2 to 3 years is out of the question for most people, either because of lack of motivation or lack of financial resources. During the economic recession, public funds for mental health facilities have been severely cut, therefore making it more difficult for agencies to serve the lengthening waiting lists of those seeking help.

It has become necessary that we seek more ways that are effective for providing short-term therapeutic interventions. Such therapeutic interventions in this volume will not be restricted to the psychotherapist-patient setting. It is the editor's view, that short-term therapeutic-type interventions in schools and organizations can be quite effective in the long run in shortening the lists of those needing direct professional help from a therapist. In recent years, probably the greatest advances in such applications have been in transactional analysis (TA).

We will also include some current short-term applications of four current psychotherapies: behavior therapy, hypnosis, Gestalt, and psychoanalysis. In addition, attention will be given to some specific populations, such as families, hospitalized psychotics, and hypoglycemics, a commonly overlooked population by physicians and psychotherapists alike. In fact, this may be the first time such a chapter has been included in a book on psychotherapy.

This volume is not an exhaustive one on short-term approaches. Even all *new* developments, if included, could fill another two volumes. Such areas as chemotherapy, orthomolecular psychiatry, physical exercise, sensory awareness, and others will have to be reserved for additional volumes.

Part I

BRIEF APPLICATIONS OF CURRENT THERAPIES

Behavior therapy is usually considered a short-term approach, more than most other therapies. Hence the longer chapter giving a more detailed account of its theory and technique. In addition, this section will include briefer applications of some more typically moderate to long-term therapies, psychoanalysis, and gestalt therapy, as well as to hypnosis, which has been used in both contexts. The common thread here is the attempt to find ways of making effective, yet brief therapeutic interventions while using existing therapy systems.

chapter 1

BEHAVIOR THERAPY

Elliott Seligman, Ph.D.

During the past several years, the public and health and mental health professionals have shown a growing interest in behavior therapy. In its earliest years behavior therapy was based on research involving animal or student subjects and clinical reports that seemed to relate only to small, easily definable problems, mainly phobias. Today, however, behavior therapy represents a truly comprehensive and relatively scientific understanding of even the most complicated or diffuse human problems. Techniques are now oriented towards change in all channels of human responses: motor, verbal, physiological, and, most recently, cognitive behaviors. While many long-term studies remain to be done, reports of controlled clinical research involving patients found in every type of diagnostic category have been published. As a result, prospective patients now look toward behavior therapy for a relatively straightforward, hopefully short-term approach to treatment.

This chapter will include the theoretical assumptions of behavioral thinking as well as the experimentally derived principles of learning on which treatment techniques are based. In addition, it will describe the most broadly used and experimentally validated techniques and discuss their application in actual practice. This description will emphasize the assessment process that precedes treatment. The approach to treatment will be illustrated by several case studies.

Although behavior therapy has been applied to a broad range of human difficulties, including psychosis, the scope of this chapter will be limited to the short-term treatment of problems of nonpsychotic adult outpatients who seek therapy voluntarily.

THEORETICAL ASSUMPTIONS OF BEHAVIOR THERAPY

Behavior therapy is based on the assumption that human behavior is objectively observable, measurable, and predictable much as are events found in the natural sciences. Research is then conducted through the use of experimental methods. An individual can best be described through a collection of measurable behaviors across various channels of information and various environmental situations. It also is assumed that no one channel of behavior or one situation represents the "real" individual, although observation of a particular channel or situation may be most helpful for prediction in a particular instance. Hence, what an individual *says* may be very different from information gained by observing his physiological or motor responses.

The second assumption basic to the behavior therapy approach is that normal and abnormal behavior is neither quantitatively nor qualitatively distinct (Ullmann & Krasner, 1969). Thus, the difference between normal and abnormal behavior begins with the "labeling" process. Behavior may be labeled "abnormal" or "undesirable" for several reasons: (1) society's custom, (2) the discomfort the particular behavior causes the patient, (3) the inefficiency of this behavior to achieve a desired goal, or (4) any combination of these factors.

It follows from this that the principles of learning that have been demonstrated with normal behaviors can be used to understand and change behavior that has been labeled "abnormal." Behavior therapy has traditionally focused on conditioning procedures to explain human learning, although the approach is not limited to these explanations and has increasingly employed "higher level" learning concepts from social and developmental psychology to explain and predict human behavior.

The ramifications of these assumptions not only affect the choice of clinical techniques but the philosophy and interpersonal posture of the therapist and patient. The concepts of a "mentally healthy" individual or a "mentally ill" individual are not employed. For this reason, a practitioner does not bring preconceived goals of treatment as would be the case in the curing of a disease. Instead, the therapist negotiates the provision of a service as a consultant towards the achievement of *mutually agreed upon goals* within ethical and professional guidelines.

PRINCIPLES OF LEARNING

Familiarity with basic experimentally derived learning principles is fundamental to an understanding of behavior therapy. Treatment techniques are derived from knowledge of learning principles. Indeed, the techniques themselves are only standardized ways of applying the basic learning concepts to common clinical situations. Because techniques must be used flexibly in regard to any particular patient, knowledge of learning principles allows the clinician to vary the techniques or even to develop a unique approach while maintaining a greater probability of providing effective treatment.

Classical or Pavlovian and operant or instrumental conditioning are the two basic paradigms most often employed to explain learned changes. In Pavlovian conditioning the subject is seen as responding (behaving) to a stimuli that presents itself in the environment. Certain stimuli (unconditioned stimuli, UCS) evoke responses without conditioning of the subject. These are mostly biological stimuli such as food or electric shock. The response to these (UCS) stimuli are known as an unconditioned response (USR). When other neutral stimuli (conditioned stimuli, CS) habitually precede the UCS they too become capable of evoking a response similar to the UCR called the conditioned response (CR). When the CS is presented without the UCS following it, the process is called "extinction" and represents a weakening of the bond between CS and CR. For example, take the case of a person trying to fix a radio with a screwdriver. A strong shock causes his hand to withdraw immediately. After pulling the radio's plug from the wall, he returns to his task. As his hand approaches the radio, his anxiety level goes up and his hand starts to shake. This response occurs even though he knows he can no longer get a shock. Here, we see the previously neutral stimulus (radio, CS) producing a similar response (shaking hand, CR) as the electric shock (UCS) when it produced the withdrawal of the hand (UCR). If the subject persists in holding his hand and the screwdriver near the radio, it eventually will no longer be capable of causing his hand to tremble. This is an illustration of the extinction of the conditioned fear response. If fixing the radio is subsequently avoided, the individual probably will remain fearful.

The term "second order conditioning" is used to explain the pairing of a previously conditioned stimulus (CS) with a neutral stimulus (CS). It is found that the neutral stimuli can produce a response similar to the one produced by the original CS which, of course, had been paired with an unconditioned stimulus (UCS). Longer condition chains have been produced in the laboratory. This phenomenon demonstrates that stimuli either through accidental pairing or inefficient training can produce responses that are inappropriate to the actual stimuli and which are far removed from the original unconditioned stimuli.

A description of operant conditioning begins with the active emission of responses by an individual. These responses have environmental consequences that will either raise or lower the probability of the response being repeated in the future. If the probability is raised, the consequences are said to be reinforcing for that individual in a particular situation. If the probability of the response is decreased, the consequence is said to be punishing. It should be noted that the classification of a consequence depends on its effect in a particular situation and may vary with the same individual in different situations. Secondary reinforcers are consequences that gain their reinforcing value through eventual pairing with other (primary) reinforcers. Hence, simplistically, money can be seen as valuable in that it can provide a primary reinforcer, food. This notion is similar to the concept of second order conditioning explained above.

Reinforcement need not be a consequence every time a behavior occurs for the individual to continue to display the behavior. If reinforcement occurs every time, the individual will reach a high rate of responding quickly but also will extinguish quickly if the reinforcements are discontinued. An individual experiencing such training may be unable to continue trying during a period of sparse reinforcement and miss out on future reinforcement. If reinforcements are given randomly in accord with how many responses the individual makes, a high rate of responding as well as a slow rate of extinction can be achieved. It is this schedule of reinforcement on which slot machines depend. Individuals trained on a very sparse schedule may well continue to play to no avail after others have given up. Schedules within which a time interval must pass before a response will be reinforced again produce low rates of responding until the time interval has passed.

David Premack (1959) has found that if an individual is allowed to perform a high frequency behavior only after he performs a low frequency behavior, the frequency of the low frequency behavior will rise and the high frequency behavior will decrease. This rather confusing postulation can be quickly understood when we remember that mother tells Johnny he can watch television (a high frequency behavior) only after he does his homework (a low frequency behavior).

Certain stimuli inform the individual what reinforcement schedules are in effect. In other words, they alert the individual to the probability that he will get what he is after if he performs a specific response. Such stimuli are seen not as evoking the response as in classical conditioning but as providing information. An example might be choosing a day when the boss comes in with a smile on his face (discriminative stimuli) to ask for a raise (response). Without the appropriate training in discriminative stimuli, an individual may make responses which are not likely to be reinforced in a particular situation, leading to frustration and deprivation.

When positive reinforcement is going to be used to increase the frequency of a response, the therapist may find the desired behavior is seldom or never performed by the patient. If positive reinforcement were delivered only when the desired response did occur, little learning would take place. Instead, a method of successive approximations (or, shaping) can be used. This involves reinforcing a response slightly closer to the desired response than the patient's usual behavior. When this occurs, the probability increases that the response will be emitted again in the future. If this continues, a higher frequency of the first approximation can be achieved. An even closer response to the desired goal is then required before reinforcement is given. By this method, the desired response is approached and reinforced.

Learning solely through a system of reinforcement and punishment can be a slow and dangerous process; it can be likened to only learning what causes physical harm by experiencing it directly. Observing and learning from the behavior of others is called "modeling." This vicarious experience can lead to development of new responses, reduction of fear connected with performing a response or increasing fear in terms of certain punished responses. Observing or even hearing about behavior and its consequences has been shown to be a powerful learning experience (Bandura, 1962). In fact, much of human learning depends on some form of this process.

Two additional concepts are applicable to the operant and classical conditioning schemes: generalization and discrimination. If an individual is trained to respond to a certain stimuli (classical conditioning) or to respond in the presence of a certain discriminative stimuli (operant conditioning), the extent to which a new stimuli is similar to the previously conditioned one will produce a fraction of the response produced by the previously trained stimuli. Discrimination has occurred when the stimuli are distinct and the response is weaker or less frequent than the originally trained response. Generalization and discrimination can occur on a large number of gradients. Certainly the physical similarity of stimuli is a factor. Razran (1961) has reported that we can generalize even a physiological response on a meaning cognitive dimension. For example, a conditioned response to the sound of a metronome generalized to the sound of the word "metronome" and vice versa.

Many human difficulties can be seen as faulty discrimination and generalization learning where individuals overgeneralize and produce responses that are not reinforced or fail to make the needed generalizations and fail to perform in new situations because they do not generalize from similar situations where they have performed successfully.

BEHAVIORAL ASSESSMENT

The application of the principles of learning in a clinical setting begins with the initial behavioral assessment by the therapist during the first three or four interviews. This procedure is often neglected by the inexperienced therapist who may have picked up a few techniques of behavior therapy and attempt to apply them to problem patients or problem "symptoms." The therapist must be aware that individuals with similar problems may be receiving different reinforcers for their behavior or may have different goals for treatment that require therapy to be adapted to the specific case. A patient also may require use of different treatment techniques because of other psychological factors that affect his or her ability to participate in or benefit from a technique. Thus, each patient's problem behaviors must be carefully analyzed to identify goals of treatment and define the problems in terms of their verbal, motoric, physiological, and cognitive components as well as the stimuli that precede them and their consequences for the patient. In most cases, the therapist must also identify the absence or inhibition of certain appropriate responses.

The first stage of assessment is the establishment of goals. Therapy is viewed as a process for making changes in behavior in a predetermined direction. The patient's concerns are taken at face value as legitimate problems to be alleviated through treatment, although the therapist often translates what the patients want to accomplish into reliably measurable entities. For instance, a patient who says he has come to treatment "to make my life happier" will be asked what changes in his behavior could achieve this. If he answers that "people would have to treat me better" he would be asked how he could change his behavior to increase the probability of this happening. If he believes he can be happier by changing his thoughts, verbalizations, physiological reactions or actions, he is a candidate for behavior therapy.

I recommend that a *Behavioral Self Rating Check List* (Cautela & Upper 1975) be used in most assessments. This form lists 73 possible types of behavior patients may wish to change. Although most patients have their own list, the survey requires them to review it. Often the patient's list has been narrowly constructed because one particular problem was causing distress and obscuring other difficulties. The expanded statement of problems also helps the clinician identify functional relationships between the patient's difficulties.

In some situations treatment cannot be initiated because the clinician cannot accept the patient's stated goals. For example, suppose a patient has the desire to continue a life of crime but wishes to feel less guilty about it. In some cases disagreement can occur when analysis reveals that certain other responses must be changed in order to alter the targeted problem behavior. Under these circumstances, the patient should be informed so that he or she can decide whether to undergo the additional changes. If agreement cannot be reached, treatment must cease, at least in relationship to the goals in question.

It is, of course, likely that treatment goals will be reexamined, revised, or expanded during therapy. When this occurs, the therapist must not imply that his expertise lies within the realm of treatment goals as opposed to treatment means.

The next phase of assessment is the empirical definition of the problems as described by the patient. In essence, the following questions are asked: (1) In what situations does the patient perform or not perform certain responses? (2) What thoughts are occurring? (3) What is the patient feeling? (4) What physiological changes are taking place? (5) What is the frequency of the problem behaviors? (6) What are the environmental consequences of the problem behaviors?

Many patients will report what seems to them the continuous nature of a problem behavior: "I am always doing it." However, this is almost never the case. Even where a relatively continuous condition is reported ("I've had a headache for the past two weeks") fluctuations in intensity always occur. Careful questioning can isolate the factors (stimuli) which are unique to the situation within which the problem arises. For example, a woman, when asked if she could distinguish a pattern to her headaches, says that they often occurred on rainy days which she says depress her. She is then asked to chart their occurrence. It turns out that she had headaches on approximately half of all rainy days. Further investigation reveals that her husband, a construction worker, was more likely to be home on a rainy day, and she had the headaches when he was or expected to be at home from work.

It is also crucial to pinpoint the consequences of problem behavior. The patient is asked how others are treating him or how he is treating himself differently as a result of the difficulties. This represents an attempt to identify those environmental changes that would tend to increase and those that would tend to decrease the frequency of responses.

The patient is asked what alternate responses would provide him with the same reinforcers. The alternative responses should serve him more efficiently and/or without the discomfort or other difficulties the undesirable behavior causes. What has prevented the patient from learning these more adoptive responses without therapy? There can be several explanations: lack of exposure, reinforcement of problem behaviors, or inhibition through punishment.

Patients are often unaware or reluctant to explore reinforcers that support problem behaviors even though they may readily accept classical conditioning or the explanation that their difficulties stem from a lack of training in certain skills. It is a common notion that if one is "gaining" from a problem behavior then it is somehow one's fault. A patient may believe that if change were truly desired, he would change but has not done it because he is lazy, selfish, or unwilling to give up the wonderful situation he has created for himself. It is the therapist's task to explain that his own view of the role of reinforcement could not be more different. The therapist understands that the patient sincerely wishes to change his behavior, is actually suffering, and is still unable to bring about changes. The therapist holds that the patient was influenced by a learning process that did not provide him with the most successful and efficient behavior to obtain goals. This may be because efficient behavior has been inhibited through punishment, reinforcement of inefficient, uncomfortable behavior, and the lack of training or reinforcement of desired responses. The patient is usually trying to obtain acceptable goals and is partially doing so but is going about it inefficiently, self-destructively, or with so much effort that he needs a specially arranged learning situation called psychotherapy. Naturally the fact that some reinforcement is gained makes change more difficult. It is only when the patient accepts this type of explanation of the reinforcers of his problem behaviors.

The clinical interview is the therapist's basic assessment tool. Although research has shown that many behavioral techniques can be applied irrespective of the particular qualities of the therapist (Wolpe, 1969) an atmosphere of friendly warmth and acceptance is most conducive to obtaining the most plentiful and accurate information. In most cases, assumptions about the role of the therapist allow him to be generally flexible, truly genuine, and even self-disclosing if he chooses. This often makes the therapeutic situation more "natural" and promotes a good working relationship between therapist and patient. If this cannot be achieved, it is best to refer the patient elsewhere.

In the course of assessment, information may be obtained from a variety of sources: interviews with people who know the patient well, observations of the patient in his or her natural environment, self-report forms, self-observation and recording of responses, and physiological measures and cognitive assessment through imagery.

After the first clinical assessment interview, the patient may be asked to complete a series of forms to provide the therapist with certain standardized information. In some cases additional forms geared to specific problems or specific behavioral techniques are used. This type of data collection has been shown to be reliable and valid (Walsh 1967, 1968; Geer, 1965; Langon & Manosevitz, 1966). In addition, it gives the patient a sense of active participation and prepares him to expect tasks outside the sessions.

Cautela & Upper (1976) recommend a general battery that includes (1) *The Behavioral Self Rating Checklist* (Cautela &

Upper, 1975) used to help establish treatment goals; (2) *The Behavioral Analysis History Questionnaire* (Cautela 1970), which provides the therapist with general background data and material such as the patient's marital, vocational, family, religious, sexual, health and educational histories, and current functioning; (3) *Reinforcement Survey Schedule* (Cautela & Kastenbaum 1967), which lists items the client is asked to rate in accord with their reinforcement value for him; and (4) *The Fear Survey Schedule* (Wolpe & Lang 1964), a list to be rated in terms of the patient's avoidance of certain environmental stimuli.

The second series of scales is more directly concerned with techniques and applies to assertive training, thought stopping, relaxation training, and covert techniques. Finally, scales have been designed to collect data on specific behaviors targeted for change: alcohol questionnaire, drug questionnaire, eating habits and sexual behavior, etc.

It has been this author's experience that the *Reinforcement Survey Schedule* is less helpful than administration of an assertive scale. Assertiveness scales usually are good indicators of the patient's ease in social situations, a factor considered relevant in almost all cases. It has been my experience that the *Reinforcement Survey Schedule* is most useful as a secondary scale particularly if depression appears to be a problem or if the manipulation of reinforcement contingencies has been chosen as a technique for change.

Self-report measures are analyzed by the therapist and discussed with the patient. These not only provide reliable information but require the patient to systematically review his areas of functioning. For the patient who has been dramatizing his difficulties or viewing life as a series of catastrophes the forms usually demonstrate the limited, although quite distressing, ground that his problems occupy. The patient should be requested to complete the forms in a manner which explains their usefulness and stresses their importance. On the other hand, undue effort should not be required of the patient. Those with academic or white collar backgrounds are more accustomed to paper work and patients who are not anxious to complete this type of homework should be assigned the forms on an extended basis with tasks divided into small parcels. Alternatively, information can be obtained through interviews.

Sometimes the therapist, with the patient's permission, will interview a spouse, teacher, co-worker, parent, or friend in an attempt to get another perspective on the patient's behavior. This may sometimes involve asking them to record the frequency of a particular behavior. It usually is advisable that the patient be present at such an interview although perhaps not as an active participant. If the patient does not wish to be there, it should be made clear to all concerned that the information obtained will be made available to the patient.

Another source of information is the observation of the patient by the therapist in the situations where the patient reports experiencing difficulty (Tharp & Wetzel, 1969). For example, where possible, phobic patients should be asked to attempt to approach the feared stimuli so the therapist can assess the extent and form of the anxiety responses and avoidance behavior. Lewinsohn, (1975, p. 49), the foremost researcher and clinician involved in the behavioral treatment of depression states:

> The necessity of observing the depressed individual's interactions with his/her family in his/her home as part of the diagnostic phase is stressed in the intake interview. The home visit typically becomes a focal point of discussion between therapist and client and requires the client to communicate and to plan with members of his/her family. The manner in which this is accomplished usually results in important diagnostic information . . . Observations are conducted during the beginning, middle and ending phases of treatment. Interactions are coded in terms of behaviors emitted by the client and the social consequences of his/her behavior.

Another means of self-report requires the patient to record his responses in the natural environment. This is often very helpful in accurately identifying the situations in which the patient's problem behaviors occur and in providing a base line against which the success of treatment can be measured. Some behavior is relatively easy to record accurately, i.e., the number of times a day the patient washes the hands. In such cases, the patient usually is asked to make a note of the situations as well as the thoughts and feelings that arise at the time. Other types of behavior are more difficult to record, such as obsessive behavior. When asked to record the amount of time or the number of times he thinks a certain thought or feels depressed, the patient may well protest that this is impossible. The therapist can explain that while it is difficult and not nearly as exact as recording external events, it can provide reliable information. This type of recording is often used during therapy as a means of measuring treatment results and modifying or continuing treatment plans (Homme, 1965). Most patients are able to keep these records if the therapist explains the need and accepts inaccuracy. Patients often report that the act of quantifying helps them control the problem behavior and that the records represent a decrease in the frequency of pretreatment norms. Occasionally, patients report that recording exacerbates symptoms and that they stopped after a few hours or days. In such cases, it is usually best to attempt to quantify the behavior by more inferential means.

Cognitive behavior modification is a subfield of behavior therapy that stresses the importance of the patient's cognitions, particularly those regarding his evaluation of his own behavior and environment. In terms of assessment, clients are often asked what they were thinking when a particular behavior occurred. Some find it hard to identify these internal stimuli. Meichenbaum (1971) has described the use of visual imagery during the assessment phase of the clinical interview. The therapist describes and asks the patient to visualize a problem situation the client has experienced. The therapist then slows down the action giving the client a chance to examine his cognitions in detail at any particular moment. This procedure not only facilitates diagnosis but provides the client with evidence of the role his cognitions play in effecting his behavior. Thus, a base is established for changing these responses. The introduction of biofeedback as a means of modifying physiological responses has had an impact on the assessment process. Clients may not be able to report physiological response levels accurately because they only have themselves as one basic physiological reference point. Patients whose physiological responses (muscle tension, etc.) are frequently at the high end of the continuum find it hard to identify small to moderate changes. As a result a patient's view of his physiological state ("I am not tense") may not correlate with actual measurement. Such physiological responses may indicate a biological link in certain problem behaviors such as tension or migraine headaches.

Most often the following measurements are employed: electromyographic recording, the patient's ability to relax his skeletal muscles, thermal devices that record the volume of blood flow, and galvanic skin response measuring perspiration. Physiological measurement before and during treatment can validate verbal reports of changes that may be confounded with the desire to please the therapist.

As the therapist gains information, he continuously forms, tests, and rejects hypotheses concerning the patient's behavior. Here, the therapist's knowledge of principles of learning is crucial to his understanding of the patient's behavioral repertoire and its environment support system.

In most cases, treatment cannot be directed to all of the patient's difficulties at once, especially at the beginning of therapy. Of course, problems causing undue distress must be addressed first. This aside, the therapist should recommend that treatment focus initially on problems that are significant enough to have some real impact but within areas where the probability of success is high. After some initial success other difficulties invariably prove more approachable.

Treatment, especially short-term, rarely directly attacks all channels of the patient's responding in regard to a particular problem, although this is probably highly desirable. Again, it is recommended that channels for intervention (motoric, cognitive, verbal, physiological) be selected for their estimated probability of success, with the channels where the greatest probability of success lies being employed first. Functional links between behaviors usually will result in changes in one mode being reflected in changes in another. However, it should not be assumed that there is a one-to-one correlation.

Within three or four sessions most therapists will arrive at an understanding of the patient's problem behaviors, the stimuli that produce them, and the reinforcement that maintains them. The therapist will have a general impression of the patient and will have formulated a treatment plan suited to the patient's difficulties and to his particular capabilities and characteristics. A summary of the case is then presented to the patient along with a treatment plan. At this point, the therapist estimates the likelihood of success. If the patient accepts the evaluation, a treatment contract is devised. It specifies the goals and means of treatment as well as the patient's willingness to undertake out-of-session homework. The therapist agrees to bring his expertise to bear on the patient's problems, to provide a certain amount of time weekly, and usually to be on call for immediate consultation.

Although at this point the therapist has arrived at a series of hypotheses to explain the situation, equally logical and empirically derived alternatives remain possible. The accuracy of the initial assessment is determined by the success of treatment based upon it. Ineffective treatment mandates an immediate reassessment.

BEHAVIORAL TECHNIQUES

Desensitization in Imagery

Many of the difficulties that bring patients into treatment involve fear and subsequent avoidance. Fear and avoidance can be conditioned through modeling, often through parents' behavior, or can be directly conditioned by classical or operant means. Once fear has been conditioned to a set of stimuli, most individuals avoid those stimuli in order to reduce the fear response. The reduction in fear serves as a reinforcement for avoidance in the future. Desensitization is the earliest documented behavioral technique for reducing fear and subsequently increasing approach behavior. The technique as it was first described by Wolpe (1958) involved the pairing of any antagonistic responses (most frequently relaxation and fear) in such a manner as to inhibit one of the responses (fear). Fearful individuals are first trained in a method of deep relaxation through a system of tensing and releasing of skeletal muscles (Jacobson, 1938). Simultaneously, patients are interviewed in order to identify the stimuli and the dimensions of their fear. For example, a patient who is afraid of dogs might be less fearful of a puppy as opposed to a full grown dog—the dimension of size is involved here. A leashed dog might elicit less fear than an unleashed one. A more complicated example is that of the patient who is afraid of "asking for a date." It might be found that he is mildly afraid of saying "hello" to a woman he would like to ask for a date and very afraid at the point of actually asking "Will you go out with me?" The therapist constructs a graded hierarchy beginning with the least fear-provoking item. This hierarchy may involve many dimensions. As an example with respect to this case, items might vary as regards: (1) closeness to the point in conversation where the date is asked for, (2) familiarity of the patient with the woman, (3) the attractiveness of the woman, and (4) other factors indicating probability of acceptance or rejection. Of course, it is probable that such a person would have difficulty on a date and would require items beyond the "asking" stage. Patients with multiple fears require multiple hierarchies or more complicated ones to insure the inclusion of all the stimuli that evoke irrational fear.

Often individuals report anxiety but are unable to identify what stimuli they are responding to. Careful interviewing may identify the appropriate variables. Patients may also be asked to keep hourly records rating their anxiety and noting their physical, interpersonal, and cognitive states. Most often patterns can be detected that will allow for the isolation of fear-provoking stimuli. Historical information concerning fearfulness of the patient's family or responses of the patient that were frequently punished can help in the identification process.

It is important to remember that stimuli to be used for desensitization may exist only as a cognition denoting a future possibility, e.g., "I may get cancer and die a horrible death." Other stimuli may be presented in the abstract by the patient, e.g., "I find I become anxious when I start to think I will lead a useless life." This cognition will then be met with the question "What would you have to do or not do to be leading a useless life?" The more concrete information obtained here would then be placed in a step type hierarchy.

The actual desensitization treatment sessions begin with inducing a deep relaxation response. Relaxation is frequently induced by having the subject tense and then release specific muscle groups. For example, the subject would be asked to hold the muscles in his hand as tightly as he could and then release the tension completely. He would then be asked to repeat this procedure with another muscle group. After some practice the subject is usually able to induce a complete state of body relaxation in a few minutes. While the subject is relaxed, the therapist describes a scene based upon the first item on the hierarchy which he asks the subject to visualize and experience. It is assumed that this item is mild enough as to allow the strong relaxation response to inhibit the mild anxiety so that the patient is able to visualize the scene without becoming anxious. Through the process of generalization of inhibition, the second scene can now be presented with an increased probability that it will not evoke anxiety. If the subject begins to feel fearful during any of the scene presentations, the therapist switches the visualization to a predetermined "relaxing scene." The subject is then asked to briefly repeat the muscle tension exercise until he is relaxed again. At this point, he signals the therapist who repeats the scene prior to the one which elicited fear. A more complete inhibition will now take place, again followed by a generalization of inhibition, and progress up the hierarchy will again continue to more fearful items.

At the end of the process the patient can imagine himself in the previously most fear-provoking scene without becoming unduly anxious. An assessment is then made of the effectiveness of the treatment in terms of the fearfulness the patient experiences in the natural environment. It is expected that the patient will experience much less anxiety in the presence of the previously feared stimulus and be able to approach the stimuli, an act which will serve to extinguish the remaining anxiety.

The clinician must consider several factors before deciding to employ desensitization. Wolpe's concept involves a model of classically conditioned fear and neglects the possibility of reinforcements for avoidance other than that of fear reduction. It may be found that a patient with a fear of riding in elevators is primarily reinforced only through anxiety reduction, and does not manipulate the social environment as a result of this problem. A second patient with the same fear controls the behavior of her husband who wants to move from the suburbs to a city high rise and also controls the couple's social activities in terms of visits involving elevators. Although such reinforcers may not have been the cause of the initial fear and avoidance they have come to support the problem. In such a case, the treatment must include, in addition to desensitization, other ways for the patient to have meaningful input into family decisions. Some reinforcers other than anxiety reduction are almost always present and the therapist must make an educated guess as to their importance in maintaining the behavior—hence the need for additional approaches to the problem.

In some cases, although the patient reports fear and avoidance of certain stimuli, the variability of the avoidance leads to the identification of certain environmental factors that seem to control the behavior. For example, a patient who reports "good" and "bad" days in regard to dizziness and fear that prevents her from traveling may be found to have had "bad" days when others are around who will then do errands for her or accompany her while, when no one is available, she experiences "good" days and travels with only mild trepidation. In this case, changes in the reinforcement contingencies may be the primary treatment. Here, desensitization may not be used at all.

Other factors to be considered before desensitization are, first, the patient's ability to learn the relaxation response. (Highly anxious patients may require extensive training. Some may not be able to learn at all.) Other techniques (e.g., implosion) may benefit these individuals. Second, the patient's ability to produce a visual image to verbally presented stimuli should be determined. Although this can be improved with practice, some individuals will not be able to do this, thus eliminating the use of this technique. Third, the patient must be able to accurately report internal states. Here, there is some danger that the patient will hesitate to report anxiety in an effort to please the therapist or may not make accurate reports. Physiological measurements should be taken where possible to confirm the patient's verbal response. Fourth, since the technique is sometimes slow, repetitive, and monotonous, the therapist must assess the patient's willingness to continue with a procedure that may not provide a sense of relief for many weeks after it has been initiated. Fifth, the technique does not require the patient to endure appreciable anxiety either in or out of the office and does not require much outside practice, a clear advantage over other fear elimination techniques.

In Vivo Desensitization

This technique attempts to directly reduce fear by gradually exposing the patient to fear-provoking stimuli. Atkinson (1973) found this approach effective, often without any relaxation training. The patient is asked to approach the stimuli to a point where he begins to feel mildly uncomfortable. He then may be asked to relax his body to remove the discomfort (Gurman, 1973) to change his thoughts about the danger involved (Meichenbaum and Cameron, 1974) or the meaning of the discomfort and to stay where he is until he feels the fear dissipate. The patient is then asked to further approach the feared stimulus until he again feels mildly anxious. The process continues until the patient is no longer fearful. This approach is often combined with modeling (Bandura, Blanchard & Ritter, 1969) where the therapist first demonstrates the approach behavior. This form of desensitization has some definite advantages over the use of images: (1) the patient is not required to learn relaxation, or to visualize imagery; (2) the probability of inaccurate reporting to please the therapist or of distracting oneself from the procedure is greatly reduced; (3) the problem of the transfer of anxiety reduction from the treatment to the actual situation is greatly reduced due to the similarity of the two conditions; and (4) the patient feels an immediate sense of accomplishment in that he actually performed a meaningful task that he was unable to perform prior to the session.

The difficulties in the use of the approach as compared to images comes mainly from the limits on the manipulation of stimuli imposed by "real situations." (1) Certain fears can only be presented in imagery, for example, the fear of growing old or sick. (2) Other fears are impractical to present in vivo, for example, fear of flying. (3) Other situations cannot be controlled by the therapist, for example, the fear of rejection during a job interview. (4) Some patients are so fearful of certain stimuli that it is not possible to present a mild enough form of the actual stimuli. In these cases it is recommended that desensitization in imagery form the initial part of the treatment which is then converted to in vivo desensitization.

Flooding and Implosive Techniques

Flooding is a technique aimed at fear reduction and employing the principle of extinction as a means of eliminating fear. If a fear-provoking stimuli is presented repeatedly without being paired with an aversive stimulus or without avoidance taking place, the conditioned stimulus will lose its power to evoke fear. The therapist determines the variety of stimuli that evoke fear. The patient is then asked to imagine these situations and to tolerate the resulting anxiety without "turning away" either by calling a halt to the procedure or distracting his attention. The therapist attempts to maximize the patient's anxiety until the presentation of these stimuli no longer evoke an anxiety response. The anxiety is then said to be extinguished. Such procedures have also been carried out (Rachman, Marks, & Hodgson, 1973) in vivo where subjects are urged to approach a feared stimuli as quickly as possible and to remain there until they are no longer anxious.

A similar procedure has been employed with patients engaging in compulsive rituals. Patients are encouraged to expose themselves to the stimuli that evoke the rituals. The therapist then urges the patient to delete or postpone the ritualistic behavior and tolerate the resulting anxiety until it has been extinguished (Marks 1973). The results of this approach have been consistently positive, however the question remains concerning which patients will chose to participate.

Implosive techniques also employ the process of extinction to reduce fear (Stampfl, 1967). Implosion, however, not only employs cues that the patient is able to report as fear provoking but also infers cues related to reported fears and finally employs cues implied in psychoanalytic theory as related to a particular personality type. This approach only uses imaged stimuli.

Differences between the cues employed in flooding as implosive techniques can be seen in the hypothetical case of a woman afraid of crossing bridges. Flooding procedure would repeatedly employ scenes of actual experiences of the patient anxiously crossing bridges. Implosive techniques would go further by inferring that the patient is most afraid of falling off the bridge either by its collapse, through an automobile accident, or by jumping. It is also inferred that the patient would be afraid of being hurt but is particularly afraid of falling into the water. This would probably be carried further as a fear of choking which drowning usually implies. Analytic cues would be further hypothesized relating to phobic symptoms in general as involved with anxiety concerning sexual impulses. The scenes would then involve all of the cues mentioned above presented in the most anxiety-provoking manner. The session is prolonged until the patient can no longer produce anxiety to the scenes presented.

Both of these techniques, particularly implosion, have been used to extinguish conditioned emotional reactions such as shame, guilt, or embarrassment that have caused the patient to inhibit social and sexual responses, assertiveness, anger, or intimate behavior. Scene presentation becomes more and more complicated and usually in the case of implosive techniques involves a horror that touches on all of the verbalized and implied fears of the patient. With extended repetition, however, even this material becomes "boring" and devoid of conditioned emotional responses which is the end of the process.

Results of flooding (Marks, 1972), and implosion (Levis & Carrera 1967; Stampfl & Levins, 1967) have been generally positive clinically with both offering a shorter course of treatment than desensitization (Barrett 1969). However, two authors (Fazio 1970; Barrett 1969) found that several patients became *more* fearful following the procedures. Although the reasons for this are not clear, in these particular cases it is predicted that if an individual's fear response is raised followed by avoidance without extinction, the treatment will serve as a traumatic fear-conditioning procedure. It is imperative then that the subject agree beforehand to continue the procedure until extinction occurs. The therapist must not back away from the elicitation of anxiety no matter how uncomfortable the patient becomes and must not terminate the session before the extinction of anxiety is complete.

Flooding and implosion are particularly useful for patients who (1) are unable to achieve relaxation responses and participate in desensitization procedures; (2) react with anxiety to so many stimuli that the shorter duration of implosive and flooding procedures is almost imperative. It remains to be empirically determined whether it is more beneficial to include the wide variety of stimuli that the implosive model requires. However, the technique offers the clinician the opportunity to include the content of psychoanalytic process in treatment along with a different method to change behavior.

The disadvantages of flooding and implosion is that the patient is required to undergo considerable discomfort. For this reason, before treatment is initiated the therapist should tell the patient why he is recommending this technique and explain the experimental rationale for the procedures. The patient should be made aware of what will be required and be given the opportunity to choose alternative approaches that might prove less uncomfortable. The contract should state that the patient will attempt to complete the procedure and spell out the disadvantages of not doing so. I have found that the technique works best with individuals who experience moderate to relatively high levels of anxiety in their daily lives. These patients are less frightened by the high anxiety elicited by the treatment and hence are less likely to prematurely discontinue treatment.

Positive Reinforcement

Positive reinforcement is a basic principle of learning employed in a wide range of behavioral techniques. A positive reinforcing event is one which increases the frequency of the response it follows. This section will describe two techniques, verbal conditioning and behavioral contracting, both of which can be seen as gaining their effectiveness mainly from positive reinforcement.

What patients say during therapy can be viewed either as a means of communication about outside events or as responses which themselves are open to modification through the conditioning process. As early as 1955, studies have demonstrated the effectiveness of selective reinforcement in increasing and decreasing the frequency of different types of verbal responses (Greenspoon, 1955). Verbal behavior can thus be shaped through the therapist's attention, facial expressions, tone of voice, and what he or she says by way of approval, disapproval, or neutrality. This process occurs whether or not the therapist intends it and it greatly influences the content of conversation during the therapeutic session and, ultimately, changes in behavior outside of therapy. Although verbal conditioning may not be the main focus of treatment, it is a factor that can never be ignored. The therapist must learn to strike a balance between eliciting information about the patient's difficulties and maintaining a genuinely sympathetic attitude without reinforcing the representation of self-punishing or pessimistic statements and complaints. Although all therapies are naturally problem focused, they also must be implicitly solution oriented. The therapist may well begin by reinforcing the presentation of all material at the first stages of treatment and then gradually withdraw the attention paid to restatement of complaints already discussed and shift the focus to solution-oriented statements.

Positive reinforcers outside of verbal ones offered by the therapist can be used to modify behavior. In fact, patients who have been in therapy often say that although they wished to change and had gained insight into their problems, they were unable to use their new insight effectively to influence their behavior. These patients then label themselves as feeling ambivalent towards change. Within the behavioristic scheme, many problem behaviors are being partially maintained in spite of their inefficiency and discomfort by reinforcement. It is no surprise then that patients do not easily shift behavior even when they are able to verbalize a more effective pattern of behavior. Using a reinforcement program for desirable behavior, the therapist attempts to tip the scales so that the frequency of the desired behavior is increased and the frequency of the problem behavior subsequently decreased.

Arrangements for positive reinforcement of desired behavior are made with outpatients through the use of behavioral contracts. These formalize an agreement between therapist and patient, two patients (a married couple, for example) or the patient and himself with the therapist serving as monitor-consultant. The agreement stipulates that the patient will receive certain reinforcers for the emission of specified behaviors, or, as in the case of a contract involving two patients, the performance of a desired behavior on the part of one patient will be contingent upon the performance of a desired behavior by the other.

The drawing up of the contract begins with the selection and operational description of the behaviors to be changed. The contract may focus on a single habit or be more wide range. It is important to choose behavior, at least at the start, that has a moderate frequency of occurrence so that reinforcement can occur. A survey of positive reinforcers, perhaps using the *Reinforcement Survey Schedule* described previously, is usually needed to determine what will be rewarding to the patient. A baseline of the frequency of the emission of the desired responses is also established before any attempt to change behavior is initiated. A contract is then negotiated, and, after agreement is reached between the parties concerned, a form is drawn up that specifies the behavior to be rewarded, the nature of the rewards to be delivered, and the mechanisms of operation on which the contract will function. A time limit that sets the duration of the contract is also included. The effects of the program are frequently and regularly evaluated by means of both verbal report by the individuals involved and the collection of data relevant to the purposes of the contract. If the frequency of the desired responses do not increase, the reasons must be investigated.

When contracts fail to work it is most commonly because (1) there is difficulty in their implementation; (2) the behaviors are not specified clearly enough or are not occurring frequently enough to provide for a rich enough schedule of reinforcers; or (3) the reinforcers are not powerful enough to affect the behavior.

Contracts can be used to change any behavior—socializing, weight loss, alcohol intake, or anger control. However, it is suggested that attempts to increase the frequency of behaviors that have a high inhibitory component (conditioned anxiety) only be employed when a method of reducing this inhibition (desensitization, flooding, or implosion) is also being used. If this is not done, the patient is placed in an intense approach-avoidance conflict that can cause considerable discomfort.

Reinforcers can vary in terms of what is practically available, (Many patients would attempt changes immediately for the proverbial million dollars.), what is ethically viable, what is rewarding to the patient, and what the parties are willing to negotiate. It is generally recommended that, if possible, reinforcers be used that the patient is not presently enjoying. Otherwise, the patient must first deprive himself of something to begin the procedure. This gives the entire contract a punitive aspect. Patients usually can be convinced that rewarding themselves with a previously denied luxury is justifiable as they clearly will have earned it. Rewards should be consumed soon after they are earned. For example, money earned through contracts should not be saved over any length of time to purchase a big item since the delay of consumption decreases the reinforcing value on the desirable behavior.

Contracts can be drawn directly between patient and therapist. Therapists often control the length of time of the session, the number of sessions per week and the fee involved. To the extent that these factors are positively reinforcing to the patient they can be included in a contract and varied on the basis on the patient's performance of desirable behaviors. An extremely socially isolated patient this author was assigned to as an intern found the attention of treatment highly reinforcing and had been in therapy for more than three years. She was habitually requesting more frequent and extended sessions. A contract was reached within which session time and frequency was earned through the performance of socializing behavior. The patient made steady gains that continued following the suspension of the contract.

Most of the time patients form contracts with themselves in which the therapist participates to varying extents. A patient may wish to reward himself monetarily for desirable behavior and deposit money with the therapist who is requested to dole out specified amounts contingent on the patient's behavior. In other situations, the patient may be able to exert enough control to reward himself for targeted behaviors without the therapist serving as monitor. Patients may reward themselves with time off from work, trips, specific purchases, or entertainment.

Contracts between couples, sometimes called "exchange contracts," (Knox, 1973) have an added quality. Here the other party to the contract monitors the behavior and affords the possibility of immediate reinforcement. In addition, such contracts tend to contain the desirable effect of escalation within the system. The desired response by a spouse serves as a reinforcer for the mate as well as a stimuli for the emission of a desired response by the mate. This in turn reinforces the spouse and serves as a stimuli for emission of another desirable response. If not properly arranged, however, the opposite effect can easily occur: the low frequency of emission of desirable behavior by one partner can quickly result in low frequency of desirable behavior by the other.

Exchange contracts may involve the exchange of chores or exchange of chores for other behavior, for example, De Risi & Butz (1975) report a case where:

> In exchange for the privilege of having four hours of "free time"
> to use as she chooses during which time Mel will babysit, Harriet
> will refrain from smoking during mealtimes.

Other contracts may involve more intimate behavior. For example, a husband may agree to show his wife more affection or attention when she agrees to more frequent sexual intercourse.

Before such contracts are drawn up, participants are asked

why the behavior in question is not presently at a high level. Often, one of the two will report that while he (or she) has thought about it, he was inhibited by the thought that the other party might not reciprocate. A contract can then be written for the exchange and participants told to perform the behavior when the thought occurs and to override the inhibiting thought.

Other patients may state that they have not thought about performing the behavior desired by the other but imagine that they would want to do so if the partners were performing in the desired way. In such cases, contracting also is appropriate. If, however, it appears that one or both are willing to perform the behavior only in order to "get what they want" from the other, it is less likely that contracting will be helpful. If contracts are made, such emotional behaviors may, in essence, become redefined so that intercourse becomes impersonal and affection becomes contrived leading to the frustration of both. In such cases, other behavioral interventions may be necessary before contracting is initiated.

It is often asked why patients enter contracts when they can perform the behavior themselves if they want to and usually reward themselves as well. In essence, what does the contract really add? First, the contract focuses the patient's attention on the behaviors he wants to change. Secondly, it provides a formal structure for change. In some cases, once the patient has entered into the contract he has limited his flexibility to remove himself from it (perhaps by depositing money with the therapist). The patient has then employed a means of external control over his actions during periods of time when desirable behaviors might otherwise have a low probability of occurring.

Another frequent question concerns the continued performance of the desired behavior after the expiration of the contract. It should be remembered here that desirable behaviors are assumed to be rewarded in the environment if they are properly and persistently performed. It is the contract that brings the responses to a level at which the individual will receive environmental rewards. It is also important that the patient be able to maintain the behavior following moderate periods of extinction as the environment rarely reinforces behavior as consistently as contracts.

This process is illustrated by the fact that many patients report that they have begun to perform the behavior regularly and that the contract no longer influences their performance. Many refer to it with a smile, indicating the humor of having once been "paid off" to do something they now enjoy.

COGNITIVE BEHAVIOR THERAPY

Cognitive behavior therapy focuses on the patient's cognitions and their modification through treatment. It is assumed within this framework that patients' thinking largely determines their behavior. This type of behaviorism should be distinguished from traditional models of dynamic therapy that also strongly stress cognitions and their modification (insight) as a potent factor in treatment. Cognitive behavior therapy focuses exclusively on cognitions as they presently occur. A history of the training of cognitions or cognitive chains may be included in the initial assessment. However, insight into this development is not seen as the essence of treatment. The contribution of this approach lies in training the patient to recognize thoughts as they occur, thoughts that are often so overpracticed that they have become automatic or assumptive. An awareness of the effects of particular thoughts on the patient's feelings, actions, and physiology is also demonstrated. This is followed by a direct attempt to help the patient change cognitions causing discomfort or inefficiency in order to reach the established goals of treatment.

Albert Ellis (1962) remains a leading figure in cognitive behavior therapy. As a result of Ellis' experience as a practicing psychoanalyst and his deep interest in philosophy, he formed the opinion that the irrational assumptions that underlie much of human thinking are responsible for emotional difficulties. If these assumptions can become more rational, the patient's beliefs and actions will become realistic, functional, and satisfactory. Although the patient may not be aware of irrational thinking habits, they can be deductively demonstrated once the assumption of the determining effects of cognitions on behavior is accepted. Ellis offers the following example: You are traveling on a crowded bus on a hot summer day. Suddenly you feel a sharp elbow jabbing your ribs. You turn swiftly, flushed with anger ready to give the jabbing individual a piece of your mind. You observe the culprit, a man with a white cane struggling to reach the back of the bus. Your anger is gone and perhaps you feel a little guilty. When asked "what made you angry?" individuals claim that the jab was responsible. This cannot possibly be so since a blind man can jab just as painfully as a sighted man. Ellis provides an answer by hypothesizing that there was an underlying assumption made that people *should* be more careful of me when I am on the bus. By setting up a moral imperative of what *should* be, the individual naturally feels enraged that such an imperative has been violated. The fact that the perpetrator is blind negates the *should* in this case and the anger disappears. Ellis challenges the rationale of this or any other *should* type cognition claiming that no one is in a position to know what *should* be in this world but rather we all can express ourselves in terms of the way we would like things to be. This includes using a should imperative applied to our own behavior. This type of thinking, devoid of moralism, leads the injured party usually to a state of annoyance or disappointment but not to one of anger or depression.

 Ellis also has given considerable attention to the tendency of individuals to perceive events as catastrophes, that is, to see events as awful, terrible, or unbearable when, in Ellis' rationale thinking system, they really are disappointing, unfortunate, or inconvenient. ("If I perform badly in the play this evening, it will be terrible" versus "it will be unfortunate." If realistically considered, no terrible consequences will follow a bad performance.) Converting negative thinking to more rationale assumptions results in a change from the emotion of anxiety and depression to those of disappointment or inconvenience.

Ellis has discerned common irrational assumptions that he believes afflict many individuals (Ellis, 1962, pp. 61–88). These include the ideas that:

> (1) It is a dire necessity for an adult human being to be loved or approved by virtually every significant other person in his community; (2) One should be thoroughly competent, adequate, and achieving in all possible respects if one is to consider oneself worthwhile; (3) The idea that certain people are bad, wicked, or villainous and that they should be severely blamed and punished for this villainy; (4) It is awful and catastrophic when things are not the way one would very much like them to be; (5) Human unhappiness is externally caused and that people have little or no ability to control their sorrows and disturbances; (6) If something is or may be dangerous or fearsome one should be terribly concerned about it and should keep dwelling on the possibility of its occurring; (7) It is easier to avoid than to face certain life difficulties and self-responsibilities; (8) One should be dependent on others and need someone stronger than oneself on whom to rely; (9) One's past history is an all-important determiner of one's present behavior and that because something once strongly affected one's life, it should indefinitely have a similar effect; (10) One should become quite upset over other people's problems and disturbances; (11) There is invariably a right, precise, and perfect solution to human problems and that it is catastrophic if this perfect solution is not found.

It must be apparent that most patients when initiating treatment do not see their behavior in terms of the assumptive cognitive determinants that Ellis postulates. The first stage of treatment involves training them to accept the notion that it is the underlying irrational assumptive universe that greatly influences their behavior including their easily identifiable cognitions. Patients are then taught to recognize examples of their irrational thinking and to substitute rational assumptions, a process that results in relief of emotional distress. Patients are assigned the cognitive "homework" of first recognizing then challenging and changing their irrational thought in the natural setting. When certain environmental situations are being avoided as a result of irrational assumptions, ("It would be terrible if I asked a woman out and she said no"), Ellis does not hesitate to assign homework involving an approach to these previously avoided situations. This affords the patient the opportunity to generate, challenge, and replace the irrational assumptions involved.

More recently Michenbaum & Cameron (1974) have developed a new concept of cognitive intervention. They have maintained Ellis' position that "thoughts" play a predominant role in determining behavior in other channels. However, they have focused away from the patient's philosophy as a disturbing factor and instead addressed himself to what he calls the role of the patients self-statements, task relevant versus task irrelevant cognitives and cognitive-coping skills. An example of this concept includes thinking during an examination, "I'm going to fail this test," a task irrelevant negative statement that substitutes focusing on the test material. The role of the therapist is to first assess and then help the patient to become aware of the role of this type of cognition in determining behavior. The patient is then trained through a process of modeling and direct instruction in more effective cognitions including the elimination of negative self-statements and their replacement with neutral and positive self-statements, the training of the thinking process to remain with thoughts relevant to the task at hand as against indulging in irrelevant thinking.

Michenbaum stressed the attention factor and its focus on the external environment as a means of reducing a self-defeating and irrelevant thinking process. Michenbaum & Cameron have also trained patients to cope successfully with anxiety-provoking situations through a technique called stress inoculation which uses images to raise stress levels and then trains the patient to omit coping cognitive responses.

The apparent advantage of this approach, as compared with the work of Ellis, is that it brings a set of variables that seem more directly relevant to what most patients consider their thinking process when they enter treatment. Probably most significantly Michenbaum has employed a controlled experimental approach to the study of cognitions and his therapeutic interventions as compared to the sole use of clinical material by Ellis.

Wolpe (1958) has particularly discussed cognitions that form brooding or obsessive thinking and has popularized a technique called "thought stopping." If obsessive thoughts are like other responses, then they too will respond to the principles of learning.

Wolpe (1958, p. 212) describes the technique:

> A thought-stopping program begins by asking the patient to close his eyes and to verbalize a typical futile thought sequence. During the verbalization the therapist suddenly shouts "Stop!" and then draws attention to the fact that the thoughts actually stop . . . the patient is urged to test the efficacy of this procedure by saying stop subvocally. He is warned that the thought will return but every time they do he must interrupt them again. . . . The thoughts in many cases return less and less readily and eventually cease to be a problem.

He explains the effectiveness of the treatment as a process of thought inhibition reinforced by the anxiety-reducing effects of each trial involving the elimination of an anxiety-producing thought.

More recently Homme (1965) developed a comprehensive system within which all thoughts are dealt with in a manner suggested by Wolpe's thought-stopping procedure. Homme introduced the term "coverant" meaning covert operant, an attempt to bring cognitions into the realm of the operant conditioner. He also has formulated the continuity hypothesis, implied in Wolpe's work, which holds that there is a continuity between these covert behaviors and overt behaviors so they can be conditioned in a similar manner, hence, the technique of thought conditioning.

One application involves the notion that the frequency with which any thought occurs can be increased if it is tied to a more frequently occurring operant. This is an application of the Premarkian principle of conditioning; however, Homme is mixing overt and covert operants. The goal is to increase the frequency of a desirable thought and subsequently decrease the frequency of an undesirable thought in situations where an attempt is being made to directly change the patient cognitions. The patient reaches a point where he has recognized the relationship of his cognitions to his behavior and can verbalize the appropriate rational or adaptive cognition during the therapeutic session. He also reports that when he is in the natural setting and his thinking seems dominated by the irrational or maladaptive thoughts he tries to use the therapy by conjuring up the rational and adaptive thought; he is unable to do so or this is a fleeting experience and he quickly returns to his irrational misery. This is explained as an attempt to pair two antagonists (the rational and irrational thoughts) and, since it is not likely that both thoughts can occur at the same time, the more practiced irrational thought will be most likely to occur. In order to increase the frequency of the rational thought, the patient is first asked to practice it when the specific irrational thought to which it is antagonistic is not occurring. If left to his own devices, this will probably not take place since as a result of the therapy the irrational thought will serve as the main cue for the patient to attempt the rational thought and this poor training system will be continued. The therapist then suggests tying the performance of the rational thought to some randomly occurring frequent stimuli in the patient's environment, such as drinking coffee or going to the bathroom. This then increases the probability that the rational thought will occur when the irrational maladaptive thought is not occurring.

The content of rational maladaptive thoughts may vary greatly in terms of each patients particular difficulties and the view taken in therapy from Ellis' more assumptive approach to Michenbaum's more specific coping approach. This author has found success with both but generally try to gear the thoughts to very particular situations, for example for a patient with insomnia: "If I cannot sleep at night I will be tired and uncomfortable the next day but I will always make it through the day." For a phobic patient: "My thinking I am going to have a heart attack will not cause me to have one." For a patient continually avoidant of asking for dates: "When I ask a woman out and she accepts I can then enjoy her company, if she says no, this doesn't mean I am an undesirable, it does mean that she doesn't wish my company. I can go on to ask others out."

Such thoughts are actually written out and patients are asked to carry them. Patients are asked not to just read the words but to think about their meaning each time they read them. Patients report that they quickly form the habit of reading the sentence following certain events. The next step is for the patient to encounter the designated stimuli, remember to think the thought, and for its meaning to come quickly to mind. Then, the thought should come to mind automatically when the patient encounters the designated situation. At this point, the situation is usually changed to another randomly occurring environmental stimuli so as to increase the generalization of the conditioning process. At some point the patient will report that the adoptive thought will "just pop into my head" at times not directly connected with the conditioning situation (generalizing along some undetermined dimensions). In essence, the patient no longer has to remember it and toward the end of this process has become a seemingly more natural part of his cognitive repertoire. The patient will then be instructed to employ the rational thought when he determines the irrational maladaptive thought is being emitted. Most patients find that the rational thought becomes much more effective in terms of reducing or eliminating the impact of the irrational maladaptive thought. Some patients report that the rational thought will "pop into their heads" automatically whenever the irrational thought is occurring. Still other patients report that the irrational thought "seems to have disappeared" and in its place the rational thought occurs and eventually becomes automatic. I have found this technique to be effective with a wide variety of patients and adaptive thought content and length. The therapist must be sure in working out the rational adaptive thought with the patient that the patient can fully accept the thoughts as true at least when the irrational thought is not prevalent as is often the case during the therapy session. Such platitudes as "stop worrying everything will turn out fine" (often offered in positive thinking literature) are rarely effective since the patient (and hopefully no one else) can really accept this thinking at any time. When this type of thought is used it is probably always immediately followed by an automatic production of thoughts indicating situations when things did not turn out fine. Second, the patient must be carefully instructed to practice the thought contingent on the designated stimulus. The temptation for some patients is sometimes overwhelming to only employ the thought when it seems appropriate, which is always when the maladaptive thought is occurring. This meets with little success and eventually leads to abandonment of the procedure.

CASE PRESENTATIONS

Case 1: Samuel

Samuel is 26 years old and had been in dynamically oriented therapy in individual and group sessions for the past five years. He had no friends and had never had a girlfriend although he had had some sexual experience with two older women who, in both instances, took the initiative. Samuel was often depressed and spent most of his time reading, listening to music, or "doing nothing." He felt inferior to other men his age and saw himself as unmanly and inept. He worried that he might make a mistake at work and be fired, that he might be embarrassed by others discovering his social inadequacies, and that nuclear war might break out. He had mild fears of heights and closed in places.

His former therapist reported that Samuel had been diagnosed as a schizoid personality with reactive depression episodes. He said that Samuel usually was passive during group sessions, and that although he often was confronted by the group for his lack of participation, he did not increase it. The doctor also said that Samuel is quite intelligent and understood and seemed to accept interpretations but he didn't integrate them into the mainstream of his thinking. He added that Samuel was reluctant to discuss his violent fantasies. In general, he had found Samuel to be a very difficult patient because of his passivity.

Samuel was given a battery of questionnaries consisting of the *Goals for Treatment, Life History Questionnaire, Assertive Scale,* and *Fear Survey Schedule.* The *Life History Questionnaire* revealed Samuel was an only child with a dominant, critical mother and a usually quiet father. Samuel felt that he always had been isolated and saw his present situation as a continuation of the pattern of childhood and adolesence.

Samuel now lives alone in a small apartment. He is a high school graduate and holds a bookkeeping job. His goals in seeking treatment were relatively clear: he wanted to enlarge his social and sexual activities, improve his mood state, and decrease his anxiety. Information from the assertive training scale indicated that Samuel was quite nonassertive at work and in his commercial dealings. In discussing these findings Samuel said he was ashamed of the aggressive fantasies that follow interactions in which he is nonassertive. He was reassured that such fantasies are not uncommon in this situation and his nonassertive behavior was targeted for treatment.

Samuel appeared to gain few reinforcers from his broad avoidance of contact with others. It was hypothesized that anxiety had been conditioned to a broad range of social stimuli which have representation in many spheres of behavior. Anxiety also seemed to be conditioned to environmental stimuli that could result in bodily harm. It was difficult to identify positive reinforcers that Samuel used to sustain the avoidance of others or the depressive thoughts. Treatment aimed at anxiety reduction and skill training was seen as appropriate. The depressive episodes were viewed as the result of a sparse schedule of reinforcement in his environment and a highly punitive, self-critical attitude probably would serve to increase the depression. An ongoing discussion of Samuel's assessment of his progress would serve as an excellent situation for new input into his self-evaluation standards.

It was decided that initially treatment would focus on expanding Samuel's social relationships. Although Samuel held regular conversations of a social nature, i.e., discussing movies, the news, etc., with four to five people at work and two neighbors, the mainstay of his personal contacts had been in group therapy. Samuel was asked to record the number, length, and frequency of his social conversations during the coming week. Samuel also was introduced to the concepts of cognitive behavior modification, that is, that his irrational philosophy as well as the self-downing internalized sentences play an important role in producing anxiety and subsequent avoidance behavior. Samuel appeared very receptive to these notions and several scenes were imaged during the session in an effort to isolate the internal sentences that Samuel used to make himself anxious. He was given Albert Ellis' *A Guide to Rational Living* to read.

After obtaining a base line for Samuel's social conversations, in vivo desensitization was employed to increase the frequency of this behavior. Samuel had a particularly hard time talking to strangers and almost never did so. His first homework in this regard was to ask three strangers for the correct time (it is almost impossible to start too small). In addition, he was asked to employ mild self-disclosure with his established social contacts by expressing a thought that involved a feeling relating to himself. Samuel experienced success with both of these assignments, and they were continued and escalated. Within three months he was easily able to initiate conversations with strangers, both male and female. He also had improved the quality of his social relationships at work and had been asked to go bowling. He went and enjoyed the evening but reported feeling anxious most of the time about his conversations and his bowling. Despite his progress, at the end of this three-month period Samuel seemed to be losing some of his initial enthusiasm. Although he had made measurable progress and was very interested in identifying and changing his internal sentences, he was disappointed that he had not changed more quickly and that his goal of having a girlfriend still seemed remote. As a result, the goal of the treatment was temporarily narrowed to focus on dating behavior. Samuel was asked to practice initiating conversations with women he thought were attractive. In the past he avoided attractive women. Samuel found this task difficult and reported that he failed to attempt to initiate many conversations.

A new treatment plan was then devised to increase the level of reinforcement Samuel was receiving for these efforts. He was asked to open a second bank account. It was agreed that all luxury items (entertainment, an air conditioner, alcohol, records, books, new clothing, a new car) would have to be paid for out of this new account. Samuel could be described as somewhat miserly; he saved almost 60 percent of his salary. The money in this new account would have to be "earned" with socializing and assertive behavior. A menu was constructed consisting of items ranked on difficulty dimensions of conversations with friends, length, and intimacy of conversations with potential dates, social activities with friends, asking for a date, and assertiveness in commercial situations and at work. Tasks were rewarded by payments from the new account in the order of their difficulty. The system worked well and Samuel showed a sharp upturn in almost all categories. He began socializing regularly with co-workers and was able to hold conversations of up to ten minutes with attractive single women. To guarantee that the reinforcers were actually consumed, it was decided that initially at least, half of each week's earnings had to be spent during the following two weeks. As Samuel was able to earn more money from the account, this spending requirement was decreased to one-fourth allowing him to save more effectively for larger items. Eventually Samuel purchased records, a new stereo, and eventually skiing equipment.

The most difficult item on the first menu was asking for a date and Samuel was not able to attempt this. Role playing was then used to sharpen Samuel's skills concerned with the actual asking. Luckily, there were women available at the hospital who were willing to participate in the therapy. Each week a different woman attended the session. Samuel and the woman were introduced and then the woman pretended to be an acquaintance at work. He became quite anxious during these sessions but after three weeks practice was able to perform fairly calmly. The response of the role-playing therapist ranged from warm to cold rejection. Following the third practice Samuel asked a woman at work for a date and was promptly rejected. He quickly asked someone else and was accepted and enjoyed the evening. His dating soon became quite regular, and he experienced only mild difficulty in asking out women from work. Samuel reported that he enjoyed the dates although occasionally he found himself "putting himself down" and becoming anxious while on the date. He was able to recognize this habit and alleviate the difficulty. The menu was periodically enlarged to include more difficult items and to pay less for items Samuel could perform with ease. Several months later Samuel reported that he had met a woman at a bus station, had a friendly conversation during the wait and the subsequent bus ride but was unable to ask her out. Role playing treatment was reinitiated. Staff women from the clinic who Samuel had not met previously were asked to participate in the in vivo desensitization procedure. Samuel would be told that a woman would be sitting alone at a certain place in or near the clinic and was part of the therapy. She would be expecting him to strike up a conversation and ask her for a date. The woman gave varying responses. After the encounter, the couple would return to the office and discuss their meeting. This treatment was effective in improving Samuel's ability to meet women and ask them out.

Within eight months the positive reinforcement menu was abandoned. Samuel had stopped socializing for the ability to buy luxuries and was really enjoying his activities. He was dating three women, one of whom he particularly liked. He was having sexual intercourse and his initial worry about how he would perform was cast aside rather quickly. He remained somewhat concerned about his social behavior and occasionally became anxious about the possibility of world catastrophes. Somewhat surprisingly he reported that he was less fearful of heights although this difficulty was never mentioned after the first sessions.

Therapy became totally oriented towards a cognitive behavior modification approach. Samuel discussed his relationships, the difficulties he was having, his relatively short periods of depression, and his hopes for the future. The author's role consisted of provoking him to question his irrational internal sentences and self-defeating thoughts.

Therapy sessions were reduced from once a week to once every two weeks and then to once a month. Therapy was terminated approximately a year and a half after it began. After 47 sessions, Samuel had established a heterosexual relationship with a woman whom he saw regularly, he was friendly with some other people at work, and had joined a bowling league and a discussion group. His periods of depression were few although they still occurred occasionally. A readministration of the *Fear*

Survey Schedule and the *Assertive Scale* confirmed and quantified the gains made in these areas. Samuel was called six months following the end of treatment. He confirmed that his gains had been maintained and that he had become more active socially and worried less than he had in the past.

I believe the factors most crucial to success in this case were (1) the use of Samuel's initial enthusiasm to effect some immediate behavior changes; (2) use of the menu to prevent a prolonged lapse into inactivity; (3) introduction of a method with which Samuel was able to identify and control his thoughts.

SUMMARY

The behavioral approach to psychotherapy represents a distinctly different view of the psychological problems and therapeutic interventions as compared to other approaches. One of the major advantages of the behavioral approach is its insistence on a quantified empirical base from which to judge itself. This provides the clinician and the patient with relatively accurate means to assess treatment results, and it mandates changes in treatment when goals are not being approached. The basic theoretical assumptions of the system that entail a learning model lead to optimism regarding the flexibility of human behavior and also reduces the stigma for those who seek to change their behavior through psychotherapy. In addition, behavior therapy offers highly individualized treatment. Although based on relatively few principles of learning, the diversity of techniques and their combination and specific application allow for a unique approach to each case.

Some readers may wish to learn more about the behavioral approach. They are referred to a number of basic texts that deal exclusively with the topic. It also is suggested that they seek supervision from an experienced behavior therapist before clinical application is attempted. As I have tried to explain in this chapter, behavior therapy is not as simple as it is widely believed to be.

Clinicians practicing other forms of psychotherapy are not faced with an either-or decision concerning the use of behavioral techniques, at least not from the behavioral point of view. Behavior therapy has been experimentally demonstrated to be somewhat effective with certain human difficulties. Although a similar burden of proof rests with other systems, no results have been conclusive and little research has been completed to identify which systems are most effective with which patients. A clinician may wish to shift from a behavioral approach to another system to increase the probability of success with different patients. Other clinicians may wish to integrate behavioral techniques to aid patients in changing their overt behavior and maintain, for example, an analytical approach to provide the patient with an understanding of the causes of his difficulties. Hopefully, future research will provide scientifically derived guidelines for these treatment alternatives.

REFERENCES

Atkinson, D. R. In vivo desensitization with college students. *Journal of College Student Personnel,* 1973, **14**(2), 141–143.

Bandura, A. Social learning through imitation. In M. R. Jones (Ed.), *Nebraska symposium on motivation.* Lincoln, Neb.: University of Nebraska Press, 1962.

Bandura, A., Blanchard, E. B., & Ritter, B. The relative efficacy of desensitization and modeling approaches for inducing behavioral, affective and attitudinal changes. Journal of Personality and Social Psychology, 1969, **13**, 173–199.

Barrett, L. Systematic desensitization versus implosive therapy. *Journal of Abnormal Psychology,* 1969, **74**(5), 587–592.

Cautela, J. R. The behavioral analysis history questionnaire, unpublished questionnaire. Boston, Ma.: Boston College, 1970.

Cautela, J. R. & Kastenbaum, R. A reinforcement survey schedule for use in therapy, training and research. *Psychological Reports* 1967, **20**, 1115–1130.

Cautela, J. R. & Upper, D. The process of individual behavior therapy. In M. Hersen, R. M. Eisler, & P. M. Miller (Eds.), *Progress in behavior modification,* Vol. 1. New York: Academic Press, 1975.

Cautela, J. R. & Upper, D. The behavioral inventory battery. In M. Hersen & A. Bellack (Eds.), *Behavioral assessment, a practical handbook.* New York: Pergamon Press, 1976.

DeRisi, W. J. & Butz, G. *Writing behavioral contracts. A case simulation practice manual.* Champaign, Illinois: Research Press, 1975.

Ellis, A. & Harper, R. A. *A guide to rational living.* Englewood Cliffs, New Jersey: Prentice-Hall, 1961.

Ellis, A. *Reason and emotion in psychotherapy.* Secaucus, N.J.: Lyle Stuart, 1962.

Fazio, A. F. Treatment components in implosive therapy. *Journal of Abnormal Psychology,* 1970, **76**(2) 211–219.

Geer, J. H. The development of a scale to measure fear. *Behavior Research and Therapy,* 1965, **3**, 45–53.

Greenspoon, J. The reinforcing effect of two spoken sounds on the frequency of two responses. *American Journal of Psychology* 1955, **68**, 409–416.

Gurman, A. S. Treatment of a case of public speaking anxiety by in vivo desensitization and cue-controlled relaxation. *Journal of Behavior Therapy and Experimental Psychiatry,* 1973, **4**(1), 51–54.

Homme, L. E. Control of coverants, the operants of the mind. *Psychological Record,* 1965, **15**(4), 501–511.

Jacobson, E. *Progressive Relaxation.* Chicago, Illinois: University of Chicago Press, 1938.

Knox, D. *Behavioral contracts in marriage counseling.* Journal of Family Counseling, 1973, 1, 22–28.

Langon, R. I. & Manosevitz, M. Validity of self-reported fear. *Behavior Research and Therapy,* 1966, **4**, 259–263.

Levis, D. J. & Carrera, R. *Effects of ten hours of implosive therapy in the treatment of outpatients; A preliminary report.* Journal of Abnormal Psychology, 1967, 72, 504–508.

Lewinsohn, P. M. The behavioral study and treatment of depression. In M. Hersen, R. M. Eisler, & P. M. Miller (Eds.), *Progress in Behavior Modification,* Vol, 1. New York: Academic Press, 1975.

Marks, I. Perspective on flooding. *Seminar In Psychiatry,* 1972, **4**(2), 129–138.

Marks, I. M. New approaches to the treatment of obsessive-compulsive disorders. *Journal of Nervous and Mental Disorders,* 1973, **156**, 420–426.

Meichenbaum, D. H. *Examination of model characteristics in reducing avoidance behavior.* Journal of Personality and Social Psychology, 1971, 17, 298–307.

Meichenbaum, D. and Cameron, R. The clinical potential of modifying what clients say to themselves. In Psychotherapy: Theory, Research and Practice, 1974, vol 11 (2), 103–117.

Premack, D. Toward empirical behavior laws I: positive reinforcement. *Psychological Review,* 1959, **66,** 219–233.

Rachman, S., Marks, I. M. & Hodgson, R. Treatment of obsessive-compulsive neurotics by modelling and flooding in vivo. *Behavior Research and Therapy,* 1973, **11,** 463–471.

Razran, G. The observable unconscious and the inferable conscious in current Soviet psychophysiology: Interoceptive conditioning, semantic conditioning and the orienting reflex. *Psychological Review,* 1961, **68,** 81–140.

Stampfl, T. G. Implosive therapy: The theory, the subhuman analogue, the strategy and the technique: Part I. The theory. In S. G. Armitage (Ed.), *Behavior modification techniques in the treatment of emotional disorders.* Battle Creek, Mich.: V. A. Publication, 1967, pp. 22–37.

Stampfl, T. G., & Levis, D. J. Essentials of implosive therapy: A learning-theory-based psychodynamic behavioral therapy. *Journal of Abnormal Psychology,* 1967, 72, 496–503.

Tharp, R. G. & Wetzel, R. J. *Behavior modification in the natural environment.* New York: Academic Press, 1969.

Ullman, L. P. & Krasner, L. *A psychological approach to abnormal behavior.* Englewood Cliffs, New Jersey: Prentice-Hall, 1969.

Walsh, W. B. Validity of self-report. *Journal of Counseling Psychology,* 1967, **14,** 18–23.

Walsh, W. B. Validity of self-report: Another look. *Journal of Counseling Psychology,* 1968, **15,** 180–186.

Wolpe, J. Psychotherapy by reciprocal inhibition. Stanford, Ca.: Stanford University Press, 1958.

Wolpe, J., Therapist and technique variables in the behavior therapy of neurosis. *Comprehensive Psychiatry,* 1969, **10**(1), 44–49.

Wolpe, J. & Lang, P. J. A fear survey schedule for use in behavior therapy. *Behavior Research and Therapy* 1964, **2,** 27–30.

chapter 2

HOW NOW: A GESTALT APPROACH

Michael Kriegsfeld, Ph.D.

To make therapy shorter and briefer appears attractive for many in our culture, and puzzling to me. One way of making something shorter is by cutting a piece of it off probably by setting an arbitrary limit. Another way of making something brief is by speeding it up to achieve a predetermined objective through pushing. Another way of making something brief or short is to pretend or judge it as if it were not as it appears. If you make something shorter by cutting it off you have made it less than it is; if you speed something up you do so through force and pressure; if you pretend as if something were brief you are living in illusion. As a Gestaltist I let be what is and work so fast that the natural process of growth and development flows without interference. For the purpose of this paper I will discuss three issues that enable me to be so concise in my practice of gestalt, namely, (1) my style of work rooted in who I am, (2) basic assumptions of gestalt, and (3) special techniques.

MY STYLE ROOTED IN WHO I AM

My 30 years of experience in a variety of settings includes work with children, adolescents, adults, in private practice, clinics, camps, therapeutic communities, ranging from neurotics, character disorders, antisocial delinquents, drug abusers, and self-destructive individuals, couples, and families. I dare to work in a direct way. My communications are simple, concrete, and specific allowing me to be vulnerable in sharing and caring. I allow myself direct communication of what I see, hear, and feel in immediate confrontation. I view confrontation (from the French confronter or Latin con frontis) as being together face to face. I am not the tabla rasa upon whom the patient will write. My communications are not to impress but to express the experience I am sharing with the other person in that moment of encounter. I focus on experiments with the clear expectations that as a trained and experienced professional, experiential data collection and awareness opportunities will lead to ever changing flexibility, acceptance of differences, and new approaches. Even in the exacting science of physics the law of indeterminancy provides recognition that the participant observer is not neutral and affects the situation. I value my choices, as well as the patients' choices, as life enhancing and appropriate. This means that I am also learning through the process. Mistakes for the client as well as for myself are part of the pattern of working through a situation. Experiments are opportunities for encouraging a flow in the process of making new choices.

As an artist I enrich my work by rooting what I do in the creative efforts of the ensemble musician who plays together with others. Unlike traditional painting or sculpture, it is only in music, drama, or dance that *two people* play together in an art form which depends on open communication, relationship, shared improvisation and disciplined practice. Gestalt therapy frees me and the other person in the same way. Each of us contributes what we are at the moment. In the image of music

I vibrate in resonance with the other. This may be in harmony or dissonance as we each contribute melody lines in counterpoint form to the relationship. Sometimes loud, sometimes soft, sometimes a steady beat, sometimes synchopated, sometimes fast, sometimes slow, sometimes out of tune either sharp or flat, ever continuing or sometimes with pauses and rests, as engage each other in the enjoyable process of playing together. Playing together can be fun, tiring, exciting, boring, painful, transparent, and clear not only to us the players but also the rest of the ensemble or group who share the experience. (See previous paper, "Play Attention: The How Experience of Gestalt," by M. Kriegsfeld, 1975, edited by Grayson and Loew.)

The first encounter is very important, and clearly a now experience. In contrast to other forms of work I begin immediately without postponement (Kriegsfeld, 1975). How does the patient present themself? What are they seeking? What are they communicating? How do they relate? What do they want from me? My own goals are self-discovery and self-acceptance, both for the patient as well as myself. Who am I? What are my expectations here and now?

To what extent have I discovered myself? To what extent do I accept myself in this initial meeting? Do I worry about impressing the referral source by living up to an image? Am I tired from working too hard? Am I anxious about clutching and holding on to a new source of income? Am I excited, bored, sympathetic, angry? Do I have an agenda or program of what is good, better, best? Do I fragment myself with pressure to make the patient become aware? "I am a pretzel" says the patient "make me into a bagel! Do you have the power and knowledge to do this?" Am I joining the patient with false hopefulness about the future? Will this become a program of what should be and energy invested in the patient soliciting and my giving advice and direction from the outside. Do I have the courage to recognize the beginning self-torture program on the part of the patient who will enlist my "help" in control and manipulation? I prefer to work with highly motivated patients.

I scnsc this not by the driving pressure to be better faster but by the degree of pain, suffering, despair, and willingness to persist in sharing real feelings. As I choose to remember God even he was insecure as he put Job through various procedures to discover through Job's faith that God was really God. Perhaps this was God's projective test for himself to discover if he was truly God and could accept this himself. In the first encounter who will be Job and who will be God?

I consider myself an expert in the process and consider the patient an expert in himself? Only the patient knows what he wants, what his needs are, what alternatives are available to him, what his endurance is, what his preferences are in values, and what choice to make in his own existence. I do not analyze, interpret, tell them what to do or be. I am a keen observer, active listener, and quick to share my experience with them. I am present at the cutting edge of life's emergency and crisis in this most precious moment of now.

I pay close attention to organismic responsiveness. Does what the patient says match what he does and feels? Breathing, voice, mannerisms, gestures, body tensions, are direct communications of the person's choice of existence. I am less interested in the content than the process. I am concerned with polarities as indications of the fragmentation and avoidances of who they are. I am especially interested in how they stop themselves from being centered, whole, and real.

Flexibility to role play and experience the various parts of themselves is the way of beginning as well as the way of terminating. Termination begins in the very first encounter and is not postponed to some future date or place. Working and playing together is voluntary and choosing continuous. The patient and I are both free to indicate our preference to continue, stop, or explore a referral. The tools of therapy are awareness and choosing what the patient takes with them whether we meet only once or more often, for an hour or extended workshop, on going weekly sessions or on intermittent occasions. To the extent that I am aware of my own nervousness, fear, public image of how others might view the situation, unwillingness to suffer my own discomfort, my own unfinished business of the past, or anticipated worry about the future I am free to choose whether to continue, how to continue, or whether to refer the patient.

BASIC ASSUMPTIONS

The basic assumptions that guide my work are related to here and now issues and feelings, "how" instead of "why," responsibility, organismic responsiveness, experience, and process. Here and now provides the framework for conciseness. The past is over with except for that part which the patient chooses to carry out as unfinished business. No amount of review or storytelling about the past will change what happened. If the patient is fixed and set as a product of the past no further work is required except acceptance of what is. The focus can be discovery and acceptance of how the patient is doing this. The future has not happened yet and I am unable to guarantee the outcome of anything even my own ability to live past the end of the session. How the patient worries about the future here and now can be part of the experience. Access to the past is through memory and access to the future is through imagination. Neither exists except through fantasy. Quickly we are into the make believe and magic of role playing the various parts. From storytelling and talking, the patient is invited to act out the parts and own the various roles, heightening the emotional experience of here and now.

Responsibility and how, are linked in the assumption that the patient creates their own response by choosing from many alternatives. How the patient chooses the response heightens the experience of one's needs, values, and acceptable options. Access to responsibility is through the choices and preferences the patient makes here and now with the full option of making new choices. I refuse to make choices for the patient. I do make choices and decisions for myself.

Organismic responsiveness reveals the true state of the individual at the present moment. How does the storytelling match with the action, behavior, and feelings? The most direct access to organismic responsivness is through coherence of the three. By paying attention to what is on the surface I have the clearest and quickest opportunity for playing in the encounter. The words "I'm o.k." can be accompanied by tears trickling down the cheek, a grin, clenched jaws and teeth gnashed, a fist clenched and pounding on a thigh, thumb sucking, nail biting, a belch, cuticle tearing, foot tapping, playing with the genitals, tripping, almost falling, etc. I inquire and call attention to this, again without interpretation or analysis. The patient, as in working with dreams, provides his own description and shares the experience. Repetition or exaggeration of the movement or gesture provides the opportunity for further experience and direct indication of interruptions or avoidances. The willingness to explore this aspect of our work quickly allows confrontation with resistance and flexibility of options. The gait, posture, movements, and actions of the individual as they go around to other members of the group in an experiment of communicating can be extremely revealing of openness and holding back. My pillows in the room as well as the couch are always ready to be beaten, stomped, punched, strangled, leaned on, kissed, caressed, stroked, etc. The essence is how the intensity of the strong expression and recognition of emotions is played out and how it matches what is being said or felt. The whisperer who experiments with yelling, the yeller who experiments with whispering, the intellectual explainer who drowns everyone with words experiments with babbling sounds, enabling new awareness of sharing and holding back.

Techniques

The most powerful tool for conciseness is group treatment as the treatment of choice. Couples, families, and individual patients have the richest opportunity through the group for growth and development, at a living tempo of their own. The attempt to make therapy brief or short as a way of avoidance of pain and suffering leads to previous identified efforts to cut off, pressure, or pretend. Obviously attention to what is here and now in the group of patients some of whom are similar and some of whom are different encourages realness and conciseness. The holistic approach does not allow for sanctioned splitting of families and couples into secret individual sessions to be followed at some future date by possible diplomatic negotiations with complicated problems of translation and talking about what has already become stale, musty, and dead.

Being yourself is easy when you hide in the clothes closet with the lights off. Talking to umbrellas and raincoats and the darkness of the clothes closet is unreal. Likewise telling secrets in individual sessions reinforces the patient's own judgment of their badness and sinfulness. It is interesting that the Catholic Church has changed the format of the confessional to an open process referred to as reconciliation.

The structure of secret individual sessions without a group suggests sanction to the patient's avoidance of their own healing process and delays the opportunity for integration and wholeness of the various alienated fragments.

Likewise with couples and family, treatment in the same group is the treatment of choice. Couples and family members who are sincerely interested in exploring and sharing themselves are quickly aware of their motives in reaction to group process. Some people are interested in control and manipulation. They will not risk being themselves as they are in order to prevent others from rejecting them. Therefore secret individual sessions become the vehicle for playing "let's pretend while I strengthen my facade and image behind which I am safe to hide even from myself." This clearly involves an intention of avoiding asking directly for what one wants, avoiding the pain of the others reaction, and the option of selecting alternative ways of determining ones' own life. I do not choose to go along with the typical ostrich syndrome, of pretending that the world disappears when one sticks his head in the sand.

In my experience I have discovered that ostriches are more likely to get sand in their ears and eyes rather than the world disappearing. Also there is truly no hiding place in the company of people who are sensitive, caring, and trained in awareness. If a patient is truly insensitive, uncaring, and not aware perhaps living in a clothes closet and being married to an umbrella does not make much difference anyway. But that is also a choice for the individual to make. My own experience clearly indicates that people who grow in their own awareness and meet the criteria of caring and sensitivity increase their acceptance of themselves as well as others. I remember my first job in a residential treatment home for children where a new resident would arrive on a Friday before the professional staff would have an opportunity to study the situation. The residents were quite able to size up the new person and describe sophisticated diagnostic signs. They alerted me so sufficiently that epileptic seizures not before noticed were noted. A more recent example is the group member whose mother had been institutionalized. He would come to group only if I agreed not to mention his mother and her condition. He chose to avoid dealing with his own anxiety and worry about his own craziness and attempt to manipulate the others in the group. As a result of his idiosyncratic manner of communicating and relating, another member of the group began to identify with the observation that he must have had a crazy mother "like mine" and proceeded with a fantasy of what she was like based on his own sense of the distress. It was of course an exacting description. Later on having grown past this avoidance the new member was able to share with newcomers the fact he did have a mother who had been institutionalized. As he put it most people just imagine their parents aberrations but he knew for a fact how disturbed she had been.

Another conviction from my experience is that when members of the group are real and direct in their discovery of themselves and acceptance of themselves this is met with acceptance and understanding from others. The group process obviously magnifies the intensity of the feelings. It is a lot easier to share homosexual strivings in a closet with umbrellas than in a group where not only group members are present but even members of the family. Only through acceptance of oneself as one is, can meaningful contact be made with others. Growth is possible only through acceptance of differences and living up to one's own expectations with recognition that others have different expectations.

I work with one person at a time using the hot seat technique and consider this to be group process. The first chair is occupied by the group member in a process of meditation and awareness of their own process. The second chair is the chair occupied by me or other members of the group as an exploration of confrontation and encounter. From self-meditation to communicating with another, relationship skills grow. The wife who eggs on another person working in the first chair "Why don't you tell your husband off?" is beginning the process of becoming aware. The use of a question "why don't you" can be explored as expressing the statement behind the question. "I too feel like you do." "I want you to solve a problem for me so that I will know that there is hope for my despair." "I would like to explore my own alternatives in a similar situation." "I hadn't been aware of similar feelings until you began to describe your own situation." These are some of the many possible alternatives for the second member to explore as their projections. Finally there is the third empty chair for role playing the various projections and introjections of "them" which provides the structure in the presence of the group for integration. In experiments of going around to each individual member of the group there is additional opportunity for exploring and accepting one's own feelings and choices. I limit feedback to statements of one's own experience and feelings, in contrast to the kind of feedback where one member tells or interprets another member. I see this as similar to my driving to Boston with a group of people, one driver at a time until we exchange places behind the wheel. I don't know of any group driving experience with five people each pulling on the wheel or stepping on the brake or feeding gas simultaneously. I have been in driving situations however with many back seat drivers who gratuitously will tell me what I should be doing even though they will not take over and drive themselves. Often I am asked what do the others do while one person is working on their awareness. They may be observing the scenery, studying the driver, noticing their own reactions, crying, out to lunch—all ways of indicating communication and relationship to their own needs and values.

The final technique which I find accelerates the process of growth is work in voluntary fashion without pressure for people to change. Growth is not a process to be pushed without disastrous results. This is best expressed by the story of the butterfly.

I remember one morning when I saw a cocoon in the bark of a tree
I remember I marvelled that imprisoned inside was a butterfly waiting to be free

I was very impatient so I warmed the cocoon with the breath of my sighs
And the butterfly trembled as he began to emerge like a miracle right before my eyes

All at once I discovered that his delicate wings were all crumpled and torn
When he still wasn't ready I had made him be born

I was stronger than nature and I made him be born

But the wonder of life has a definite plan
So he died in my hands
By the will not of God
But of man

Every man has moment and I'm waiting for mine when I am finally free

But I mustn't be hurried
Give me life
Give me time
Like the butterfly

Refrain:

Not so fast Not so fast
Let it grow Let it last
Nature knows when and why
Think about the story of the butterfly*

REFERENCE

Kriegsfeld, M. The obsessive-compulsive personality: The case of Marion. In C. Loew, H. Grayson, & G. Loew (Eds.), *Three psychotherapies.* New York: Brunner/Mazel, 1975.

chapter 3

BRIEF USES OF HYPNOSIS

Henry Grayson, Ph.D.

A large majority of the population and even a significant number of mental health professionals continue to think of hypnosis as something magical. Instead, it is simply an altered state of consciousness, which is a very natural and easily learned human process.

While there are many levels of induction in hypnosis, we are only concerned with the lighter trance states for short-term uses of hypnosis. For long-term uses of hypnosis such as in hypnoanalysis or in the recall of deeply repressed memories one might need to do work to obtain deeper and deeper hypnotic levels. For short-term uses, however, all that is necessary is something more akin to the hypnogogic state, which is that natural state most everyone experiences just as they are beginning to doze off to sleep—that state that is halfway between sleeping and waking. It is characterized often by a light floating sensation in some people or in others it might be more of a feeling of weightedness or heaviness in the body. Both are simply indications that the person is very deeply relaxed.

The value of working in this state is that a person is much more open to suggestion or to the input of various stimuli than he or she would be in his natural waking state. There are, of course, some exceptions, for there are some people who are quite suggestible in any state. For such persons we do not need to use such induction techniques as we will be describing, but rather we need only to find what suggestion or to what kind of approach are they highly suggestible.

For example, some may be more responsive to an authoritarian figure, while others may be more responsive to just a kindly, fatherly sort of person. Some may need the intensity of emotion, such as a strong confrontation. Others may respond to a simple warm caring suggestion. For yet others responsiveness can only be engendered in a trusting long-term relationship while others might respond best to a stranger.

The purpose of this chapter is to focus on a few short-term applications of hypnosis. The applications we will focus on will be: 1) hypnosis for the use of habit control, such as smoking and overeating, and 2) for the development of skill and the improvement of self-confidence and self-image. However, before discussing these specific applications, I would like to describe more generally how I introduce the hypnotic process to a client who comes into my office, and to relate several possible induction techniques that might be relevant to different kinds of personalities.

When a person comes into my office requesting hypnosis or when it seems indicated to me for a person that I have already been working with, and I suggest it, I am concerned to know what the client himself or herself knows about hypnosis. I would like to know what their associations are, what kinds of information or misinformation they might have concerning hypnosis, and what kind of magical expectations might be attached to it. I have found that the majority of people have been exposed to hypnosis primarily as part of a magic act that a stage performer carries out and so consequently carry with it feelings of magic and a loss of power for themselves. This misinformation causes many people to come expecting that the hypnosis will be a miracle cure and that I will be the miracle worker with them; or it causes other people to be frightened of it, and they fear extreme loss of control and vulnerability, thinking that I will do something to them that will be frightening or harmful. It is extremely important that such misinformation be clarified at the very beginning of considering work with hypnosis.

I view hypnosis not as something that I would do to another person, but rather I will simply teach the person certain techniques and skills which, if they practice them, they will simply do for themselves. It will be a state that they will create for themselves, thereby increasing their power and expanding their levels of consciousness rather than a decrease of power in themselves or attributing it to an outside person or source. I emphasize this point strongly and repeat it many times because I feel it is extremely important in the success of the use of light trance states in short-term work that the client take full responsibility for his or her changing. Contrary to the belief of many of my analytical colleagues, hypnosis is not a way of infantalizing someone, and does not, when used in the way that I am prescribing, put one into a more dependent state. In fact, it contributes to the exact opposite: the significant increase in ego control and responsibility taking. I think it is important that I make clear to the client that I am not going to work any miracles, that I will *not do to* him or her, but rather, I will simply teach him a process or a technique, which he can use in his own behalf as he chooses, and when he chooses. I will simply work as an instructor, guide, or tutor to aid him in the developing of this particular natural skill. Instead of giving up part of himself to me, he is really becoming more aware of and able to use another of his own resources.

Let us turn now to several induction techniques, which I will relay just as I would to the client.

INDUCTION PROCEDURE I

Just lie down wherever you would be most comfortable, either on the couch or on the carpet, whichever place you would find more familiar and more comfortable for you to relax. Give attention to making yourself comfortable where you are, be aware of any places on your body in which you feel any kind of discomfort, and feel free to move around or at any time to make yourself more comfortable. And give attention to your breathing, allow it to deepen, to become slower and more regular . . . slower and more regular as you allow it to deepen and deepen . . . and now begin to scan your body for any signs of muscular tightness or tension . . . start with the tip of your toes and gradually scan all the parts of your body . . . and as you come to any place where you feel tension just concentrate on that spot and gradually let the tension go . . . just let it relax . . . and as you relax that spot move on to another where you feel tension . . . focus on it and just let the tension go . . . relax . . . just relax . . . and when you've relaxed that spot move on to yet another . . . any other place in your body where you feel muscular tightness . . . and let the tension go and just relax . . . just relax . . . allowing yourself to breathe deeply . . . and regularly . . . and in your own rhythm . . . just become more and more relaxed . . . just relax . . . just relax . . . In just a moment I'm going to count down from ten to one slowly. And with each descending number you can become more and more relaxed, so that by the time we get to one you can be very, very deeply relaxed . . . as deeply relaxed, perhaps more deeply relaxed than you have ever been . . . Ten . . . just relax . . . just relax . . . nine . . . deeper . . . and deeper . . . eight . . . becoming more deeply relaxed . . . more and more relaxed . . . seven . . . deeper and deeper . . . and deeper . . . six . . . becoming very, very relaxed . . . five . . . still more relaxed . . . more and more relaxed . . . five . . . deeper and deeper . . . four . . . very relaxed now . . . very, very relaxed . . . four . . . deeper . . . deeper . . . and deeper . . . three . . . just relax . . . relax . . . just relax . . . two . . . deeper and deeper . . . and deeper . . . and deeper . . . and one . . . now finding yourself very, very relaxed . . . feeling so deeply relaxed . . . feeling so good just to be sustained by the couch or by the floor . . . requiring no effort of any kind . . . just allowing total relaxation . . . being totally relaxed . . . so deeply relaxed . . . very deeply relaxed . . . breathing becoming slower . . . and deeper . . . and more rhythmical . . . and you become more and more relaxed ... Now in just a moment as you remain in this deeply relaxed state, I am going to give you the suggestion that we agreed upon. I would like for you to repeat it after me, each piece of it, either aloud or silently to yourself as you may choose. But in either case I would like for you to repeat it after me, so that you are also clearly giving the suggestion to yourself (At this point I will begin to give the agreed upon suggestions, which we will discuss below).

Induction Procedure II

Another induction procedure is one that might be used for persons who have a little bit more difficulty in letting go, or who appear to have a bit more tension in their bodies, particularly in their face, so that this one variation might be added to the above technique in a useful way. It should be included after scanning the body for signs of tension, but before the use of the descending numbers:

I'd like for you to open your eyes very, very wide. Roll your eyeballs way back in your head ... roll them back as though you were trying to look at something on the top of your head or on your forehead ... Roll them back, that's it, farther ... farther and farther. Straining ... straining, as though you're trying to see what it is up there ... trying to see what it is on the top of your forehead ... as though there's a little speck there ... or something that you are trying to see. You're trying to see the hair on your head ... whatever it is that you're imagining, but strain ... roll the eyes back farther and farther so that you can see what it is that's there ... Straining, straining ... straining as you roll your eyes back ... back ... trying so hard to see. And now as your eyes just become so tired from straining, just let them come to rest ... let them close ... let them relax ... and just feel the peacefulness of your eyes relaxing ... just relax ... and feel the relaxation go through your whole body as your eyes relax ... just relax ... it feels so good ... just to relax ... to let your eyes relax ... and to relax all over ... just relax. Now once again, open your eyes wide, roll back your eyeballs again, once again trying to see what it is on the top of your head or on your forehead ... Roll your eyes back, roll them back, straining, straining ... roll them back farther and farther and farther . . . straining, tensing, straining . . . Trying to get them to go back even farther . . . even farther than they are now . . . Straining . . . Straining . . . Straining . . . Trying so hard to see what it is up there . . . Until again those eyelids become so heavy they just want to close . . . And there they come to rest . . . Just let them come to rest . . . Just let them relax . . . And feel your whole body relax . . . feel how much it relaxes as you let your eyes relax . . . Just relax . . . allowing them to come to rest . . . just allowing your whole body to relax . . . just relax.

INDUCTION PROCEDURE III

In addition to, or instead of the focus on the breathing, scanning for signs of tension, and the numbers—as in Induction Procedure I—you might substitute for any one of those, or add in addition to them the following:

Find a little spot on the ceiling or the wall in front of you as you lie in your relaxed position. It might be a little speck. It might be a little nail head. It might be a flaw in the wall or in the ceiling . . . But just find a spot . . . something that you can focus on that's very small and just concentrate on that. Don't take your eyes off of it, but just focus on that one spot. Concentrate on it, hold your eyes there, and don't let your focus move away. That's it . . . just focus on that one spot . . . Total concentration . . . just on that one spot . . . You might feel the urge to take your eyes away because they might be getting tired . . . but don't respond to that urge . . . just let your eyes remain totally focused . . . totally focused on the one little spot that you have selected . . . Just continue to focus . . . concentrating entirely just on that one spot . . . You might begin to feel a bit of strain . . . that's all right . . . just let yourself continue to focus even though your eyes might begin to be a bit tired at this point. Just concentrate on that one spot . . . and relax . . . Concentrate and relax . . . Don't divert your eyes away . . . just focus on the one spot . . . concentrate there and relax . . . just relax . . . Just continue to focus until your eyes become so tired and strained that they just must come to a rest . . . that you just must let them close . . . and let them relax . . . That's it . . . just let your eyes relax . . . let them relax from all the strain . . . let them close . . . let them come to rest . . . And as your eyes relax . . . feel your whole body relaxing . . . becoming so relaxed all over . . . the tension going and feeling so relaxed . . . feeling so relaxed (If at this point it appears that the individual needs some further relaxation instruction, this may be repeated or any of the ones described above may be added to aid in further deepening the relaxed state).

There are many other variations of induction procedures that could be presented, but I think these will suffice for the person beginning work with hypnosis. Variations within these can also be made, however, just in the way that you give the instructions. You may find that one individual will respond best to a very relaxed, slow, mellow kind of voice—one that is soothing—generally, most people do.

Occasionally you may find that a person is not responsive to this procedure at all, but is much more responsive if you are giving the instructions in an authoritative way. So, I might in a very cool, matter-of-fact, forthright way, simply tell the person to lie down, and to relax, and to give attention to the breathing. But I would say it in a manner that is much more brusque, much more direct, quicker, and almost as though I am giving a command. Occasionally you might find someone who will relax simply by your telling them to lie down and relax, and relax deeply. And with yet another person you might use none of the above procedures described, except perhaps to just continue to say, in a soft, slow voice: "Relax . . . just relax . . . relax . . . more deeply now . . . relax," and so on. You might continue this for five or ten minutes with nothing but the word "relax." Clinical sensitivity and perceptiveness on the part of the therapist will be necessary to ascertain which approach would be more effective for which person.

HYPNOSIS FOR HABIT CONTROL

Most people find habits of long duration very difficult to change. The habit itself might be expressing some emotional need that has not be yet been resolved from childhood developmental experiences. In such instances the internal conflict may need to be worked out in order for the person to be successful in changing the habit.

Second, habits may be continuing as functionally autonomous behavior, that is, they originally began in response to a childhood adaptation, but the need for the adaptation is no longer necessary. The dynamic need does not yet remain as a present motivating force. In such instances hypnosis can be most effective in the changing of the habit. I recognize the distinction between the two is often very difficult to ascertain. Sometimes the answer to the question only comes as the result of trial and error. It is also true that habits exist out of unresolved dynamics that might also be changed by way of hypnosis or other procedures with no ill effects, and often without any kind of symptom substitution, as has been previously assumed (Spiegel, 1967).

Some habits are more easily dealt with by hypnosis than others. Smoking, for example, is a much easier habit to control than overeating, because in smoking one simply stops the behavior and there are no ill consequences of it. However, in excessive eating, one cannot totally stop eating or else the person will starve to death. This makes for a much more complicated procedure and requires a greater length of time in working with such habit control.

First, I would like to give attention to the use of hypnosis for stopping smoking. When a person comes to my office requesting hypnosis to control the habit of smoking I will proceed as described above by asking what they currently know about hypnosis or what associations they have with hypnosis, and will clarify my perspective in contrast, perhaps, to the one that they bring as I described above. I explain to them that hypnosis is not something that I will do to them, but rather I will teach them the process that they can use, which will increase their strength and will power in a significant way in order to stop smoking. I might ask them to imagine an old-fashioned balance scale and one side is weighted down with stones representing the habit of smoking, and the other side has no stones on it at all, or very few, so that the balance is tipped totally towards one side. I explain to them that if they were to give themselves a suggestion in a normal waking state, it would be something like taking one of the stones at a time and putting those on the opposite side of the scale. And so it is a very slow, arduous process to take every stone, one by one, and move it to the other side of the scale, and overbalance the first side.

In hypnosis, however, by putting oneself in the deeply relaxed state, or a light trance state, one can take handfuls of those stones and place them over to the other side. This will significantly increase the person's effectiveness in exercising his will in controlling his habit. I explain to them then that what I will be doing is not changing them myself, but rather, I will teach them the skill that they can use to control the habit. I instruct them on the process of deep relaxation, of putting themselves into a light hypnotic trance, at least two to three times a day for the first week, and at least daily for the second week or two. After the first week they are to report back to me for one additional session. At that point, if they have not been successful in being able to use self-hypnosis alone, then I will tape my instructions during the session and give them a tape with my voice giving the relaxation and the instructions for hypnotic induction. Some persons may need this external guidance to help them focus for awhile, until they can internalize the process for themselves. Most people are successful in stopping smoking with no more than these two sessions. Herbert Spiegel (1970) has reported, for example, that 20 percent of 271 hard-core smokers have remained without smoking for over 6 months with only one session using the suggestion that we will give below.

Once these options are clear I will explain to the person the suggestion that we will use so that he will know the suggestion in advance. Then we will add to the suggestion anything that the person feels he or she particularly wants to be included in the suggestion. For the very beginning we are enlisting the ego involvement of the person in the process, even the taking responsibility in negotiating with me for the appropriate suggestion. The basic suggestion that I will offer is the following syllogism: *I really want to be good to myself. Cigarette smoking is harmful to me. Therefore I will not smoke.* If the person wishes to have any other suggestion added at this point, then we will discuss it. Some people, occasionally, who are concerned about weight gain, will want something to do with that included, such as "nor will I overeat fattening foods as I stop smoking."

Once we have completed negotiating the suggestion, then I will proceed with the induction procedures described above. When the person is deeply relaxed I will proceed to give the suggestion above as we have negotiated it together. When I have completed the suggestion, I will ask them to repeat it after me, either silently to themselves, or aloud, as they may choose, so that they are beginning to incorporate the suggestion as coming from them, not just from me. They will begin to develop the habit of giving themselves the suggestion while in the hypnotic trance state. Once we have completed the suggestion, first my saying it, then the person repeating it following me, I will give them the suggestion that they will be able to repeat this experience of putting themselves into this deep relaxation simply by giving attention to whatever the instructions were that we used. In this state they will be able to give themselves a suggestion, and it will make a strong impact upon them, one that will aid them in controlling the habit of smoking. Once we have completed this second suggestion I tell them that I will begin counting from one to three very slowly; they will become increasingly alert and awake and ready to carry on as they normally would with no side effects of any kind. It would go something like this:

> One ... you are becoming more alert now ... two ... you're becoming increasingly present and alert ... three ... and now coming back to the present ... fully alert ... ready to carry on as usual.

Then I will wait silently for another minute or two as they gradually open their eyes and begin to be present. If they do not start talking after a minute or so, I may start talking slowly to make the transition a very gradual one, not one in which they will be startled or shocked from their state.

At this point I will discuss with the person how they experienced the relaxation, how deeply they did or did not seem to be relaxed, how they felt in the process, and how they felt giving themselves a suggestion. I will further reiterate the need to relax themselves and give themselves the suggestion for at least two to three times a day for the next week and make an appointment for the following week. I clarify that this will be the final appointment and the only necessary one for stopping smoking. Some people may be astonished by the brevity, thinking they will need to come for a number of times, or want to become dependent on hypnosis. Instead of being seduced into this, I tell them that I have already taught them all that they need to know in order to be able to stop smoking. They now know how to give themselves deep relaxation instructions; they know how to put themselves into a light trance state; and they know how to give themselves the appropriate suggestion. We will simply follow up with one more session to make sure the process is going well and refine it in any way that is necessary. I do not tell them at that point that we will put the instructions on a tape if they are not successful in using them. I wait until they come the following week, and if they have not been successful then I will tape the instructions and explain to them that they may use those in the same way that we have described.

Hypnosis can also be used for the control of excessive or compulsive eating habits. In smoking the goal is to stop totally. In overeating the goal is not to stop totally, but rather to develop a different habit of moderation and a different choice of foods. I explain this difference to the person seeking hypnosis as well as the other explanations about hypnosis that every patient hears. This kind of habit control requires more sessions than trying to stop smoking. I think no compulsive overeater will be surprised by this statement. With these patients I also explore the attitudes and beliefs about hypnosis which they bring. I spend time clearing up any misconceptions about hypnosis, taking away any of the magical elements, and clarifying the personal responsibility taking. I explain in particular the importance of the use of self-hypnosis and the increased will power that the use of this procedure will add in the control of their habits. As with the control of smoking, I do not use hypnosis for aversive conditioning, but rather base the suggestions used upon a very positive, self-enhancing responsibility-taking based position. So, time is spent with the client working out together the nature of the suggestion and the exact content of the suggestion which is to be used in the very beginning and at subsequent times.

A first suggestion to be negotiated might be something like the smoking suggestion:

> I really want to be good to myself. Eating fattening foods and excessive quantities of any foods is harmful to me. Therefore, I will eat appropriate foods and eat with moderation.

If the person has binges with specific foods, we will probably include those specifically in the suggestion as foods that would be avoided. For example, if a person consumes a great number of cookies, we might say, "Therefore I will avoid quantities of food, particularly fattening foods, such as cookies."

In controlling one's eating habits it is extremely important in the use of self-hypnosis to go into light trance states at least two times daily, preferably four times daily: morning, noon, night, and bedtime. Sessions are usually spaced about a week apart at which time we explore how the person has been able or not been able to use the self-induction procedures. As with smokers, if the person has not been able to do the induction by himself or herself, then we will produce a tape of instructions, which they will take home and play for one to two weeks at each of their practice sessions, in order to integrate the capacity to produce a trance state for themselves. In a sense the tape serves as a temporary transition object for the client.

After one or two weeks practice a different kind of relaxation may need to be taught. One may need to change the approach in order for it to work better for a given individual, or the suggestion may need to be changed in order to fit the change and needs of the client. If a person begins to have difficulty with inappropriate eating at particular times of the day, or if the kind of foods change, or the settings or situations become clearer, these will need to be refined and to be included as a part of the suggestion. With patients using a tape, these new suggestions will need to be included.

Most people are successful in losing or beginning to lose significant amounts of weight by using this process. However, often a person may come to a plateau or reach a level of resistance beyond which they do not want to reduce their weight; or they begin to have trouble in controlling the diet. It probably means that clear changes in the body image are occurring that are producing psychological or social conflicts for the individual. In order for the person to be successful in continuing to reduce, attention must be given to these issues in depth. While they can be talked about to some degree, the use of hypnosis is also relevant in the working through of such issues. For example, as a woman begins to lose weight, she may begin to imagine that as she loses more weight she will become more sexually attractive. Or perhaps she is already beginning to get more responses or advances from men. While at one level she may find this exciting and desirable, on another level she may experience it as frightening. She may stop losing weight as a protection against the fears that this situation would bring up. We can explore this by having her imagining the various situations that might occur—both those that she would hope for and those that she would fear—and ask her to describe those in the most minute detail, no matter how rational or irrational they might be. Then, to deal with those aspects of the situation that may be more frightening, we can create an image together of an opposite solution and have her create it in the greatest detail while in the trance state. Initially I might describe it in detail for the client and have the client create the image silently in her own mind. Gradually I would have her create it out loud, so that I could hear the exact content of the imagery. While producing the positive imagery in this form, it will begin to counteract some of the negative expectations that could become self-fulfilling prophecies. But by creating the positive images repeatedly while in this trance state, the person will become more acclimated to the possibility of a new way of being. By this kind of practice it will become familiar and therefore easier for the patient to repeat while in a conscious waking state.

Another issue to deal with might be the body image change itself. A number of ways are valuable for the person to become accustomed to the change in body image. I might encourage the person to spend time looking in the mirror, both clothed and unclothed, to become aware of the changes that are there in the body. I might have the person take a picture of himself or herself when still heavy and take new pictures as the weight is lost and then compare them in the most minute detail. Motion pictures or videotape can also be used for this purpose. I also encourage the person to be aware of different kinesthetic feelings. He might even go through exercises with himself to note how he feels when climbing stairs, or when bending over to pick up an object, or when running, or when carrying things, or when engaging in sports. Women in particular are very much aware of differences in the way they feel when they are trying on clothes while shopping in a store. It is particularly relevant when they are trying on smaller and smaller sizes. I might also encourage the clients to touch their bodies in order to sense the difference, in order to feel the arms, the hands, the face, the thighs, the buttocks, the calves or ankles, and to experience the difference in the amount of flesh that would be in these various spots. Then while the person is in a light trance state, we might ask them to imagine themselves as even thinner than they are now and to imagine themselves in a positive situation. It can be useful while the person is in a trance state at home to continue this process of creating positive images in connection with imagining oneself thinner.

The work characteristically will proceed with attention varying from a focus on the food intake itself to focus on body image change and the psychological and social implications or consequences of such changes. Lack of attention to any one of these three areas can result in failure.

USES OF HYPNOSIS FOR INCREASING SELF-CONFIDENCE

To work on creating increased self-confidence in the client, the process is not much different than those described for habit control. While it may be a process that is target centered for a person engaging in a specific task, it may be used in conjunction with other forms of therapy or as an adjunct to ongoing therapy being carried out by another therapist.

The basic concept here is that we are constantly producing images inside ourselves in relation to specific behaviors we engage in. These behaviors may be positive or they may be negative, and often they occur without the person being consciously aware of them. The person will act on this image and to actualize it in behavior, not really knowing that it had originated in a fleeting thought or a fleeting image prior to the behavior. It is as though the person has been programmed like a computer to respond in a certain way, even to think in a certain way, and to image in a certain way, and then act on these thoughts and images. We can teach the person who is ready and motivated to use self-hypnosis to change this pattern in the ways that he or she would like. For example, a young man feels frightened and lacks confidence in meeting new women. Before going he may habitually create images of being rejected or of behaving in such a way that he will make himself unattractive or appear foolish, and then consequently act in such a way as to make this occur. With self-hypnosis he can learn to create an image of himself that when meeting a woman he is talking, walking, and standing in a confident manner and appears self-assured and interesting. He might even imagine himself saying various things that to him would be interesting, and would be the kinds of things that he would wish to say in an actual situation. Creating this positive image in advance can serve the purpose of getting an inner experience before actually engaging in the outer behavior, which will form a foundation for engaging in the new behavior. It is not unlike the principle of astronauts going through simulated flights in their rocket before attempting to take the actual flight to the moon. We in a sense are helping the person take simulated flights in his or her own head, which will then be incorporated gradually into the self-image of the person. Often, resistances to change may occur, particularly a desire to hold on and to act out old, negative images of oneself. These, of course, can be worked with in whatever therapeutic modality the therapist is skilled in using for such work. However, it can also be combined with self-hypnosis, which can speed up the process significantly in many instances.

Let me give an example of one young man, a pianist, who would find himself in the midst of his practice sessions with tense hand muscles and almost cramped at times, thereby making it impossible for him to continue practice. Occasionally this would happen before a concert, which would interfere tremendously with the quality of his performance. He was able to use self-hypnosis first of all in his practice sessions to create deep relaxation. I instructed him to engage in this process prior to starting his practice session. After relaxing himself, I instructed him to imagine himself in a very relaxed position in his most favorite place. It might be some place on vacation on a beach, or it might be in his favorite chair, or it might be floating in a water bed. The place needs to be the one that is the patient's own association to the deepest relaxation. After he creates this image in his mind, I suggest to him that with this feeling throughout his body, he then imagines himself sitting at the piano playing while continuing to feel the same kind of relaxation in his neck, shoulders, arms, hands, and fingers: to imagine himself playing, shifting back and forth between the image of relaxation, and the image of himself playing at the piano. After he goes back and forth between these images, say, 10 or 20 times, which can occur quite rapidly, then he is instructed to bring himself slowly out of the light trance state and to proceed with practicing. If at any point he begins to experience the tension again, he was instructed to stop practicing, leave the piano bench, lie down once again, and relax, and repeat the process of the paired associations just described above.

Once he was able to master this quite well while lying down, he then had to simply stop practicing at any point he felt the tension begin. But while remaining at the piano bench he was to create the same relaxed scene and pair the relaxing scene with the practicing and the picturing of himself practicing in this relaxed manner. Gradually this became easier and easier for him so that he was able to do it almost within one or two seconds, and eventually just with an instant thought in his mind.

One young woman had great fear every time she was approached by a man that she would like to meet. She found herself behaving "stupidly," playing dumb, and not at all showing her intelligence and her charm that was characteristic of her with her closest friends. As we talked about it, she stated that her main fear was that if she would behave naturally that the man would not like her. With some exploration we were able to see that she imagined herself behaving and feeling in such ways very often. This was particularly true when she was going to a party or to a bar where there might be an occasion to meet desirable young men. As we explored further we discovered that even as a man would approach her a negative image formed in her mind about herself and her performance. This would then become acted out as soon as the man approached her. By having her go into a light trance state and then to create images of herself functioning in the way she would ideally like to function, and to do this on repeated occasions, particularly prior to going into the feared situation, she was able to create a positive image of herself. As she created these images repeatedly in her own mind, they carried over into her behavior in a gradual way, which was gradually incorporated into her personality.

REFERENCES

Spiegel, H. Is symptom removal dangerous? *Am. J. Psychiatry,* 1967, **123,** 10.
Spiegel, H. A single-treatment method to stop smoking using ancillary self-hypnosis. *Int. J. of Clinical and Experimental Hypnosis,* 1970, **18**(4), 235–250.

chapter 4

A SYSTEMATIC APPROACH TO BRIEF THERAPY FOR PATIENTS FROM A LOW SOCIOECONOMIC COMMUNITY

**William C. Normand, M.D.,
Herbert Fensterheim, Ph.D.,
Susan Schrenzel, M.S.S.W.**

A major task for the professions concerned with mental health is to provide more adequate services for the poor. One approach to this task has been the establishment of new kinds of clinical centers, such as walk-in clinics, reported by Bellak (1964), Colemen and Zwerling (1959), Jacobson and associates (1965), Normand and colleagues (1963), and Peck, Kaplan, and Roman (1966). However, the danger exists that such centers will tend to follow traditional patterns of treatment, rather than to develop the new and more flexible approaches that are needed (Albee, 1965).

Since its inception in January 1962, the Walk-In Clinic of

the New York Medical College-Metropolitan Hospital Center has been concerned with these problems. The clinic serves mainly a low socioeconomic population and has been attempting to develop new approaches to meet the clinical problems posed.

Clinical experience in this setting has led to a reformulation of goals of treatment. The clinic undertakes to provide immediate professional intervention in a problem situation in which, to greater or lesser degree, psychological disturbance is involved. The goal is not to "cure," but to ameliorate symptoms and to re-establish the previous, more effective state of equilibrium or, hopefully, to achieve an improved equilibrium state. The intervention is limited to six visits, but referral for various forms of extended care is available.

The term "problem situation" is purposely nonspecific to indicate that the clinic is not limited to meeting crisis situations. Included among problem situations is psychologically disturbed behavior which is primarily a consequence of the nonoptimal nature of the environment in which most of our patients live. To produce disturbed behavior, of course, the environmental stresses must interact with the particular personality, and treatment dealing primarily with the personality organization is included. Nonetheless, the most effective therapeutic approach frequently involves changing the environment rather than changing the person.

In this perspective the concept of "intervention" takes on a broad meaning. The immediate, short-term intervention may involve primarily one of the various forms of brief psychotherapy, as described by Bellak and Small (1965), Coleman (1960), Rosenbaum (1964), and Wolberg (1965). However, it may also focus on environmental intervention. A wide range of such interventions is available: vocational rehabilitation, job finding, intervention with community agencies, to name only a few. These environmental interventions may be used alone, used as adjuncts to psychotherapy, or used as the major intervention modality with psychotherapy being adjunctive.

Thus, there are many different modes of intervention available to serve as the core of the treatment plan. Indeed, the number of possible modes of intervention is so great that it becomes a problem to decide which method of intervention would be optimal in a given case. The present paper is addressed to this specific issue: to increase the effectiveness of a walk-in clinic by providing a means for the systematic selection of the most appropriate intervention technique. To achieve this end, the authors have been experimenting clinically with a modification of the diagnostic process that would allow for such systematic selection.

THE DIAGNOSTIC MODEL

The model being presented has evolved out of experience in treating patients of low socioeconomic class, and it was formulated with the intent of avoiding two of the more obvious potential hazards of brief therapy. The first hazard is the reliance on an exclusively "common-sense" approach that ignores the knowledge of personality dynamics developed over the past half-century. Overemphasis on personality dynamics, on the other hand, leads to the second hazard (more common in psychiatric clinics at present), which consists of leaving out of account the hard realities with which the poor are burdened. This tends to restrict the interventions to traditional forms of psychotherapy, brief or long term, and the potential power of other types of intervention is lost.

To avoid both hazards, and to aid in selecting the optimal intervention technique, the diagnostic model that has been developed makes use of two different kinds of formulations for each patient. One is a dynamic formulation, which stresses the characteristics of the patient, of the environment, and of the interaction between them. The second is an action formulation, a working hypothesis, which is primarily concerned with treatment strategy rather than with the characteristics of the disturbed behavior.

DYNAMIC FORMULATION

The dynamic formulation is similar to that customarily made in a psychiatric clinic. It attempts to achieve an integrated survey of the current psychopathology and of the strengths and weaknesses of ego functions and of the current environment, including supportive as well as pathogenic features.

The formulation emphasizes the symptomatic picture and minimizes the genetic aspects. The emphasis on symptoms is mainly for the purpose of determining and describing target symptoms so that the goals of intervention may be concretely and specifically delineated. For the same reason a description of the equilibrium state that existed just prior to the current disturbance is needed. Often, it is not essential that the current problem be thoroughly understood in relation to past events. However, though often minimized, genetic aspects are not ignored. Sufficient history is taken to provide at least tentative conceptualization of the genesis of the current dynamics.

Perhaps the major change introduced in this dynamic formulation, a change more of degree than of kind, concerns the emphasis on the patient's current environment and life situation. Although the extent of this emphasis varies from case to case, a rule of thumb is that equal attention is paid to environmental aspects and to intrapsychic forces. This is necessary, not only because of the possible role of a nonoptimal environment in the precipitation of disturbed behavior, but because an understanding of the specifics of the life situation may be important in determining the appropriate intervention technique.

To help achieve the integrated survey of intrapsychic and environmental variables, the initial interviews were jointly conducted by a psychiatrist-social worker team. Despite the overlap in the concepts used by the two team members, it was found that the interaction of the perspectives of the two mental health professions did serve to bring about a more comprehensive formulation that maximizes the chance of ferreting out an avenue of approach to brief therapy. If a collaborative approach is to be used, the joint interview is an economical procedure. It eliminates the need for a second interview with the other professional and avoids redundancy in data gathering; and it shortens the time required for consultation between the two professionals without sacrificing the closeness of the collaborative effort.

ACTION FORMULATION

The action formulation, or working hypothesis, is derived from the dynamic formulation. The action formulation is intended to be an explicit blueprint for action, as suggested by Ewen Cameron (1953), and it describes the general strategy that is to govern the therapeutic interventions. It is basically a working hypothesis, stated in deliberately oversimplified terms, which attempts to relate intrapsychic and/or environmental aspects to the disturbed behavior (target symptoms) that is the major concern.

The working hypothesis is action oriented. No claim can be made that it is either complete or completely accurate. It is based on the dynamic formulation, which itself is limited. However, it is not intended to be such a completely accurate statement; it is intended to lead to planned and integrated action. If this action is effective, i.e., if it relieves the target symptoms and restores an equilibrium state, the treatment goals are accomplished. If the action is not effective, there is the option of formulating a new working hypothesis, which leads to a different set of planned and integrated interventions. Thus, the therapeutic strategy may be deliberately and systematically changed.

The main point to note is that, although it is framed in terms of the patient and his life situation, the working hypothesis is not primarily about the patient. It is the dynamic hypothesis that attempts to explain the patient. The working hypothesis is about the therapeutic plan and the strategy and tactics to be used.

An aid to action, the working hypothesis is formulated in terms of one of four "levels": situational variables, ego functions, emotional conflicts, and character structure. While it is evident that all four levels are significant in every patient, it must be remembered that the working hypothesis is not primarily about the patient. The purpose of this conceptual tool is to indicate where the major, although not necessarily the exclusive, intervention will take place. It indicates the core of the therapeutic tactics, for each level "connects" with a different kind of intervention.

The terms that designate the levels are used in their common meanings and do not need elaboration except perhaps in the case of "ego functions." With reference to the action hypothesis, the term refers to tactics that involve support, modification, or strengthening of specific ego functions, including both autonomous functions and mechanisms of defense. An example is given below in which a defense mechanism was restored to effective functioning. Another example involves counseling a profoundly homosexual young Negro woman to obtain training with which she could get a desired job. This played a part in relieving the depression with which she had presented herself and contributed to a better adaptation in her generally troubled life setting. Ego defects based on organic disorders often are formulated at this level. These various types of ego disorders are treated by generally similar tactics, which involve various means of improving particular ego functions or recognition and acceptance of ego defects. Frequently, adjunctive interventions in the environment help to achieve or reinforce the desired changes.

Selection of the other levels also tends to lead to specific types of intervention. A formulation at the "environment level" leads to environmental modification. In one case the core of the intervention was to find a new apartment for the patient. In another case, the husband was called in, and attempts were made to modify his behavior in order to relieve a stress on the primary patient.

A formulation in terms of "emotional conflicts" tends to lead to verbal psychotherapy, often brief insight therapy, as the major intervention. For example, a 48-year-old grocery clerk of Italian background presented with "attacks" of pain in his arms, accompanied by moderate anxiety. The initial interview indicated that the pain resulted from muscle tension and was a conversion symptom. It was determined partly by his attempt to struggle against his identification with his mother, who had "the shakes" due to Parkinsonism, and partly by his need to control his rage at his sister and brother-in-law with whom his mother (to whom he was pathologically attached) was residing. The patient was made aware of these concepts, and he stopped treatment after five visits, symptomatically much improved.

A "character disorder" formulation often serves to limit action in the Walk-In Clinic and may lead to the use of chemo-therapy for symptom amelioration as the primary mode of intervention or to immediate referral for long-term treatment, analytic or supportive, or to referral to a social agency for long-term casework. In these cases it has been found that ser-vice can sometimes be rendered to other members of the pa-tient's family in helping them to cope with the problems that arise from the patient's disturbance.

It must be noted that action is not limited to the single indicated level. However, when action is taken at another level, this is supplementary or ancillary to the main core of action at the level indicated by the hypothesis. In this way the integrated nature of a whole series of actions is maintained and coordi-nated.

In the conceptual model presented, a series of interven-tions are at the disposal of the therapist to help reach the goal of relieving target symptoms and restoring a state of equilib-rium. A modification of the diagnostic process allows for a systematic choice of the intervention technique to be used and for the integration of different interventions. The model may be clarified, and its strengths and weaknesses more specifically illustrated, by considering its use in a particular case. The case chosen is not the most dramatic nor the most successful in the authors' series, but it is typical of the severe social and psychological pathology with which the clinic deals and of the setting up and achieving of limited goals.

CASE ILLUSTRATION

The patient was a 31-year-old Negro woman, separated from her husband, with one child. She was very anxious and tense and was frightened that she was going crazy. These symptoms were precipitated when the guidance counselor at her child's school told her that her child was disturbed, that the disturbance was because the mother spent so little time with the child, and that for the sake of the child she must stop working. This meant that she had to apply for Welfare. The symptoms appeared during her last day of work and rapidly exacerbated.

The history revealed that she was the oldest of nine children and was brought up in the South. When she was twelve, her mother moved to the North leaving her to care for the family with little help from the father. Five years later the patient herself moved North, worked hard for long hours, and eventually brought up four of her siblings and put them through school. She had married at the age of 19 and one year prior to her present disturbance had separated from her husband because he had been drinking excessively for some time and she had become "fed up." During the marriage, there had been an incident where she had been in jail for several days for stabbing her husband. Just prior to the current disturbance, she had been employed as a laundry worker and had to travel an hour each way to work. She would leave home at seven in the morning and return home at seven in the evening, while her six-year-old son was left to cope for himself. During the evening, she would speak to friends on the telephone, an activity she would have to give up when she went on Welfare. The clinical evidence, including brief evaluation by a psychologist, indicated that she had a basically psychotic personality and was presently decompensating.

The dynamic formulation stressed her unresolved dependency needs, feelings of deprivation, and the resulting rage and guilt, her intense fear of loss of control of her aggressive impulses, and the consequent danger to herself or her son. These, combined with difficulties in sexual identification, made the role of woman and mother intolerable. Her work and the telephone partially removed her from this role and at the same time helped her to maintain the image of being good. Ego strengths and environmental support were not very adequate.

The need to work in order to maintain her compensation and the need to be good served as the basis for the action formulation. What was implied by the school authorities was that she would be a "bad" mother if she did not stop working. This is what made her give up her job. Possibly she felt guilty about even wanting to work. It was the equation that work equals being bad that made it impossible for her to use this much-needed defensive technique and that set off the decompensation.

The formulation was made at the level of ego functions, and counseling became the major intervention technique. The aim of the counseling was to reassure her that she wasn't bad because she wanted to work and that she could be "good" if she worked part time (for contact with the school guidance counselor did indeed indicate that her child had severe problems). Ancillary action was taken at the environmental level through intervention with other agencies, but this was still based on the core concept of breaking down the equation that work equals bad. An employment agency was contacted to help her find a job. The social worker made this contact rather than having the patient make it, for the intent was to demonstrate in action what had been said in words: that it was all right to work. The school counselor was contacted and the patient's need to work was explained. This served to remove the reinforcement of the work-bad equation.

In the second interview a few days later, she was compensated and did not want to return for further treatment. The ego defense was restored and the former equilibrium re-established. An attempt at a follow-up contact was made several months later, but the patient had moved and direct communication could not be established. However, it was learned from the school counselor that the patient had sent the child to live with her mother, who could spend more time with him, and that she herself had returned to full-time work. The fate of the child could not be followed up in this case although obviously important from the viewpoint of prevention (an important aspect of the walk-in clinic, but beyond the scope of this paper).

DISCUSSION

Although in this instance the target symptoms were ameliorated and the previous equilibrium (somewhat changed) was restored, it does not mean that the working hypothesis was verified. It appears that the therapeutic intervention did restore a previously effective ego defense, but it is difficult to be certain what made the treatment effective. However, the working hypothesis did contribute an organized focus of activity. The contacts with outside agencies were coordinated with the goals of the counseling sessions. There was even a basis provided for deciding whether the patient or the social worker should contact the employment agency.

Implicit in the model that has been presented are concepts of limited goals and of a treatment approach that does not follow the psychoanalytic treatment model (though psychoanalytic theory is used in formulations) but that is comparable to the way in which people use a family doctor. Treatment is geared to the presenting problem, and often is not definitive. The patient feels better and stops coming. The illness may recur and the patient can return for additional therapy; or exacerbations in the course of a chronic disorder can be dealt with as they occur. This is consistent with the desires and expectations of most of our patients. In the case presented, the patient terminated before the therapists were ready to stop, a common event in the Walk-In Clinic.

This frame of reference makes it easier for the therapist to help the patient. One of the strengths of the model is its influence on the therapist. Often a therapist dealing with poor people feels overwhelmed, particularly when hit with the real problems of living under deprived circumstances. Depression, a common symptom in this clinic, may serve as an example.

Typically, the depression stems from the ego's awareness of inability to cope (Bibring, 1953). Low socioeconomic status contributes essentially to this depressive process. In the developmental phases deprivation fosters ego weaknesses, and the forces with which the adult ego cannot cope are frequently in themselves overwhelming. Thus the psychodynamic forces are intimately associated with the environmental circumstances and the therapist himself may see no way to deal with the problems. Hence, the therapist himself begins to feel frustrated and helpless in facing what appears a limitless sea of irremediable misery and may detach himself from his patients or continually set goals that cannot possibly be achieved. What the diagnostic model does is to structure the clinical situation for the therapist. It sets limits that permit him to direct his action meaningfully to what is possible and feasible.

A difficulty arises from the fact that therapists are usually analytically trained and oriented. Many years have been spent in sensitizing themselves to the expressions of emotional conflict and character structure. Person-environment interactions tend to be interpreted in a way that illuminates intrapsychic processes, and working hypotheses tend to be formulated at the "emotional conflict" level and psychotherapy chosen as the optimal treatment method. The model presents two barriers to this stereotyped approach. The fact that other levels must be considered with each working hypothesis tends to bring about a more flexible approach; and the fact that the social worker is present for the purpose of stressing the environmental-social perspective, whether or not the social worker himself has been trained in psychotherapy or psychoanalysis, also leads toward a greater flexibility.

A possible weakness of the model lies in the absence of explicit guiding principles for the selection of the level to use in the action formulation. However, the problem situations are variegated and complex and specific principles might restrict the flexibility of action. The careful evaluation by the joint psychiatrist-social worker interview of the strengths and weaknesses of both ego and environment does facilitate finding a course of action that is possible in the circumstances.

Although a diagnostic model has been presented, reference has also been made to the limited-goal, professional-intervention type of brief therapy that it serves to coordinate and guide. Both the diagnostic and the treatment methods are part of the emerging pattern of new kinds of engagements that are developing between mental health professionals and the poor they are now attempting to serve. The treatment techniques in themselves are not new. What is new is the attempt to facilitate their systematic and flexible use as an aid to providing high-quality mental health services to the poor.

REFERENCES

Albee, G. No magic here. *Contemp. Psychol.,* 1965, **10,** 497–498.

Bellak, L. *Handbook of community psychiatry and community mental health.* New York: Grune & Stratton, 1964.

Bellak, L. & Small, L. *Emergency psychotherapy and brief psychotherapy.* New York: Grune & Stratton, 1965.

Bibring, E. The mechanism of depression. In Phyllis Greenacre (Ed.), *Affective disorders.* New York: International Universities Press, 1953.

Cameron, E. A theory of diagnosis. In H. Hoch & J. Zubin (Eds.), *Current problems in psychiatric diagnosis.* New York: Grune & Stratton, 1953.

Coleman, M. D. Emergency psychotherapy. In J. Masserman (Ed.), *Progress in psychotherapy,* Vol. V. New York: Grune & Stratton, 1960.

Coleman, M. D. & Zwerling, I. The psychiatric emergency clinic—a flexible way of meeting community mental health needs. *Amer. J. Psychiat.,* 1959, **115,** 980–984.

Jacobson, G., Wilner, D., Marley, W., Schneider, S., Strickler, M., & Somner, G. The scope and practice of an early-access brief treatment psychiatric center. *Amer. J. Psychiat.,* 1965, **121,** 1176–1182.

Normand, W., Fensterheim, H., Tannenbaum, G., & Sager, C. The acceptance of the psychiatric walk-in clinic in a highly deprived community. *Amer. J. Psychiat.,* 1963, **120,** 533–539.

Peck, H., Kaplan, S., & Roman, M. Prevention, treatment, and social action: a stragegy of intervention in a disadvantaged urban area. *Amer. J. Orthopsychiat.,* 1966, **36,** 57–69.

Rosenbaum, C. P. Events of early therapy and brief therapy. *Arch. Gen. Psychiat.,* 1964, **10,** 606–612.

Wolberg, L. The technic of short-term psychotherapy. In L. Wolberg (Ed.), *Short-term psychotherapy.* New York: Grune & Stratton, 1965.

Part II

APPLICATIONS TO
SPECIFIC POPULATIONS

Depression, anxiety, and other psychiatric symptoms have often been the theme of many longer term therapies, sometimes having little success with certain patients.

Psychotics have often received only chemotherapy while hospitalized, which means that only one cause of the problem is being treated. Dr. Aiello's chapter offers another viable option supported by a solid theoretical base: the use of short-term group methods. New information regarding hypoglycemia offers much more speedy relief from depression, anxiety and other symptoms to certain patients, which is the contribution of Dr. Osterritter.

Therapy often can be shortened significantly if the whole family is involved rather than one patient who returns to the family with the same conflicts. Transactional analysis is the approach of the authors in Chapter 7, which they believe may further shorten the time for necessary interventions.

chapter 5

SHORT-TERM GROUP THERAPY OF THE HOSPITALIZED PSYCHOTIC

Thomas J. Aiello, Ph.D.

It seems that psychosis is a sad perogative of the human species (Mahler, 1968). To enter into the world of unreality can be a trip for some but when you feel there is no coming back, it is another story. The story, for the clinical population I work with, the poor disenfranchised minorities of the Bronx with meager socioeconomic resources, is grim. Our group lives on the edge of disaster in a rapidly deteriorating inner city. Family ties are frail, decent housing is scare, social resources are limited, decaying neighborhoods are expanding. The streets are not safe. The city is becoming psychotic.

Where is there hope for a psychotic in a psychotic city? The answer lies with each other. Group approaches to the treatment of the psychotic person, even though short-term, offer nurturance and support, which our patients have been deprived of all their lives. Group approaches relate to the core disturbance in psychosis, i.e., the absence of the mother's tending to the infant in a consistently satisfying manner so as to be need fulfilling and tension relieving (Mahler, 1968). Mahler has theorized three phases in the process of development: autism, symbiosis, individuation-differentiation. Failure of satisfactory development at the symbiosis hurdle, which involves the mother's pleasurable and satisfying relatedness and bonding with the infant so as to provide a "safe anchorage" and launching pad for "hatching" from the omnipotent system into the external world, eventuates in "faulty or absent individuation" (Mahler, 1968).

This is not to suggest that a developmental lag or fixation at the autistic level is less debilitating; in fact, it is more so. Passage through this phase requires breaking out of the autistic shell. The infant makes his initial bond to the external world by not yet recognizing the separate existence of the mother. A misstep in this process delays entry of the infant into the symbiotic orbit with its consequent pleasure and satisfaction (as opposed to frustration and pain) in relating to her. "Hatching" into external objects and the reality world occurs under the umbrella of the omnipotent duality that the mother/child union fosters. Mahler (1972) refers to this development of relatedness to external objects as a process of "spilling-over of his interest in the mother onto inanimate objects," (p. 335) which are associated with the mother. The dirty, smelly old blanket has reached its fair share of recognition by Winnicott (1953) and others for its contribution to the course of individuation-separation. While transitional objects are initially designed to maintain both heavenly bodies as one, they eventually become separate as a result of two basic facts of life: first, the mother's recognition and acceptance of their separateness, and second, the growing infant's experience of satisfaction and pleasure in the world of external objects. In essence, positive, nuturing infantile experiences are fertile ground for the internalization of growth-inducing processes that are precursors of differentiated and integrated levels of self and object relatedness. A bad, depriving, humiliating, persecutory life experience results in eventual isolation, decompensation, and a giving up of the self in search of a magical solution to pain, panic, and despair.

The psychotic process involves a fixation or regression to the symbiotic stage of development where primary undifferentiated self-object representations result in primitive splitting, fragmented identification, lack of awareness of ego boundaries, and impaired reality testing (Kernberg, 1976; Volkan, 1976). The depressive psychotic suffers from early severe disappointment and/or abandonment by the love object, coupled with a lack of belief in being able to find one in the future. The schizophrenic has grown up in an atmosphere of "emotional and spiritual poverty" with unstable parents who themselves were not capable of supporting the growth of individuation and stable identifications in their offspring (Jacobson, 1964). Under these conditions the only survival option is a wish for union with the omnipotent magical mother (good object) who will defend against the painful, destructive mother who is split off and projected onto an external object (Jacobson, 1954). Self- and object-identifications are fused and boundaries breakdown. Primitive splitting is a characteristic process marked by a remarkable lack of ambivalence; affects become primitive, intense and diffuse (Kernberg, 1976).

The eruption of a psychotic episode singles the collapse of a fragile structure in desperate need of repair. Hospitalization serves the purpose of removing the patient from a currently stressful environment into a presumably safe haven. The issue of whose benefit the hospitalization of the identified patient serves (i.e., spouse, family, or community) is merely being alluded to, since it does not fall within the scope of this paper to enlarge upon this theme.

When an individual decompensates, support and stabilization become the first order of business, and if motivation and ego-strength allow, rebuilding structure. This task begins on a small scale. The potential for increased growth and differentiation is limited by the realities of past and present social, economic, emotional, and hereditary predispositions. Since it is through the process of internalization that the development of stability and structures can occur, it follows that the basic condition required for recovery is based on the psychotic person's reentry into a symbiotic orbit and eventual "hatching" from the mothership into his individuated and separated path. The reader should bear in mind that I am addressing myself to a continuum of development, having as its end-point separation-individuation. It is increasingly clear that in order to avert psychosis, the symbiotic stage must be entered via autism, must be nurturing and fulfilling, albeit sufficiently frustrating to encourage passage from "lap-babyhood to toddler-hood" (Mahler, 1972). Blanck & Blanck (1974) succinctly summarized the basic characteristics required for growth through internalization processes (introjection, identification, and ego identity) as basic trust (Erikson, 1968), "good enough mothering" (Winnicott, 1953), and "in an average expectable environment" (Hartman, 1958).

It is generally accepted by psychoanalytically oriented group psychotherapy theorists that the group as a whole represents the pregenital mother figure:

> I have speculated that, on the deeper genetic-regressive level, the group entity becomes for the individual the symbolic representation of a nurturing mother (cf. such terms in popular usage as 'mother earth' or 'motherland'). In a broader sense, the hypothesis can be advanced that the universal human need to belong, to establish a state of psychological unity with others, represents a covert wish for restoring an earlier state of unconflicted well-being inherent in the exclusive union with the mother (Scheidlinger, 1964, p. 5).
>
> A group activates in the adult individual traces of the preoedipal mother image and the fears connected with it . . . (Durkin, 1964, p. 79).

We are immediately aware of the implications of this view. Internalization of the group as a whole can potentially engage a psychotic patient in another opportunity to reengage with the preoedipal mother. Indeed it is another attempt to recoup a symbiotic relationship and move forward developmentally from whichever level of fixation he seems to be stuck at in his unfulfilled symbiosis. Therefore, our model for recovery and growth through groups assumes that internalization processes will function to enable the psychotic person to interact once again with the good, nurturing, fulfilling mother, absorbing support, solidarity, and affection. Modeling oneself after group standards, values, and norms (the reality of the group), promotes the development of reality testing and a sense of reality for the individual. The rudiments of a self-concept and a fragmentary grasp of other than self-relatedness is promoted. Belonging to a group, commits oneself to a group by investing an incomplete self into a structured, cohesive, corporate body. "The group" conveys a sense of self: "my group is me." Group identification catalyzes individual identification. Reunion with a nurturing mother, creates another opportunity for support, stabilization, and ego repair. Furthermore, since this sense of belonging to a group is directly related to the concept of cohesiveness, we recognize its importance as a central unifying group concept in our approach to the group treatment of the psychotic. Frank (1957) defines cohesion as the attraction of the group for its members, a coalescing in search of unmet needs from a nurturing mother. The group as a mother symbol nurtures its members through mutual understanding, acceptance, and respect. This is its anchorage, which its members must achieve before they dare expose themselves to attempt at practicing their skills in the external world.

SELECTION OF PATIENTS AND TREATMENT ORIENTATION

The area of selection of patients is one of the most critical junctures in group treatment of the psychotic. We must keep in mind that most patients will be hospitalized and in the group only from four to six weeks (usually meeting on a three times a week schedule). The range of pathology is so extreme, the severity so extensive that careful judgment must be exercised in selection processes. Severely regressed individuals fixed in their autistic state cannot possibly develop a sense of belonging with people who have promptly recovered from their acute psychotic state. In addition, among the early recoverables differences emerge about an interest in integrating the experience, of becoming psychotic, into their lives or disregarding it as circumstantial. Indiscriminate lumping of diverse groupings leads to inactive, boring, depressing, and despairing group experiences. Hope is deflated in both members and leaders.

As we have suggested, adaptation to psychotic illness can be dichotomized along a continuum with polarities at integration and sealing over (McGlashan, 1975). The integrative response style conveys a greater degree of openness and curiosity about personal conflicts and anxieties. There is a greater sense of "interpersonal involvement, therapeutic engagement, and empathic interchange" (McGlashan & Levy, 1977). By contrast the sealing-over style is more close-minded and less aware of inner conflicts, tending to project them externally. They prefer to deny the experience, using it as if it were an isolated event due to external causes.

This three-fold classification suggests group approaches for each pattern of adaptation. Nonverbal, motorically-oriented activity groups, of not more than four persons is advisable for the severely regressed, autistic and symbiotic psychotic (Youcha, 1976). The focus of participation is to bring each member into orbit with another person, be it the leader, another member, and ultimately to the group as a whole. Since their lack of definition of the self is so severe, it is expected that the process of breaking through the shell is prolonged long-term work.

For those individuals engaged in sealing-over defensive styles, it is suggested they be placed in activity groups geared to working on concrete tasks and projects. Bondings between members, the leader, the group, and the activity objects occurs within the context of structured tasks. Within this framework, support and guidance is provided in dealing with frustrating situations, emerging in the natural course of an activity so as to increase their sense of mastery and ego functioning. Task groups can be distributed along ego function dimensions (Bellak, et al 1973), having as their goal the strengthening of particular dysfunctional aspects of the ego. Obviously these groups will not only benefit sealing-over people, since integrative and regressed styles possess dysfunctional egos as well. However, since these groups are not primarily insight oriented, it seems to be of particular advantage to the sealing-over style to be placed in this type of group. The basic function of structured groups is to confront in their particular way the ethos of helplessness, by successful activity, and solidarity, which is endemic to the hospitalized psychotic.

For those who are integrative types a group psychotherapeutic approach is suggested. Our goal is to enable the patient to increase his self-awareness and promote changes in the behavior patterns that lead to psychotic breakdown. By recognizing the symptoms and/or behavior patterns that occurred during the period of decompensation, we seek to provide the patient with initial insight into the cluster of forces that collectively precipitated his breakdown and thereby learn and practice adaptive changes in behavior required to alter a pathological course of events. When a patient informs the group that her depression began with a sinking feeling in her chest when she was concurrently feeling very much alone, we have achieved a major insight. This becomes the focus of our work with her, i.e., to help her develop and enlarge her circle of social relatedness by giving her feedback about the maladaptive social behavior patterns she manifests in the group that interfere with her achieving more fulfilling relationships. Opportunities are created within the context of group interaction for new behaviors aimed at acquiring more gratifying relatedness. In addition, particular emphasis is placed on her recognizing the danger signal for decompensation, e.g., sinking feelings in the chest, so she can seek immediate help in order to avoid a collapse.

This psychotherapeutic approach is focused on understanding the precipitating factors in the patients descent into psychosis. There are two sources of information we draw on to further self-awareness: verbal and behavioral. Behavioral awareness grows amid the interaction patterns manifested in the group. We assume, in line with Rabiner et al. (1970), that dysfunctional behaviors that lead to decompensation will be replicated among fellow group members. Observation and feedback are utilized to increase insight and keep track of these repetitive behaviors until they begin to yield.

Our goals are two-fold: to restore functioning and to help patients change dysfunctional behavior patterns. Neither should we ignore the goal common to all of our psychotic groups, i.e., developing cohesion and a sense of belonging and solidarity with a benevolent, nurturing symbiotic mother. Four to six weeks of hospitalization is insufficient to stabilize a psychotic structure; they require more sustenance. It seems to me that after-care groups are essential in order to help stabilize the patient and put an end to the revolving door pattern of admission, discharge, and readmission. When a patient has a beneficial group experience in a hospital, he will recognize its value as a treatment option when it is offered to him in an after-care facility. The positive transference to the mothering group, where he finally received the nurturance he required for stability, will spill over to the after-care group and be instrumental in his making a positive connection. I am afraid without this fusion, we can only expect repeated hospitalizations. The psychotic patient cannot be left alone. When isolated he will likely decompensate. He must reconnect with another symbiotic orbit in order to receive the kinds of satisfaction required for his stabilization and growth. I am suggesting that some people may require this for variable lengths of time until they can function on a more or less recovered, separate basis. Furthermore, we may reluctantly have to consider treatment over the course of a lifetime for those who simply cannot achieve a level of recovery that allows for a separate individuated level of functioning.

Leadership

When working with people who function on more regressed, disorganized, and primitive levels, group contagion can increase to a level where the leader himself becomes vulnerable to the relentless impact of extreme, deviant behavior on his unresolved personal conflicts. Consider that for the most part, the professional staff involved in direct service to patients is younger and less experienced. They become all the more susceptible. A helping hand is needed in the arena in the form of a co-therapist. When both leaders are compatible in their working relationship, mutual support is provided. One leader can take up the slack if the other therapist becomes temporarily incapacitated as a result of a severe countertransference reaction. The value of sharing perceptions in furthering understanding of dynamic and process variables as well as correcting distortions is vital.

From the patient's view two doctors are better than one so more help seems available. Since internalization is one of the crucial factors in growth, two leaders afford the patient different models to identify with diverse aspects of his self. When working with minority groups, leadership pairs who are ethnically, socially, and sexually different are highly effective. I recall the delightful exclamation of "God damn!" by a highly intelligent black patient who was confused and disorganized in his thinking, when he realized that one of the group leaders, a light-skinned black man, was also black. It was as if his being stretched across the room linking-up with the therapist. For a more comprehensive discussion of the co-therapy relationship than I can offer here, I suggest McGee & Schuman (1970).

A distinct advantage provided by a co-therapy team occurs when one member belongs to the inpatient staff and the other leader is on the staff of the after-care service. When the after-care service leader conducts groups at his home base, and his patients in his ward group are assigned to one of his after-care groups upon discharge, he becomes a vital link in the continuous flow of care from hospitalization to posthospitalization. This concept, with such intrinsic merit, is most difficult to implement when territorial disputes and status issues arise. (That is, in the hallowed tradition of psychiatry, the outpatient practitioner maintains higher status by clinging to his outpatient role.)

Specific leadership attitudes and behavior (including technical procedures) are indicated if we recognize that the psychotic suffers from serious limitations in the integration and development of his self- and object-representations. A remote, passive, and ambiguous mirrorlike leadership approach that promotes abstinence in an effort to become the object of transference distortion is ill-advised. The problem here is that this approach, which has its place with neurotic and high level character disorders, has as its goal increasing anxiety and promoting regression in order to work through early infantile conflicts, is grossly misplaced when applied to psychotics. They are much too vulnerable to anxiety and regression with consequent primary process flooding, which is the antithesis of growth and restructuring. This does not mean that we necessarily act as suppressors through supportive and psychopharmacologic techniques. But rather, we attempt to work through in the here and now the core conflicts that lead to decompensation through the medium of the nurturing mother-group. A balance must be struck between activity, gratification, and frustration. Actively reaching out to gratify a patient occurs within the context of promoting a foothold on a higher level of functioning.

Jane Z. in the midst of her anger at one of the group leaders (her individual therapist was the co-leader) abruptly left the group treatment room. Both leaders wanted her to discuss her feelings about her intention to terminate group therapy. However, she believed she no longer needed to share her problems with the group, since she now was able to confide in her individual therapist. Immediately after her flight from the group her individual therapist followed her, and both therapist and patient returned to the group together. Subsequent discussion brought out the group theme directly related to her acting out. How could she and other members, including two people new to the group, meet their needs in the group when they had to share their relationship with the leaders. The corollary of this theme is the question, can my peers help me? That is, is helping-power solely invested in the authority of the doctor-leader, or can it be distributed among the group members? By providing gratification of her unconscious wish, pursuing her in her flight reaction that is viewed as an attempt to have her therapist/ mother exclusively, she is encouraged to return to the group where she can begin to confront the conflicts she has in moving from "lap-hood to toddler-hood." For her to learn that fellow patients and peers can also be a source of nurturance and fulfillment she must be secure in the availability of her mother. From this example we can tease out two additional principles in the group treatment of the psychotic. The interaction pattern in the beginning sessions of a group is directed towards the leader that he accepts and absorbs, (promoting cathexis between patient and leader) and thenceforth redirected towards the group members (redistributing the cathexis of attachments between the members). Thus this patient's primary attachment is to the leader/mother, which she tried to make adhesive. As a result of this connection the leader is now in a position to influence her to move out beyond this dyad, into the world of peer relationships. In her effort to please and submit to the parental relationship, in order to satisfy her need to maintain the mother-child union, she is being gently pushed into expanding her horizons of relatedness and connectedness so that she will obtain satisfaction of her needs from her peers.

   The second point I want to make is that while we are dealing with transferential reconstructions of the early maternal relationship, the intervention (interpretive and modeling) of the leaders is focused on the present day reality of the patient. Hence, we do not seek to induce regression to full-blown transference psychosis, but rather to utilize the transference manifestations occurring within the group as a means of understanding and working through their conflicts in achieving object relatedness. Thus a depriving, nongratifying, passive, silent, ambiguous stance by the leader, (in its extreme form the Tavistock leader) while having merit with the better structured and integrated neurotic patient, seems to me contraindicated as a therapeutic position in working with the psychotic.

Beginning the Group

Groups are conducted on wards that are usually subdivisions of geographical units. This means that therapy within a group occurs within a larger system. The effectiveness of any therapeutic program, including group therapy obviously, requires that the leadership of the unit endorse and support the specific activity. Lack of support, or lukewarm acceptance is equivalent to a death blow, since the chief's ambivalence will leak through the ranks. Staff will consciously or unconsciously sabotage the project. Patients will not appear for group because an x-ray or lab test was inadvertently scheduled for the same hour, or they may be scheduled for activities off the ward, and so it goes.

Group sessions should be scheduled on a three times a week basis at the same hour, if possible. Frequency helps build cohesion and intensity. Given the brief span of time patients will be hospitalized, greater frequency of sessions per week increases the number of therapy sessions available for accomplishing the work that needs to be done. Sessions should be held regardless of the number of patients appearing for a given session. Since our patient population lives on the threshold of chaos and disintegration, regularity, consistency and follow-through are characteristics that help provide a stable structure for the development of safe environment which is nurturing and growth producing.

Group-centered theorists including Bion (1959), Ezriel (1950), Foulkes (1957), and Whitaker & Lieberman (1964) have enlightened us about the powerful influence of group as a whole on individual members. Their thesis is that an interplay occurs between unconsciously determined individual needs, tensions, and behaviors arising within the context of the group setting. This interaction promotes group development, which is influenced by the individual and in turn influences the person. Linkage of members occurs through the expression of common themes which become group themes, tieing together loose threads of thought, affect, and behavior (Ezriel, 1950). It is the elucidation and clarification of group themes, as they impinge on individual behavior, which facilitates group members inclusion into the group as a whole. This in my opinion is a powerful factor in the development of cohesion, since it recognizes a sharing of needs and conflicts. As intermember and member–subgroup or group conflicts are clarified and resolved, participation in the group becomes a positive experience. When intermember attractiveness increases, group cohesion escalates and with it the sense of belonging.

In connection with our understanding of common group themes, we have arrived at a point where we can describe the major concerns in a group's development. Bennis & Shepard (1956) indicate group members proceed from a dependency position through intimacy issues and eventual independence of the leader. Shutz (1966) theorizes three successive phases of group integration, which are recapitulated in all interpersonal relationships: inclusion ("in or out"), control ("top or bottom"), and affection ("near or far"). The basic assumptions of Bion (1959) derived from his work with study groups, suggests a high degree of overlap with the formulation of Bennis & Shepard, and Shutz. He suggests that a group is operating under any one of three basic assumptions at a given time: dependency, fight or flight, and pairing. The common denomination for these theorists is that the initial phase is characterized by dependency issues. The psychotic patient has been uprooted from his home, transported onto a hospital ward, locked behind doors, stripped of his clothes and issued unattractive hospital clothing, prescribed meals, eaten at preordained times; a schedule of living completely determined by external authority figures. There is no question about the fact that he is placed in a dependent position. These situational factors compound his sense of being overwhelmed by forces (internal and external) that he could not control. No doubt the matrix of the hospitalization experience determines his initial response to his psychotherapy group. He is made to, and does experience feelings of helplessness, loss of autonomy with a consequent lack of a sense of responsibility for himself. It is evident, therefore, that the initial concerns of group members is with the sense of helplessness, heightened dependency feelings, and a search for some benefactor who will rescue him from the persecution he experiences.

The search for a messiah can be utilized for its therapeutic advantage by providing a motive for the patient's enlistment in the treatment process. I am in agreement with Scheidlinger (1964) who considers all stages of group treatment with schizophrenics centering on the sense of strong identification with the group as a whole in order to gratify his wish for reunion with a nurturing mother. Along with gratification from the group, collective norms, values, and reality testing take hold and can influence him to recognize the necessity for his participation in his recovery process.

The hospital, the doctors, and staff are viewed as bad objects who are tormenting the patients and if only they could go home, back to the good parent, they will feel better. The dominant strategy of the initial stage is to engage the therapist in a rescue effort. I recall an initial session in which a patient's plea for help after vividly describing his terror and despair when perched on a ledge in a suicide attempt was greeted by a request for a day pass by the next responding patient. It is typical of the psychotic to respond to highly affective, anxiety-inducing material with concrete statements in a defensive response. I find it helpful to establish as a group norm the prohibition of requests for day or weekend passes and medication change in the group. These can be dealt with by the individual therapist after the group. Requests of this nature are individualized rescue effort strategies (which on a latent level may be transferentially significant) and are highly disruptive of group interaction.

The fundamental task in the initial phase is to provide the patient with a sense that they can be helped through the group. Their initial efforts to form a tie with the leaders are accepted, accompanied by the recognition that they too must participate in the helping process. Through his tie with the leader internalization and modeling of the leader's relatedness to the group occurs, which fosters member interaction and relatedness to the group as a whole. Hence, the patient begins to experience a sense of acceptance, not only through the person of the leader, but also from his peers. This is all the more significant, since peer acceptance is divested of the reservation-limiting therapist acceptance; namely it is an aspect of our role function. Peer acceptance makes other sources of gratification available. Nurturance and identification can spread from dyads to the group as a whole. This view of the goal of the initial stage of group development correlates with my original thesis; namely, the psychotic requires reengagement at the symbiotic stage of development in order to promote stabilization and eventual growth. In addition to this fundamental position, the therapist is attuned to the recapitulation of conflicted behaviors that lead to the patient's decompensation and begins the process of working them through within the group.

Troublesome Role Behaviors

Once the group is underway we can predict the appearance of specific role behaviors by individual members that can be troublesome for the group therapists. This discussion, while not inclusive, will be concerned with the monopolizing, disruptive, hallucinatory, silent, and potentially violent patients.

THE MONOPOLIZING PATIENT.   Invariably makes his entrance during the first session. We assume he suffers from overriding anxiety which he handles by continuous chatter and interruptions. His behavior is intended to absorb the interest of the leader and the group. Without this incessant activity he believes he would fade into the woodwork and disappear. Unconsciously it appears to be an attempt to incorporate the group before it can incorporate him. The group at one and the same time, welcomes him into their midst since it relieves them of their vulnerabilities and is turned off by him, and because they are excluded from becoming engaged with the group. Hence, the monopolizing patient is detrimental to the development of cohesion in the group; he must be stopped.

There are two alternative approaches to deflecting this narcissistic involvement: through the group members and by the intervention of the leaders. The former method requires the leaders turning to the group and asking them for their reactions to the monopolizer or interpreting their defensive posture in allowing him to go on and on. In the early life of a group, these approaches are not likely to succeed because the monopolizer acts out the unconscious resistance of the group to sharing the leaders and relating to each other. Consequently the development of the group has not yet jelled into a cohesive mass strong enough to thwart him. Due to these circumstances it is incumbent on the leader to actively intervene. He can do so by structuring the activity level for the patient. This is done by informing him that the leader would like him to remain quiet for the next 5, 10, or 15 minutes in order to give the other members an opportunity to talk, an explanation which is not demeaning and is quite acceptable to the monopolizing patient. The therapist must persist and be consistent in this intervention. If this technique is not effective, then seating oneself next to the problematic patient is suggested. The therapist thereby, gratifies the monopolizer's need to be at one with the leader. At the same time the leader can control the interruptions by talking to him, touching him, and gently reminding him of the need to allow others to speak and control his impulse to discharge his anxiety by verbalization.

THE DISRUPTIVE PATIENT. Our understanding and techniques for handling the disruptive patient who is so impulse ridden that he cannot contain his anxiety without external controls, directly parallels our discussion of the monopolizer. Repeated requests for cigarettes, coffee, and passes, and going to the bathroom, walking about, changing seats, attempts at leaving the group room, etc. are serious interruptions to the flow of interaction. To include a disruptive patient in a psychotherapy group is highly questionable, since his extreme narcissism is a serious threat to the development of cohesion. Placing two disruptive patients in a group is disastrous. Should sitting next to the patient and attempts at steadying him by touch fail, the leader may have to resort to asking the patient to leave the room for 5 or 10 minutes at a time until he can regain control of himself and reenter the group under those conditions. If repeated attempts at this technique fail, including lengthening the time span, one has to reconsider the patients suitability for the group. Whenever this drastic technique is resorted to, the leader should recognize the necessity to explore their reactions with the group and the designated patient.

THE HALLUCINATORY PATIENT. The task of understanding the confusion that accompanies the individual with a thought disorder, delusions, and hallucinations is made clearer when we recognize that the latent theme of the group contains the basic threat menacing each member at that given moment. If the leader identifies bizarre statements as attempts at communication, and as associations to the theme gripping the group, then we have opened a pathway to connecting with the patient who is presumed to be out of contact with reality. I am not suggesting that every statement is understandable, but rather the stance of the leader is one of openness and exploration with the confused patient. This model progresses to the group and acts as an inducement to include him in the group rather than isolate him in the withdrawn world of his bizarre ideation. When the leader's activity serves to integrate the hallucinating patient into the group, he will be struck with wonder at the reality basis of his idiosyncratic patterns. In addition, he will be gratified to see other patients relating to him, testing reality, and utilizing his association to expand their level of awareness.

THE SILENT PATIENT.   The silent patient represents the inclination in the group to withdraw into the autistic shell and not relate to anyone but oneself. He epitomizes the flight reaction from the anxiety aroused in the group as a result of interpersonal conflicts. The leader cannot afford to let this behavior style pass unattended. Silence with the psychotic person begets more silence. The same understanding applies to the silent subgroup and group. Long periods of silence are more than likely associated with withdrawal tendencies than reflective thought. For the psychotic, withdrawal and isolation which is reinforced in the group, can only lead to further dysfunctional behavior.

Again, the responsibility falls on the leader to intervene with the silent patient in the early phase of the group. When cohesion has developed, members may reach out to silent members, but the leader cannot depend on this occurring at all times. When members do seek out silent members it is incumbent on the leader to affirm this behavior. The silent subgroup or group must be challenged by the leader, since this is reflective of avoidance behavior in the group, which is self-perpetuating the longer it continues.

THE VIOLENT PATIENT.   With current medication practices and screening procedures for the psychotherapy group, violent patients are not usually encountered. What we do understand about violent patients is that their frustration tolerance is rather low. In a group setting, when they are not obtaining a satisfactory response to their feelings from the leader, a group member, or even the whole group, feelings of helpless rage can erupt resulting in a physical assault. We are witness to a total dissolution of the sense of self—feeling wiped out is at a low threshold for our poorly integrated patients. At that point the only means available to reestablish one's fragmented self-image is to become assaultive. In other words if a potentially violent individual is able to make contact on a verbal level, recognizing his being as a person, the need for contact through a physical assault can be prevented.

Attention must be paid to the need for response in the violent patient. This is his fundamental problem, learning to become aware of his needs and communicating them so as to effect a more satisfying response. This issue joins the violent patient with the group, since this is one of the fundamental tasks the group members must learn. In addition, it is important to explore the sources of threat leading to the unresponsiveness of the member or subgroup, and, when applicable, group as a whole. If the violent person's conflict centers around the leader's lack of response to him, and there is a reality basis to this perception, then it is important for the leader to explore his countertransference attitudes. The degree of self-disclosure by the leader can be limited to here and now feelings and thoughts as they relate to the particular incident. There may be some disagreement on just how much does one reveal. I believe the crucial issue is that attention must be paid to the patient's need for contact and this should be responded to on a reality basis. By recognizing the reality basis of the patient's grievance, the leader in one fell swoop furthers the working alliance, strengthens the differentiation of self from the object, and validates his reality testing and judgment. This kind of interaction captures the essence of corrective experiential learning which is vital for the violent patient and for the group members who of necessity share these feelings. Angry feelings and impulses do not destroy the object- self-identity but can have a strengthening constructive outcome.

Termination

It is inevitable, from a process point of view, that our last words be reserved for termination. Separation issues are extremely pertinent since the parameter, which we are continuously facing in dealing with the hospitalized psychotic, is the short-term treatment program. Discharge from the hospital, which has been so eagerly sought, is now looked upon with dreaded anticipation. It should be obvious to the reader that the specter of separation, reviving feelings of loss, abandonment, and frustration, ruptures the fragile structure of the fragmented self. Since our patients at discharge are in the midst of a process of repair through "therapeutic symbiosis" (Searles, 1973), it is not surprising that intense feelings are aroused. Psychotic patients manifest the average person's vulnerabilities in extremes. Separation and loss are perhaps life's most stressful events. Particularly for the psychotic, separation hits hard.

Separation issues revolve about being able to survive in the external world. Some deny any possibility of threat about leaving the group and hospital and reentering their social milieu. Others are clearly frightened, feeling they are going into an environment they could not cope with when they entered the hospital. Still others feel more optimistic on a realistic basis, about their abilities to adapt to the external world. All face the loss of the symbiotic mother and as I have discussed, require after-care treatment in groups.

The focus of the leader's interventions in dealing with termination issues is to relate to the anxieties aroused as a result of separation. This applies to the departing member as well as those left behind. This is a crucial juncture when separation anxiety is heightened and after-care treatment can be sold to the patients. Its endorsement is recognized and pushed by the leaders who can offer the present group experience as a testimonial. The group as a whole can also be enlisted in this effort.

We take advantage of the positive transference to the group, which usually exists at termination endowed with healing power, to further the implementation of our therapeutic goals (after four to six weeks of hospitalization). We would be naive to think that stabilization and integration can be maintained without further therapeutic work. If the group is fortunate enough to have a therapist from the after-care agency as one of its leaders, then the transition to an after-care group is made easier.

For the group to lose its members (sometimes two or three patients leave within a week), poses a considerable threat to the very existence of the group. Patients who remain must not only deal with their ambivalent or split feelings about losing members who are highly significant as real and/or transferential objects, but also they must face the potential dissolution of the group. This evokes in those left behind feelings of anger, despair, and an overriding urge to leave the group. It is a painful reminder of the hurt that comes with losing the symbiotic mother. Patients talk of transferring to another ward or hospital, going home to their mothers or children, look forward to their own discharge, etc. in an effort to replace the lost object. In other words, they are in flight from the scene of a disaster.

The general tendency of departing and remaining members is to deny the reality of separation. It is startling to witness a member leaving and not a word is uttered by anyone, sometimes the leaders included—denial is rampant. It is so difficult to repeat what feels like the hasty or abrupt ouster from the omnipotent orbit of the mother. A patient who feels left behind wonders if he will be missed, if at his grave someone ("all I need is just one person") will be there. Visions appear of the lonely, desolate graveside.

The primary task of the leader is to confront the group with the loss of the members. Leaders who are susceptible to being overwhelmed by their own feelings of loss become desperate about the impending collapse of the group. They grow depressed and feel impotent and disillusioned about working with psychotics in an inpatient service. Vestiges of unresolved conflicts concerned with our passage through the symbiotic mothering period of our lives will make its appearance during these high intensity periods. Leaders may feel they cannot offer the group anything at the nadir of the group's existence. My rejoinder is that what the leaders can offer to the group is the group itself. Members die, leaders die, but the group lives. The group is the object with which they can remain cathected. In maintaining this connection the blow of separation is lightened. Members will resist reinvesting in each other and the group because of the pain of separation. Here the leader can serve as a model as he relates to separation issues by dealing with them and simultaneously maintain his connection to the members and the group. The members need to know that the group will continue and after a couple of meetings by themselves, they will add new members. The leaders should declare their intention to remain connected and committed to the group. With this experience, patients will have the opportunity to learn that separation does not require the loss of the mother but instead a continuation of the growth cycle.

BIBLIOGRAPHY

Bellak, L., Hurvich, M., & Gediman, H. K. (1973) Ego Functions in Schizophrenics, Neurotics and Normals: A Systematic Study of Conceptual, Diagnostic and Therapeutic Aspects. New York: John Wiley & Sons.

Bennis, W. G. & Shepard, H. A. A Theory of Group Development. Human Relations, 9:415–437.

Bion, W. (1959) Experiences in Groups. New York: Basic Books.

Blanck, G. & Blanck, R. (1974) Ego Psychology: Theory and Practice. New York: Columbia University Press.

Durkin, H. (1964) The Group in Depth. New York: International Universities Press.

Erikson, E. H. (1968) Identity Youth and Crisis. New York, W. W. Norton.

Ezriel, H. (1973) Psychoanalytic Group Therapy. In: Group Therapy, 1973, An Overview, ed. L. Wolberg and E. K. Schwartz. New York: Intercontinental Medical Book Corp., pp. 183–210.

Foulkes, S. H. (1957) Group Analytic Dynamics with Specific Reference to Psychoanalytic Concepts, International Journal of Group Psychotherapy, 7:40–52.

Frank, J. D. (1957) Some Determinants, Manifestations, and Effects of Cohesiveness in Therapy Groups. International Journal of Group Psychotherapy, 7:53–63.

Hartmann, H. (1958) Ego Psychology and the Problem of Adaptation. New
York: International Universities Press.

Jacobson, E. (1954) Contribution to the Metapsychology of Psychotic Identification. J. American Psychoanalytic Association, 1:239–262.

———. (1964) The Self and the Object World. New York: International
Universities Press.

Kernberg, O. (1976) Object Relations Theory and Clinical Psychoanalysis.
New York: Jason Aronson.

Leopold, H. S. (1976) Selective Group Approaches with Psychotic Patients
in Hospital Settings. American Journal of Psychotherapy, 30:95–102.

Mahler, M. S. (1968) On Human Symbiosis and the Viscussitudes of Individuation. New York: International Universities Press.

———. (1972) On the First Three Subphases of the Separation-Individuation
Process. International Journal of Psychoanalysis, 53:333–338.

McGee, T. F. & Schuman, B. N., The Nature of the Co-therapy Relationship.
(1970) International Journal of Group Psychotherapy, 20, 25–36.

McGlashan, T. H., Levy, S. T. & Carpenter, W. T. (1975) Integration and
Sealing-over: Clinically District Recovery Styles from Schizophrenia.
Archives General Psychiatry, 32:1269–1272.

McGlashan, T. H. & Levy, S. T., (1977) Sealing-over in a Therapeutic Community. Psychiatry, 40:55–65.

Rabiner, E. L., Wells, C. F. & Yager, J. (1970) Psychiatric Admitting Units:
A Critique and Proposal for Their Rehabilitation. Unpublished manuscript.

Scheidlinger, S. (1964) Identification, The Sense of Belonging and of Identity
in Small Groups. International Journal of Psychotherapy, 14:291–306.

Schutz, W. C. (1966) The Interpersonal Underworld. Palo Alto: California
Science & Behavior Books.

Searles, H. F. (1973) Concerning Therapeutic Symbiosis. In: The Annual of
Psychoanalysis. New York Quadrangle. The New York Times Book Co.

Volkan, V. (1976) Primitive Internalized Object Relations. New York: International Universities Press.

Whitaker, D. S. & Lieberman, M. A. (1965) Psychotherapy Through the
Group Process. New York: Atherton Press.

Winnicott, D. W. (1953) Transitional Objects and Transitional Phenomena.
International Journal of Psychoanalysis, 34:89–97.

Youcha, I. Z. (1976) Short-term In-Patient Group Formation and Begin-
nings. Group Process, 7, 119–137.

chapter 6

HYPOGLYCEMIA

John F. Osterritter, M.D., M.P.H., Ph.D.

Hypoglycemia is defined as an abnormally diminished amount of glucose in the blood. Usually, however, the term is used more generally to refer to the complexity of symptoms, a syndrome, that occurs when the central nervous system is deprived of the amount of glucose it needs to function normally. It sometimes is called neuroglypenia, reflecting the insufficient supply of glucose to the nervous tissue. Its symptoms may be somatic and psychic.

Hypoglycemia can be classified in many ways as to etiology and the classifications are as numerous as the authors writing on the subject. For the purpose of this presentation it is sufficient to divide its etiology into two categories, organic and reactive. An anatomic lesion or disease frequently can be identified in the organic form while in the reactive variety a demonstrable pathologic defect may not be apparent; however, some malfunction of the normal physiology does exist. Only functional hypoglycemia, one of the reactive types, is consid-

ered here.* The term "functional" in medicine is a euphemism
meaning the cause is unknown. Some consideration of a probable etiology of functional hypoglycemia is discussed later.

Functional hypoglycemia is rejected as a clinical diagnosis
by many clinicians, both physicians and psychologists. Some

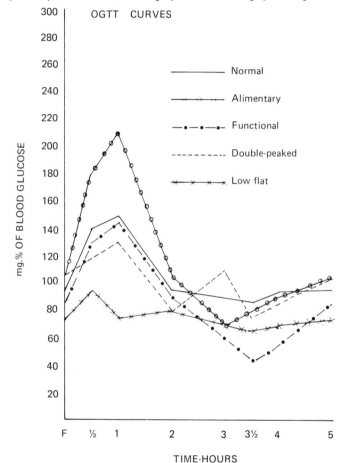

Figure 6–1. Curves of functional hypoglycemia and a normal.

*Figure 6-1 shows a normal 5 hr. glucose tolerance curve and four
different types of curves often found in reactive hypoglycemia.

consider it a rare disorder, one not likely to be discovered with any regularity in routine practice. Others interpret the results of an oral glucose tolerance test (OGTT) as a variation of the normal and because of the nature of the symptoms and the patients complaints they are called neurotic. Many of these patients may well be neurotic but by removing the physical or organic component of the illness they are better equipped to handle their neuroses. When patients in psychotherapy are found to have a functional hypoglycemia and it is properly controlled, they almost always make better progress in their therapy.

Hypoglycemia as an entity had been known but it was first described as a clinical syndrome by Seale Harris, Professor of Medicine at the University of Alabama. He noticed that some of his nondiabetic patients presented symptoms not unlike those of patients who had diabetes and had taken too much insulin for regulation of their blood sugar. This constitutes a state of hyperinsulinism. He made this observation in the early 1920s shortly after the discovery of insulin. In a 1924 article in the Journal of the American Medical Association Harris wrote: "I realized that I had seen many non-diabetic patients who had complained of the same symptoms: i.e., hunger, weakness and anxiety neurosis." Hypoglycemia can be described as follows (Rabinowitz, 1972)

> Hypoglycemia occurs whenever the input of glucose into the blood stream does not keep pace with the rate of its removal by peripheral tissues. Nervous tissues are exceedingly dependent upon an adequate and continuous supply of glucose for the maintenance of normal function. Consequently, the most dramatic manifestations of hypoglycemia, whatever its cause, are usually neurologic and psychiatric. Hypoglycemic episodes can mimic almost every neurologic and psychiatric disorder: local nerve palsies; hemiplegia; paraplegia; convulsions; visual disturbance; episodes of aphasia; thick speech, or prolonged sleepiness; restlessness; negativism; personality changes; emotional instability; maniacal behavior; coma; catatonia; and acute paranoid delirium can all be observed.

Williams textbook of Endocrinology (1968) refers to hypoglycemia as

> ... the most common type of spontaneous hypoglycemia, has been described variously as functional hypoglycemia or hyperinsulinism, nervous hypoglycemia, hypoglycemic fatigue, and reactive hypoglycemia. Persons with this disorder tend to be emotionally unstable, tense, anxious, and very conscientious. They have various manifestations of a hyperactive autonomic nervous system, including hypermotility of the gastrointestinal tract. Psychosomatic problems are common.

Note that 50 years ago Harris specifically referred to "anxiety neurosis" just as the current textbooks refer to neurologic, psychiatric, and emotional disturbances. Anthony et al. (1973) studied 37 patients with reactive hypoglycemia and found that they had significantly abnormal scores on the Minnesota Multiphasic Personality Inventory (MMPI) for both hysteria and hypochondriasis. Seltzer (1974) & Conn (1955) emphasized that functional hypoglycemic patients appeared to have an unstable autonomic nervous system as part of a general psychosomatic disorder and that they tended to overrespond to stimuli. Abrahamson & Pezet noted that they had an increased "sensitivity to external stimuli, crowds, noise, sensations of taste, and smell. Treatment affected reversal of these sensitivities. In 1966 Salzer, a psychiatrist, found that 40 percent of his patients had a reactive hypoglycemia which produced symptoms that mimic neuropsychiatric disorders, including psychoneurotic anxiety and depression and depressive reaction.

The refusal of so many trained clinicians to accept functional hypoglycemia as a real clinical entity becomes more significant when it is recognized that anxiety and depression as clinical syndromes outrank all other diagnostic problems in general medicine. Its incidence in the United States today is not known. Even an estimate would be nothing more than a guess. The Department of Health, Education, and Welfare in a response to a question regarding the prevalence of hypoglycemia answered the Executive Director of the Hypoglycemia Foundation with: ". . . unpublished data from the Health Interview Survey show that an estimated 66,000 cases reported in household interviews of the civilian, noninstitutional population during fiscal year 1966–67 . . . This represents 49.2% of those interviewed."* (See also Jung, Khurana, & Corredor, 1971.)

The signs and symptoms of functional hypoglycemia are numerous and varied. Any number of them might exist in any one individual, but for any one patient the cluster of symptoms tends to remain relatively constant. They result from the release of epinephrine from the adrenal medulla with resultant stimulation of the autonomic nervous system and the decrease of glucose to the brain and other nervous tissue causing a form of anoxia. Signs and symptoms of hyperepinephrinemia include sweating, headache, lightheadedness, hunger, weakness, tremors, shaking, cold moist skin, palpitations, confusion, irritability, and anxiety. Those of the central nervous system can be drowsiness and stupor, depression, insomnia, clonic convulsions, amnesia, visual disturbances, paresthesias, slow cerebration, transient hemiplegias, disorders of speech or gait, inability to concentrate, poor memory, inappropriate behavior, slow cerebration, and others. Fatigue, exhaustion, nervousness, irritability, depression, anxiety, and lack of concentration are the most frequent complaints of these patients.

The etiology or pathologic physiology of this syndrome is not clearly defined. Dr. Harris postulated hyperinsulinism as the cause and it did serve as a working hypothesis but this mechanism, while found in a few patients with functional hypoglycemia, is not present in the majority of cases. Furthermore, the psychic manifestations so frequently seen in functional hypoglycemia usually are not seen in diabetics with regular occurrences of hypoglycemia due to improper dosage of insulin.

Tintera (1955) presented evidence and suggested that the

*Personal communication with the author.

etiology of functional hypoglycemia might be a mild to moderate adrenal cortical insufficiency. The symptoms of decreased adrenal cortex function are similar and include fatigue, insomnia, inability to concentrate, restlessness, irritability, depression and apprehension. The association of depression and a relative adrenal insufficiency has been noted by several clinicians working in this field.

Marks & Rose (1965) make the following statement:

> The rate of transference of glucose across the blood-brain barrier is largely independent of the blood glucose concentration and is constant over a wide range. The factors concerned with and regulating the rate of transfer are still largely unknown, but it is known that neuroglycopenia develops at higher blood sugar concentrations in hypoadrenal and hypopituitary, than in normal subjects, and that neuroglycopenia, unresponsive to the elevation of blood glucose responds to the administration of hydrocortisone.

Thorn (1950) noted that adrenal cortical insufficiency causes the individual to be more sensitive to the action of insulin, and symptoms of hypoglycemia are manifested at levels of blood sugar higher than in other persons. There is substantial evidence to indicate that the corticosteroids or lack thereof have something to do with the etiology of functional hypoglycemia but the exact mechanism remains to be clarified.

Yudkin's (1971) observation on the intake of sugar and functional hypoglycemia is most interesting in view of the fact that practically all of these patients crave sweets and devour them in large quantities. He says, "We believe some people, but not all, are susceptible to a high sucrose intake, and we believe it acts hormonally." He found that high sucrose in the diet slightly increases the production of insulin but it increases the output of the hormone 11-hydroxycorticosterone by fourfold. This hormone is manufactured by the adrenal cortex. Yudkin is of the opinion that the adrenal cortex gradually becomes overworked and overstimulated while on a high sugar intake, and eventually it cannot cope with the overload and a relative adrenal cortical insufficiency develops.

The average patient seen in the office and eventually diagnosed as having functional hypoglycemia is young to middle age. Almost always they have been to three or four physicians who performed "complete physical examinations and blood studies." Usually thyroid hormone determinations have been made and sometimes an electroencephalogram performed. The vast majority are told that everything is normal except that perhaps the blood pressure is a little low; "you are fine," or "it's all in your head . . . just nerves," or they may be told that they are neurotic. Frequently psychogenic drugs either as tranquilizers or antidepressants or both are prescribed; many have been prescribed amphetamines. Usually they are advised to carry some candy or sugar cubes with them at all times.

The chief complaint of these patients invariably is fatigue; even after a "good night's sleep" they awaken exhausted and find it difficult to get up. They give a history of an intermittent feeling of lightheadedness, or as if they are going to faint, but never do. Their complaints are of fuzzy vision, poor memory, lack of concentration, depression for no known reason, rapid mood swings, behavioral changes, and hyperirritability. They describe a pressure in the chest just under the sternum with no radiation to the shoulders or arms, palpitations, abdominal or epigastric bloating, cold or sweaty hands and feet, and inappropriate periods of perspiration. As the symptoms progress they tend to withdraw from society preferring to be alone rather than with others, even those whom they especially like. Increased sensitivity to external stimuli develops. Most of them like salt and some have a craving for it often eating pretzels, potato chips, or french fried potatoes because of the salt and, of course, unconsciously also obtaining carbohydrate. Some patients will eat the salt plain, licking it from the snuff box portion of the hand. A large number of them give a history of diabetes or alcoholism in their families. Most have mild to severe allergies.

It is amazing how often they can identify the time when they first began to notice symptoms developing. Almost always they commence shortly after a period of unusual emotional or physical stress. It may be a death of someone close, a divorce, separation or broken romance, an illness or operation (infectious mononucleosis is often mentioned), a pregnancy, a very trying school term, etc.

The desire for sweets is common and almost all patients comment on this; most have a craving for them. They find early that eating something sweet helps to prevent the onset of symptoms and to relieve those that have developed; it "gives them a lift" for a time. But the feeling of well being is not sustained and a "drop" occurs leaving them worse than they were originally. Even following a large satisfying meal the need for something sweet can be overwhelming. A sugar addiction develops: they devour ice cream, cookies, cola, orange juice, and junk food for their desire for a quick lift is uncontrollable. Only occasionally does one find that the complex carbohydrates are used to satisfy their need.

Sometimes alcohol can fulfill this desire in these patients. This may occur very early in life. It is not rare to have them describe the intake of tremendous quantities of alcohol commencing at the age of 12 or 13. The enormous increase over the past several years in the sale of very sweet wine to young people is significant. Fortunately, many of them recognize that the large consumption of alcohol can be dangerous and discontinue it, then turn to the sugars. Alcohol itself is a hypoglycemic agent and almost all alcoholics are hypoglycemic. At Alcoholics Anonymous meetings the standard refreshment is coffee with sugar, pastries, doughnuts, or something similar. Honey or sweet fruit juice cocktails replace martinis and manhattans.

Reactive hypoglycemia can be classified as that associated with early or mild diabetes mellitis, "alimentary" hypoglycemia, and functional hypoglycemia. Patients whose blood sugar is elevated to a very high level, 300 to 350 mg percent during the first or second hour of a OGTT, then falls to a low point during the third to fifth hour are considered to have a reactive hypoglycemia which may be associated with or described as early diabetes. Alimentary hypoglycemia as the name implies occurs in people who have something wrong with their gastrointestinal tract, usually they have had a gastric resection. The OGTT of this form is somewhat similar to that of the early diabetic but the apogee may not be as high. This kind of hypoglycemia is being seen more often in persons without a history of gastrointestinal surgery and then must be considered as functional.

The OGTT of functional hypoglycemia does not fit the fixed curve of the other two forms of reactive hypoglycemia. Over the years it was generally agreed by those working in the field of diabetes that a blood glucose level of 50 mg percent must be reached before a diagnosis of functional hypoglycemia could be entertained. Now it is recognized that if an absolute level of blood sugar during a five-hour OGTT is to be diagnostic, that value is most likely 40 mg percent. However, it has been reported that 23 percent of the normal population will have a blood glucose level below 50 mg percent and in some instances the value may drop to 35 mg percent or even lower and the subjects remain asymptomatic. Whether this is to be interpreted as a variation of the norm or the OGTT of asymptomatic functional hypoglycemia is an open question.

The patient with functional hypoglycemia will display signs or experience symptoms during the five-hour OGTT somewhat similar to those that he experiences in everyday life. It is not necessary for an absolute low blood glucose level to be reached; a relative low level from a previous high one can produce symptomatology. A decrease of blood glucose of 100 mg percent within one-half to one hour of a previous high can cause symptoms to develop. In some instances the nadir may be no lower than 70 mg percent or even higher. Thus rapid drops in the blood glucose as well as absolute lows is significant in diagnosing functional hypoglycemia. Usually the fasting is normal, and an apogee is reached within the first one-half to one hour of the onset of the OGTT and a nadir lower by 100 mg percent or more is reached by three to three and one-half hours. Frequently symptoms occur about this time. A typical curve of functional hypoglycemia is characterized by a normal fasting blood sugar and sometime within the five hours of the OGTT there is a decline in the blood glucose followed by a rebound eventually approaching the fasting level. The decline usually occurs between the second and fourth hours but may appear as early as the half hour. A decrease of blood glucose 20 mg percent below the fasting level anytime during the OGTT is considered by some as a curve of functional hypoglycemia.

A low flat curve is occasionally seen, so called because of its appearance. the fasting blood sugar is normal, but after the glucose is ingested the zenith of the curve may not be more than 10 to 20 mg percent above the fasting level at the first hour. It then falls to the fasting value or a little below and meanders aimlessly throughout the five hours with little fluctuation. This is sometimes interpreted as a normal curve, but if the subject has symptoms during the test it is a functional hypoglycemia curve.

It is possible to have a functional hypoglycemia and yet show a normal OGTT. "The subjects vary periodically in their emotional reactions, eating habits, etc. and consequently different types of glucose curves may be obtained at different times, even in the same subject. It may be necessary to perform several glucose tolerance tests, each lasting 4 to 5 hours to demonstrate the hypoglycemia" (Williams, 1968). A patient may develop symptoms during the test and a hypoglycemia per se may not be recorded on the curve. If the history of this kind of patient is suggestive of functional hypoglycemia and the diet is poor, dietary therapy should be tried.

If the OGTT is to be meaningful it must be performed accurately. In preparation for the test a diet that is high in carbohydrates, 250 to 300 grams per day, is eaten for two and preferably three days before the test. Medication and cigarettes are prohibited from the onset of the fast until the completion of the test. Only water may be ingested. The minimum number of determinations of blood glucose during the test should be eight: fasting, ½, 1, 2, 3, 3½, 4, and 5 hours and any time that the subject may develop symptoms.

The diagnoses of functional hypoglycemia must be made only after all other forms of hypoglycemia have been eliminated and any specific mental or physical disease excluded. Fasting hypoglycemia must not be confused with functional hypoglycemia. The fasting variety occurs after prolonged fasts, while the reactive functional form is postprandial and associated with the ingestion of food. Fasting hypoglycemia is not common but when it does exist it usually is of organic origin with a pathology amenable to treatment to relieve the hypoglycemia and the associated symptoms.

The therapy of functional hypoglycemia is directed toward the correction of any emotional problems and a high protein, low carbohydrate diet with frequent small feedings. There is no place for the so called megavitamin therapy in the control of functional hypoglycemia. Care must be taken that the patient does not focus on the physical aspect of his problem to the extent that he denies that which is really psychological. Sometimes a patient will latch onto foods as their salvation, overeat, and gain weight. When this happens it should be a signal to the therapist that he may be dealing with a severe psychological disturbance.

Functional hypoglycemia can and should be treated by responsible physicians and psychologists, lest the patients fall prey to the many unscrupulous practitioners who charge exorbitant fees and gouge them for large quantities of money by performing unnecessary tests and selling them numerous vitamins and food supplements. The truly concerned clinician can help these patients by removing a somatic parameter that may be hindering psychotherapy. [Whether a patient in therapy has functional hypoglycemia or not good dietary habits should be explored.] Functional hypoglycemia must not be used to cover up other mental or physical illnesses but if it does exist it should be controlled.

REFERENCES

Abrahamson, E. & Pezet, A. *Body, mind and sugar.* New York: Holt, 1951.

Anthony, et. al. Personality disorders in reactive hypoglycemia. *Diabetes,* 22:664, 1973.

Conn, J. W., and Seltzer, H. S. Spontaneous hypoglycemia, *Am. Journ. of Med.,* 19:460, 1955.

Jung, Y., Khurana, R. C., and Corredor, D. G. Reactive hypoglycemia in women: results of a health survey, *Diabetes,* 20:428, 1971.

Harris, S. Hyperinsulinism and dysinsulinism, *JAMA,* 1924, **83**:729–733.

Marks, V. & Rose, F., *Hypoglycaemia.* Oxford: Blackwell, 1965.

Rabinowitz, D. and Margolis, S. Hypoglycemia, in *The Principles and Practice of Medicine.* (A. M. Harvey, R. Jones, A. Owen, & R. Ross, eds.) New York: Appleton, 1972.

Salzer, H. Relative hypoglycemia as a cause of neuropsychiatric illness. *Journal of the National Medical Association,* 1966, **58**:12–17.

Seltzer, H. S. True versus false functional hypoglycemia. *Public Health Reviews,* 1974, **3**:341.

Thorn, G., *Textbook of endocrinology,* (R. H. Williams, Ed.), Philadelphia: Saunders, 1950.

Tintera, J. The hypoadrenocortical state and its management. *N.Y. State J. Med.,* 1955, **55**:1869–1879.

Vinicor, F., Faulkner, S., & Clark, C. M. Reactive hypoglycemia. *Hospital Medicine,* 1975, **11**:65–79.

Williams, R. *Textbook of Endocrinology.* Philadelphia: Saunders, 1968.

Yudkin, J. Sugar: dangerous to the heart? *Medical World News,* 1971, **12**: 38–47.

chapter 7

A TRANSACTIONAL ANALYSIS MODEL OF BRIEF FAMILY THERAPY: FIRST STEPS

Edward M. Gurowitz, Ph.D., C.P.T.M.
Nancy E. Gurowitz, C.M.
Nanci-Ames Curtis, M.D.

This paper grew out of a series of discussions among the two transactional analysis (TA) therapists and a family therapist interested in transactional analysis and its short-term applications. We wanted to see what we could do with our idea that, in TA terms, the family provides the original scripting situation, which should make family systems intervention a potent tool for facilitating long-term script change.

At the risk of oversimplification, family therapy sees the family as a social system: the process or dynamic generated in a family creates an entity that is greater than the simple combination of the individual dynamics of its members. System components (family members) are assigned roles and functions, often corresponding to what TA calls game positions. Frequently one member, the identified patient, is designated as "the problem," in much the same way that an individual may focus anxiety on a symptom as a way of dealing with a psychoneurotic problem. The family therapist intervenes in the family, utilizing the theory that when systems dynamics are restructured individual change and growth will follow. Simply put, when the family environment is changed so that it becomes less toxic or counter to growth and more nourishing and growth-promoting, family members will change and support each other's changes. (For a more complete account of Family Therapy, theory and practice, see Minuchin, 1974.)

When we began seeing TA group or individual clients in family therapy as well, it quickly became apparent that the intervention styles of the two modalities were quite different. From the family therapist's point of view, the TA therapist overemphasizes individual change, works too much with the identified patient, buys into the family system, etc. The TA therapist encounters that he sees the family therapist falling short of cure, setting up new adaptations rather than autonomy, creating a system whereby people learn to live more comfortably with their script rather than change it, etc. Since both TA and family therapy are clearly effective and valid therapies in the hands of potent therapists, we felt that, despite the disparity in styles, a common ground of TA and family therapy, combining the potency of both, could be designed. We began the search by combining theoretical models, and this led to a model of intervention.

THEORETICAL MODEL

We began with the assumption that the family is based on an interlocking of mother's and father's scripts in a symbiotic fashion. This symbiosis will have healthy and unhealthy aspects and may include complementary and/or competitive compo-

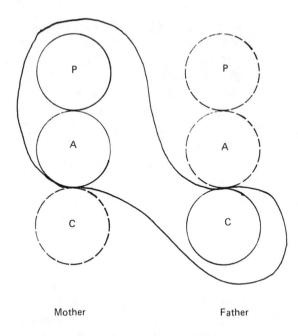

Mother   Father

Figure 7–1.   Diagram of the symbiotic relationship between
Father's Child and Mother's Parent and Adult.

nents (Schiff, 1975). A simple example of such a symbiosis is
shown in Figure 7-1.

When a child is born, he is automatically in a (healthy)
symbiosis with mother (Fig. 7-2A), and thus may compete
implicitly with father for his place in the symbiosis, as well as
possibly forming a new (unhealthy) symbiosis with father (Fig.
7-2B). As subsequent children are born, new symbioses form
and old ones shift, both between the parents, between parents
and children, and among the children. In a family of four there
is the possibility of a large number of symbioses, and family
members become so interlocked that no one seems able to move
independently. Satir (personal communication) has said that a
good test of any system is to "sculpt" it (portray the dynamics
by arranging the individuals' bodies in attitudes symbolic of

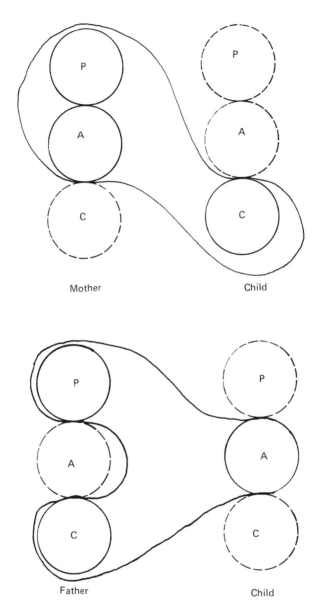

Figure 7–2.   Family symbioses. A. Healthy mother-child symbiosis.
B. Father-child symbiosis.

their roles) and then see whether everyone can leave to go to the bathroom without the system collapsing. In a highly symbiotic family, the structure is destroyed if anyone leaves it to meet a need of his own. Thus the trade-off of individual autonomy for symbiotic "security" builds an interdependent network whose members feel they have to maintain the status quo to prevent the (apparently) life-threatening collapse of the system.

A family establishes a network of symbioses according to what its members perceive as "survival conditions," and so they are deeply invested in maintaining it. This exactly parallels the way an individual establishes a life script that is resistant to change. A family system is, however, far harder for a therapist to deal with: when several people have a stake in maintaining it, each intervention designed to weaken a part of it and produce individuation will be met by strenuous efforts on the part of family members to repair the breach. The therapist is more heavily outnumbered than in individual work where his potency is only pitted against the efforts of the client's Critical Parent/Adapted Child axis to keep the client's script from changing. For this reason, family therapists often opt for behavior change or social control rather than script change. It was our conviction that through the combination of TA concepts and methods with those of family therapy, we could work with families toward full individuation and autonomy (script change) as well as growth of the family system.

INTERVENTION MODEL

We defined our goal as restructuring the family system such that the parents start rescripting the children along healthier, more productive lines and that family members support them in making changes in the direction of autonomy. To promote this we use four levels of intervention, exactly comparable to the levels of intervention with an individual.

STRUCTURAL INTERVENTION. We make a collective structural analysis of the family as well as examining the ego states of the individual family members. The most productive way we have found to do this is through the use of the egogram (Dusay, 1971). We first work with individuals' egograms and then help the family as a whole to construct one or more family egograms. We have found that the family egogram may or may not represent the simple sum of the egograms of the individuals. Also of interest is whether one individual contributes disproportionately to some part of the family egogram. Much of this can be here-and-now work as the therapist creates stresses, divisions, etc., by his intervention, and the individual's and family's responses to new stimuli are revealed.

The use of structural analysis in this way stresses and makes use of the family's unit strength and also begins work on individuation by focusing also on the members' functioning and contributions. Symbioses also are readily apparent as ego state functioning is compared, and these can be pointed out using TA concepts in such a way as to maximize everyone's "OK-ness." "I see you do a lot of the thinking and problem solving, John. Your Adult is really important to the family, but what about your Child? Do you ever feel that part of you is neglected?" This recognizes and strokes John's real contribution and also recognizes and validates his Child needs.

TRANSACTIONAL (STROKE) INTERVENTIONS. Here, as in structural interventions, we have found the use of a diagram very helpful, in this case modified versions of the Stroking Profile (McKenna, 1974). We obtain pictures of the individuals' stroke economies and of the collective pattern as well as work with the family as a whole to change dysfunctional patterns.

Diagramming stroking profiles, like egograms, involves working largely with the clients' Adult and Little Professor. As issues are uncovered, however, engagement of the Child, establishment of Child-Child, Parent-Child, Adult-Adult and other dialogues among family members can proceed. Intervention in the session is designed to change patterns of stroking and transacting in the family, to help family members contract for new ways of being together, to decipher family patterns, and to uncover individual script material. Family therapists, for example, have long been aware of the benefits to children of self-disclosure on the parents' part and of the bringing to light of family "secrets." Again, the focus on stroking and transaction patterns facilitates this process. The ready understandability and applicability of TA concepts helps the family do much of this work for themselves rather than have the therapist point out patterns, interpret, etc. We have also found that changes in stroking patterns accomplished by here/now work in sessions or through homework often yield surprisingly large results in a short time, thus easing much of the pain and "hooking" all of the family into therapy, a perennial problem in family therapy.

GAME INTERVENTIONS.   Game work is often easier with families than with individuals, since family games are generally more obvious, more repetitive, and more readily recognized by family members. Also, where a new client may take several group or individual sessions to begin initiating games, families generally show them from early on, indeed from the first transaction of an intake session. In game analysis, as in any form of TA therapy, the Drama Triangle (Karpman, 1968) is a most useful tool. Family members readily recognize their primary roles and position changes, and it is easy to identify payoffs, cons, and other game components.

SCRIPT INTERVENTIONS.   We believe there is a family script in addition to the individual scripts and family counterscript as well. However, we have yet to work out a systematic theory of script interventions on a systems level. Clearly individual script material is revealed at the structural, transactional, and game level, and is dealt with. Other script interventions include the introduction of concepts such as the gallows laugh (Steiner, 1967), the use of sweatshirts (Berne, 1972), and pointing out and working with rackets (English, 1971). Our main intervention at this level has been to identify these and make reference to them, but we have not developed any consistent form of intervention at the Child or redecision level other than those used in TA individual or group therapy. As noted earlier, it is at this level that the family network solidifies most tightly against the therapist's intervention.

Conclusion

The combination of TA and family therapy methods provides a potentially powerful tool for script cure of family members, although the dynamics of script intervention in this model remain to be clarified. Family systems intervention provides the TA therapist with an excellent model for working with a family as a whole, especially in a crisis or adjunctive to the ongoing personal therapy of one or more members, and for the family in which there is no major problem or crisis but whose members want to create a more nourishing atmosphere for themselves.

References

Berne, E. *What do you say after you say hello.* New York, Grove Press, 1972.

Dusay, J. M. Egograms and the "constancy hypothesis." *Trans. Anal. Journal,* 1972, **2**(13), 37–41.

English, F., The Substitution Factor: Rackets and Real Feelings Part I. *Transactional Analysis Journal,* 7:4, 1971, 27–32.

Gurowitz, E. M. A TA model of family therapy. Paper presented at ITAA Summer Conference, San Francisco, 1975.

Gurowitz, E. M., Gurowitz, N. E., & Curtis, N. A. TA and family therapy. New York, Workshop at Eastern TA Conference, 1975.

Karpman, S. B. Fairy tales and script drama analysis. *Trans. Anal. Bulletin,* 1968, **7**(26), 39–43.

McKenna, J. Stroking profile: application to script analysis. *Trans. Anal. Journal.* 1974, **44**, 20–24.

Minuchin, S. *Families and family therapy.* Cambridge, Ma.: Harvard University Press, 1974.

Schiff, J. *Cathexis reader.* New York: Harper & Row, 1975.

Steiner, C. Treatment of alcoholism, *Trans. Anal. Bulletin,* 1967, **2**(23), 69–71.

Part III

THEORETICAL AND TECHNICAL DEVELOPMENTS IN BRIEF APPROACHES

In the attempt to make therapy more efficient and to bring about changes more quickly, new theoretical stances and techniques have evolved. From the specific programs of assertive training to the technology of videotapes to contracts for change—all aim at making the therapy more target focused and the results quicker.

chapter 8

SHORT-TERM CONTRACTUAL GROUP TREATMENT AND WORKING THROUGH

William H. Holloway, M.D.

Transactional analysis (TA) was originated by Eric Berne (Berne, 1961; 1964) as a means for establishment of symptomatic control by means of goal-oriented brief psychotherapy. With his background of psychoanalytic training and expertise, Berne also recognized the essence of working through for the resolution of conflicts between narcissistic desire and neurotically patterned adaptive mechanisms so he extended transactional analysis to include script analysis for that purpose. Berne's contributions were unique in that he devised a system for understanding communication, which was readily comprehended by the patient, placed the power or responsibility for attainment of change in the hands of the patient, diminished the potential for improper handling of transference and countertransference, and included an outcome that is the equivalent of personality reconstruction, which is the alleged result of thorough psychoanalysis. It also provided for the application of these principles to the less extensive goals usually sought in brief psychotherapy for individuals, groups, and families, which are often referred to as reeducative and supportive.

If I were to say the same thing in the jargon of TA it would go as follows: Berne developed TA to be applied by persons for the purpose of establishing social control by the process of decontamination of the Adult ego state while engaging in contractual group treatment. The foregoing was accomplished through the processes of structural analysis, transactional analysis, and game analysis. Once the person cured himself or herself of the troublesome symptom then script analysis was undertaken for deconfusing the Child ego state. The patient sets the goals and is responsible for attaining them. The therapist provides information and confrontations while observing the patient's communication and interpersonal transactions. When the conflict between the Free Child and Adapted Child are resolved, the patient will, by decision, attain the state of script-free autonomous function.

For many reasons, clinicians who have been trained in other traditions have not incorporated transactional analysis into their practice. Because colleagues tend to see TA as simplistic, they do not become aware of the potential for its application as an in-depth psychology—even in brief therapy. My purpose in this chapter is to identify the process of working through as it is dealt with in the context of short-term contractual TA group treatment.

In psychoanalytic psychotherapy there is a general pattern consisting of the therapist enhancing the patient's tendency to misidentify contemporary persons as if they were authority figures from the past. Whatever the presenting complaints or incapacitation there is an assumption that as the transference relationship is intensified the unconscious significance and primitive intent of the patient's responses will emerge with such consistency that it will be possible to interpret the meanings. As the impact of these meanings is experienced by the patient, he or she will acquire an emotional insight and a resultant ability to shift cathexis and restructure the intrapsychic operations. Within this process the original complaint will be ameliorated or disappear.

Many clinicians have doubted the need for a patient to wait so long before gaining relief from the symptom complex and Berne eventually espoused that view in his admonition "cure them now and find out why later." He invested himself in the development of a pragmatic system to first attain symptom relief and to then go about the task of correcting the narcissistically originated intrapsychic difficulties.

Obviously, if one believes that the symptom complex represents an unchangeable consequence of basic conflict, then they would not be inclined to explore Berne's approach. In recent years, however, there is increasing evidence that various direct behavioral and interpersonal experiences can and do result in remarkable changes in a short time, not necessarily followed by some other symptom replacement. Analytically oriented clinicians are increasingly willing to inquire into the systems used by others.

Berne (1961) and followers (Harris, 1967) relied on the knowledge that psychotherapy involved an interpersonal learning experience that also involves modification of behavior. There is also the inspirational aspect involving persuasion, hope, trust, and self-mastery. Finally, there is the awareness that humans are capable of abstract reasoning, prediction, and anticipatory decision making. Berne's work is also consistent with the concepts of development of intellectual function proposed by Jean Piaget.

From all of this Berne proposed a decisional model to account for the development of patterns, otherwise identified as psychopathology, and that the adaptations that resulted in contemporary function had their origin in decisions intended to maintain survival. The failure of a person to reasonably predict consequences and to misinterpret events is the consequence of the intrusion of archaic ideation and strivings and intrusion of primitive authority instructions on the perception and interpretation of events and the response, generally described in TA as contamination of the Adult ego state.

As background for understanding the dynamics included in TA concepts, Berne hypothesized that the mind as an entity could be subdivided into three organs, viz, the *Archeopsyche,* composed of primitive strivings and the feelingful events of early life; the *Exteropsyche,* composed of the recorded instructions and actions of the authority figures; and the *Neopsyche,* which is the data processing, probability estimating, and decision-making apparatus. Pictorally, he showed these organs in this physical relationship.

Berne then described the dynamic behavioral realities that derived from each of these organs as ego states. Thus an ego

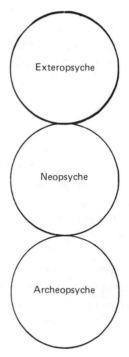

state is a behavioral manner of being at a given moment in time accompanied by a correlated feeling and style of thinking. Those ego states dominated by the influence and instruction of the exteropsyche were labeled *Parent,* those related to data processing were labeled *Adult,* and those influenced intensively by feeling and impulse were labeled *Child.* Thus giving use to the diagram with which most persons are now familiar.

Earlier, transactional analysis was preceded by structural analysis. The patient learned to identify ego states in the self and others. The identification is made by observing and listening, and focuses especially in word content, inflection, emphasis, posture, facial expression, and movement. The reason for learning to identify ego states is that there is a greater accuracy of prediction of the likely behavior through understanding ego

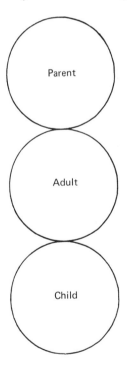

states than by any other method. Certainly here the concepts of superego, ego, and id though useful for explaining action, are not available for accurate prediction.

As a patient understands ego states, there then follows transactional analysis in which the lines of communication can be drawn between two or more persons. In this stage, the identification of complementary, crossed, and ulterior transactions is learned along with some basic rules of communication. It is especially important that one comprehend ulterior transactions since they contain hidden messages often based in narcissistic strivings and frequently result in the manipulative and exploitative behavior and its consequent disappointing or destructive consequences that Berne identified as games. Within games, there is always the experience of emotional displeasure of varying degrees, related to deferred and partial gratification of narcissistic needs.

Once a person understands ego states and transactions, then game analysis is possible. Thus a person is provided with intellectual tools with which to be alert to past self-defeating behavior and to create and choose new options that thwart the gamey behavior.

Games are considered to occur because of intrusion of parental and child influences on the data-processing, problem-solving Adult ego state. This intrusion is called contamination and is outside of the person's awareness. By using structural, transactional, and game analysis, the patient becomes aware of the contamination and then will function with increased awareness and consequently diminished deception and exploitation. The following diagrams portray contaminated and decontaminated Adult ego states:

With decontamination of the Adult ego state and the exercise of options rather than habitual response, the patient will have established social control. In so doing, he or she will avoid painful manipulative and somewhat symbiotic dependency relationships. Simultaneously, because effective problem solving is established there follows behavior for more effective gratify-

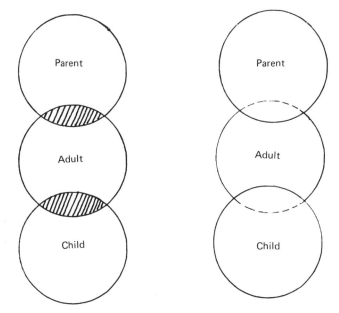

Parent and Child Contamination of A   **Uncontaminated Adult**

ing of needs and in consideration of others. The goal of deconta-mination of the Adult ego state is the establishment of social control.

Beyond contamination of the adult is the issue of deconfus-ing the Child ego state. Within the archeopsyche and its deriva-tive Child ego states, reside two groups of opposing forces. On one hand there are the narcissistic, acquisitive, expressive, in-quisitive, creative and destructive forces that are behaviorally identified as the Free Child. On the other hand, there are the learned, stylized, oppressed, programmed, and often stultifying forces by which young persons learn to survive with partial gratification which are behaviorally identified as Adapted Child.

In his early work, Berne saw psychoanalysis as the means to attain deconfusion of the Child and later he described the process as script analysis. A life script is an unsatisfactory life plan based upon the decisions of a very young person experiencing survival-threatening stress. The script is unsatisfactory in that it is characterized by repetitive unpleasant feeling experiences and recurring difficulties in interpersonal relationships. The term life script was useful to identify the personal fairy tale that dominates one's life.

In the process of deconfusing the Child and decontamination of the Adult the result is a realignment and congruence of thought, feeling, and behavior. This is also the end result of thorough psychoanalysis through the process of "working through."

Working through implies that one becomes consciously aware of the distortions of transference processes as they exist in all aspects of one's life. In psychoanalysis, this occurs by first facilitating an intensification of the transference relationship with the therapist and then by timely interpretation one identifies the nature and intent of the unconscious processes. Eventually, this extends to transferencelike distortions in relationships other than that with the therapist.

While clinicians using transactional analysis acknowledge the existence of transference, the method for working with it is quite different. The essential difference is that the patient is the one who decides the pathway of the therapeutic interaction and the therapist follows. Consequently, the TA clinician does not accept the power which the patient attempts to thrust on the therapist.

This difference is accomplished by the establishment of a treatment contract with an explicit goal for change. The patient bears the responsibility for defining the change intended and to describe the behavioral evidence that will indicate that the intended change has been accomplished. One definition of a treatment contract is as follows: The contract defines the working relationship between patient and therapist and contains the patient's statement of an intended change that will be accomplished by a future decision.

In contractual treatment, whenever the patient evidences transference and reliance on the therapist to direct the way, the therapist can refer to the contractual goal which was previously specified and ask how the patient will attain that goal. The therapist does not have a responsibility to get the patient to the goal. He or she has only a responsibility to identify the ways in which the patient avoids attainment. Generally, this involves the confrontation of incongruities in a nonaccusative manner. Therapists who demonstrate investment in facilitating goal attainment, will be experienced as warm, caring, and trustworthy. They will also continually encourage the patient to explore creative alternative pathways rather than the habitual. Thus, the patient will recognize her or his personal potency in self-fulfillment rather than seeing the power as derived from the all-knowing therapist.

Contracts may be directed at either social control or the attainment of autonomy. In the first instance, the consequence is effective problem solving and in the second, one additionally develops the capacity to fulfill and protect the Free Child by the use of the Adult rather than relying on the rules within the Parent and the stylized patterns of the Adapted Child. Autonomy results for the resolution of internal conflicts between Parent and Child and those between the narcissistic striving and learned patterns of partial gratification. This is quite similar to reducing the id-superego conflicts and establishing ego resources to provide adequate outlets for id impulses.

The autonomous person is not one who relates to others with callous disregard while fulfilling personal desire. Rather, he or she is a person who accepts full responsibility for inner feelings and choices and is responsive to others and the environment and thus is generally satisfied and frequently experiences intimacy and joy.

Another aspect of the contractual process that I have not as yet mentioned is the effect on countertransference. By countertransference, I mean the tendency for the therapist to unconsciously identify the patient as a significant person from the past and to then manipulate or exploit the patient while seeking to fullfill narcissistic needs. When the goal is specified by the patient, the therapist who is willing to keep the goal in mind will have less opportunity for countertransference distortions to cloud the therapeutic work.

Thus with the use of contract, there is a device that provides for a different method of handling transference processes and for diminishing countertransference. The net result is the attainment of desired changes in less time than in other psychodynamic approaches.

REFERENCES

Berne, Eric, *Games People Play,* New York; Grove Press, 1964.

Berne, Eric, *Transactional Analysis in Psychotherapy,* New York: Grove Press, 1961.

Harris, T. A., *I'm OK—You're OK,* New York: Harper & Row, 1967.

chapter 9

INTRODUCTION OF VIDEO TO A SHORT-TERM THERAPY GROUP

John Gladfelter, Ph.D.

Transactional analytic approaches to treatment permit and support a varied and open-ended application of methodology to promoting change. The blending of videotape methods with group therapy provides an additional dimension to treatment and requires the therapist to have a solid foundation in both group theory techniques and in video methods. The therapist using both methods will need some time to incorporate his own personality into the blend so that he brings his full potency to treatment without technical interference. This combination can be effective especially as a short-term treatment approach.

The view being presented requires the therapist to experience the video equipment as an extension of himself in both hearing and seeing; the equipment becomes a means to an end, namely that of change in the patient, rather than an end in itself. A therapist using video will find that it becomes as natural as one might experience the driving of an automobile while doing therapy. It is, in fact, easier and much less dangerous.

Reprinted from John Gladfelter, "Introduction of Video to a Treatment Group," *American Journal of Videology,* 1978, **1**(2).

Equipment for doing video work in therapy is simple in operation and scope. One needs a large television monitor with a 23 inch diagonal screen, a reel-to-reel tape deck with slow and stop motion, a zoom camera with a solid tripod, and a simple mixer with several microphones. The camera and tape deck are beside the therapist's chair, the monitor is opposite the therapist in the group circle, and the microphones are spaced around the group circle. Space for seating eight or nine people is possible with the monitor taking a space on a small table so that everyone in the circle is able to see it with minimal discomfort. The monitor is in the circle and is turned on, as is all of the equipment, so that when entering the room, each group member can see a picture on the monitor. The video deck is usually turned on but not recording until the therapist chooses to record. Often as people enter the room they want to see themselves and seat themselves in particular relation to the camera and monitor. Some choose to see the monitor while others find a seat near the monitor in hopes that they will have difficulty in seeing themselves or being seen.

If a therapist is beginning to use video in his treatment groups for the first time he will find some accommodation is necessary in the group before a normal treatment process can continue. It is useful to tell the group members a session or two before introducing video to the group that you plan to do so. Then, when the equipment is in the group, group members have an opportunity to see themselves, talk about their thoughts and feelings and discuss their reactions with the therapist and each other. Often some play with the equipment such as zooming in and out, panning, and experiencing the feelings of seeing one's self is helpful before the usual treatment process begins. A playful atmosphere is an important part of this first exposure to video and enhances the positive attitudes and feelings necessary to effective use of video.

A brief explanation of how the equipment will be used is important in relieving some of the anxiety that people generate in themselves when something novel is introduced. They can be told that the equipment will be used to help them see themselves as others see them and will be used only with their agreement and with a clear contract as to how it will be employed. They should be told that the equipment will be used regularly during the group sessions, that the therapist will be videotaping their work during the group session, and that it will be used in playback if it is a part of their working contract. This means that there will be videotaping of all of the group session. Only those segments chosen by the therapist and the patient are used. Technically, this means that the therapist will be using a single hour tape over and over again and will not store or use the tape for any other purpose than treatment. Tape rewind after an hour of recording is a matter of a few moments and can be done without interfering with the ongoing treatment process. This is important information to convey to the group members to allay their fears of the tape being used against them in some way. This repeated reuse of tape avoids the need for legal release forms and other potential legal complications. Tapes of current manufacturers are remarkably durable and will last for hundreds of recordings and replays before picture quality drops below useful levels. This regular use, however, means that the recording heads on the video tape deck should be cleaned weekly and tape pathways checked for debris in order to maintain tape life and recording stability. If videotapes are to be made for training or supervision, release forms of some sort are necessary and should be devised through the assistance of an attorney. A bulk eraser for videotapes is also useful for erasing the contents of a videotape after groups are over for the day.

Therapists who are not accustomed to viewing videotape should take the opportunity to review segments of their recorded tapes after group sessions in order to become accustomed to looking and listening for particular data. In particular, therapists using transactional analysis will find the recognition of ego states, script signals, games, and the like remarkably easy and fun. Learning to look with video comes with practice and looking at tape is valuable time spent in developing the skills of looking. Taking the time after each session is the best time to look since much of the material will be fresh and clear. With added monetary investment, the therapist can obtain a special effects generator and a second camera to use for obtaining split screen images of himself and the patient while doing therapy. This is particularly useful if supervision is planned.

Groups are usually uncomfortable about videotape use initially, but accommodate within two or three sessions and usually are not mindful of video after that unless it is used in their personal work. It is the decision of the group therapist to introduce video into his group treatment and not a democratic decision on the part of his group. It is usually necessary to listen to the discomfort of group members about video and valuable to be aware of the information related to personal discomfort as an integral part of the life script of the person.

Individuals often ask for replay of their treatment work on their own after the initial accommodation period. It is often useful for people who are particularly uncomfortable with video images to operate the equipment themselves and they should be encouraged to do so briefly to decrease their fears. For patients who refuse to work while being taped, there is the option of pointing the camera at others in the group during the work or pointing the camera at the therapist.

There are occasional therapists who find the equipment intrusive after a period of time and often give up on using video in treatment. This problem arises when there are technical details which are not understood or solved or when the therapist begins competing with the equipment for effectiveness or information. The solutions are usually basically supervisory in nature and depend on an experienced therapist who knows both video and treatment well. Closets throughout the country are full of video equipment which therapists purchased and do not use because of their unwillingness to work through their discomfort. Video equipment available in the last five years is remarkably stable, flexible, and foolproof. The useful rule for

whether video equipment can be used in a particular setting is
can the patient in the group be easily seen and easily heard. If
the therapist tolerates bad lighting and a noisy environment for
doing treatment, it is unlikely that equipment can adjust for bad
situations.

After the therapist has added video to his treatment approach, new members coming into the group will need some
time before they are ready to use it in their treatment. They will
need to be informed of the use of video in the group and have
opportunity to ask questions about it. They will have ample
opportunity to see themselves early in the group as one way of
becoming familiar with their image on the screen. Other group
members can be very supportive of the new group member and
often recount their experiences of first seeing themselves. In this
writer's experience, there has not been an occasion in which
members of the group were lost from treatment as a result of
video.

The therapist first using video should take the time to view
himself on video at length and explore his own feelings and
thoughts before using it in the group. The experience is one of
the most fascinating possible. Seeing one's self is decidedly
different from the image in the mirror and the therapist will
need to give himself permission to really look and take time
looking before doing any extensive work with video. Stop motion, slow motion, and regular speed images are all useful and
important in becoming accustomed to one's own appearance. It
is often helpful to work with a supervisor or friend who will
operate the camera so that the therapist will see other tapes
than what he might choose.

In keeping with the treatment philosophy in transactional
analysis, the patient will work from a treatment contract. This
means that in initial contract work, the therapist may offer to
incorporate video into the treatment operations he will use and
inform the client as to how video can help. Specific contracts
involving video are contracts in which the patient may see
and/or hear himself complete the treatment contracts he works

on. He may choose segments for replay or the therapist may use segments of the work for reviewing. He may also use segments of his treatment work to get feedback from other group members. The patient does not know how video can be useful and so must learn from the therapist as to what he can look for, how to look, and where to look. This means that ample time is required and that some amount of teaching is valuable for both the individual patient and the group.

In the development of treatment contracts, video is valuable as a means of confronting the client with his reluctance to make a contract. The therapist, aware that the client is unwilling to make a contract, may offer to play back to the client the process of the contract work. This material is fed back via instant replay as important adult information and not to pressure or "game" the client. The client then may choose to work further on making the contract, stop work, or use the information as a resource for formulating what he wants to work on. It is important to check ego states of the client so as not to give information when the client is not working from his Adult ego state. This initial contract information is useful in enabling the therapist and the client to spot ways in which the client defeats himself or rebels against change. The client himself can often serve as therapist and devise ways to confront the self that he sees and hears on the screen. These early tape segments are often full of material of which the therapist should be aware. (Such things as "stoppers" not OK miniscript drivers, discounts and cop outs are usually obvious during these early videotapings.) For transactional therapists in training, the videotapes are rich in resource material for supervision.

Treatment operations are basic to effective transactional treatment and video can be introduced and employed in all transactional operations. Several operations will be described and video methods will be discussed as they apply to each operation. Examples will be included to clarify the use of video. Treatment operations that are not traditionally transactional analysis will also be described and their use with video will also be discussed. It should be pointed out that this chapter represents only a very small segment of the applications of video in group treatment and that a later book by this author will detail the extensive applications possible.

Specification as an operation involves the focusing on specifics in the life experience and feeling of the client that he has been unaware of and has avoided. With video, the therapist can bring into sharp detail the vagaries and caution that the client uses to keep himself protected from his own awareness and others. An example is when the client seems to be unable to describe what he is feeling or what it is that he wants to work on. The client says "I feel that everyone rejects me and I don't know what to do." Instant replay of audio and video of that remark will often clarify for the client how he avoids being specific about his feeling and about the choices that his awareness gives him. He may see the expression on his face, the tone of his voice, or the mannerisms he displays and discover the next step he must take to change. Serial repetitive replays of the short segment without comment of the group or the therapist are potent sources of information to the client. It is important also to be very sure that the client agrees to see the replay before the material is presented. He makes a contract with the therapist to see the video material before it is replayed, and if he chooses not to see it, his choice is respected. It is useful for the therapist to assist the client in looking and offer stop motion or slow motion views of particular behaviors that the client might not ordinarily see. When the client is aware of the specific experience, feeling, or change that he wants to work on it is also useful to review his statements on video so that he can further strengthen and enhance his potency in making the specific changes that he chooses.

Confrontation is useful for it allows many of the inconsistencies and incongruities in the client to be clear. The confrontation with video also allows the client opportunity to operate from adult information that he obtains from the video tape. Video is a potent ally for the Adult ego state in clients and the information he obtains is useful in making adult choices and adult contracts for change. When the client says "I'm going to give up feeling sad," the video replay will readily disclose the smile on his face, the crossed fingers, and the "no" in the nod of his head. Immediate replay of these data will effectively present to the client for his use the manner in which he discounts his verbal statements and confront him with the discrepancy between words and behavior. To effectively use video in confrontation the client will need time to evaluate, process, and decide on choices that evolve from the data arising from confrontation. Repeated replays of data are useful for time allows additional room for thinking. By the nature of video replay, almost everything done with video might be considered confrontation; however, other treatment operations by the nature of video and the treatment contract are possible.

Illustration with video is most effectively conducted by presenting longer segments of video tape in which examples, samples, and excerpts demonstrate for the client his use or misuse of his transactions. When the client makes a contract to be aware of playing games and stopping the games, a segment in which he hooks the gimmick of another group member can be effective in illustrating his game. A very effective use of illustration with video is a client who says "I now make a contract to be direct with other members of the group, not discount others, and give positive strokes to others in the group now. I like you Jane, and I particularly like the way you smile at me, like right now." A replay of that short segment will give strong positive reinforcement for continued effective change and give potent illustration for him on replay as to the validity and usefulness of his contract. The segment will also be useful to other group members as an illustration of contracts and change possibilities. Video replay makes possible replay of incidents and interchanges in the group that allow support for change. Illustrations of discounts, games, script signals, and other transactional processes are readily identified with video.

Confirmation is very much a part of video utilization in a

therapy group. The videotape segments of client's work are replayed for the person to view, integrate, and use as a part of his change. When the client is able to see and hear his changes and explore further change, the video system has amply validated its use. There are few other methods in therapy that allow such immediate confirmatory evidence for the client. Changing in transactional analysis is so rapid and so concise that the full effectiveness is not always appreciated by the client or the group. It is a highly effective confirmation of work to replay segments of redecision work, impasse resolution, decontamination, particularly when the clear decision point is available for the client and the group to see. Several viewings also enable other group members to learn from the process and contract for themselves for later work. The client says "I am not depressed, I have decided that I will not depress myself any longer, that I will have fun and enjoy myself, and that I will enjoy my effectiveness and potency in talking with my friends." When he hears his strength, his pleasure, and sees his own pleasant face, clear lines, and positive appearance he has much to confirm and reinforce his change. The immediacy of reinforcement is important in curtailing and avoiding later doubts or questions that might arise. The replay also allows other group members to see the changes in the person and add to the reinforcement of the video image.

Although not transactional operations, support and reassurance are effectively a part of video use in a group. In support, replay of positive stroking by other group members and with the opportunity to stroke himself, the client has many chances to use video. Replaying the positive smile of the client and his ability to think and feel are supportive segments which he can use. When he sees and hears himself giving himself permission to feel, think, and listen, he gains powerful support for his permission from himself as well as others. Hearing and seeing other people who are supportive of him is also valuable in replay in reinforcing the support. Reassurance is much related to support but has the additional value of being parental and clearly positive. Reassurance from the therapist that is clear, simple, and potent can be replayed. Statements from other members of the group also are valuable in providing repetitive and consistent support. The positive facial, voice, and body characteristics of the therapist and other group members on videotape may be as important as the verbal statements such as "You can do it," "You're O.K.," "You can take care of yourself."

Prior training in video is worthwhile to any treatment method and is particularly valuable in transactional analysis. The therapist needs to first have an opportunity to play with the equipment at home to get over the shyness of the child in the therapist that is seeing and hearing himself. This play also offers a chance to learn to operate the controls and gadgets easily. Loss of self-consciousness takes a while and with practice the therapist can become highly skilled in recording, rapid replay, stop motion, slow motion, and tape handling. The time to do this is individual and should not be hurried. It is also important that the equipment be handled in a fun way without fear of breaking something. Video workshops can often give a solid beginning for those interested in equipment types and equipment use. Learning to look and look everywhere is an important part of the first learning process. Breaking social looking taboos is important and again are best learned from an experienced video therapist. Only under unusual circumstances can a cameraman other than the therapist be of help in doing therapy with video. In most instances the additional person in the group or in another room becomes a problem for both therapist and group. If the video equipment is being used to make teaching tapes or other similar use, then other kinds of equipment and other arrangements can be considered. If therapy is the goal, then the therapist must learn to use the equipment as an extension of himself.

chapter 10

ASSERTIVE TRAINING

Elliott Seligman

Assertive training calls upon a loosely packaged combination of techniques based on learning principles and designed to increase the patient's assertive responses. As defined by Lange & Jakubowski (1976) assertiveness is:

> ... standing up for personal rights and expressing thoughts, feelings and beliefs in direct, honest and appropriate ways which do not violate another person's rights. The basic message in assertion is: this is what I think, this is what I feel. This is how I see the situation.

Originally Wolpe (1958) described assertiveness as an antagonistic response to anxiety that fit in well with his desensitization concept. During the past five years others have become interested and a great many books and articles have been published on the topic (Smith, 1975; Fensterheim & Baer 1975; Alberti & Emmons, 1974). The concept of an assertive response has been expanded to include not only standing up for one's rights but expressing one's preferences in a nonmoralized way, becoming less sensitive to criticism, not feeling guilty or being manipulated, and the expression of intimate or positive feelings without hesitation or embarrassment. In fact, the concept has become so broad that assertive training has developed into a system of interpersonal relations.

The above definition, then, does not completely describe what has come to be considered "assertive"—one could feel shattered by most criticism and still express those feelings directly. Additionally, assertiveness encompasses the assumption that the assertive person does not attempt to impose moralistic concepts on the behavior of others regarding what *should be.* He does, however, directly express his preferences in terms of the way he would like things to be. For example, a mother is acting moralistically when she says to a child, "You are a bad girl. You didn't clean your room and so I have to punish you." She would be acting assertively if she said "I am angry that you have not cleaned your room and so I am not letting you go out today." The assertive person habitually speaks the "I" language as opposed to the "you" language.

Another assumption intrinsic to assertiveness is that the assertive individual basically believes that he is worthwhile and does not condemn himself for lack of intelligence, competence, or self-sacrifice although he may be self-critical and wish to change some behavior related to these areas. In terms of Rogerian (Rogers, 1950) concepts, he has a positive self concept or, in popular terms, has high self-esteem and confidence. The individual who has established this assumption does not become flushed with anger when morally criticized ("that was a terrible thing to do") because that kind of criticism does not cause him to question his basic self-worth. Instead, he may choose to modify his behavior and point out to the critic that what he did was something that the critic personally objects to but was not, in and of itself, "terrible." Additionally, self-perception that is both positive and stable readily permits the expression of positive and intimate thoughts. By doing so, the assertive person risks less than the individual who does not have a positive, stable self-image. If rejected, he does not relabel himself "worthless" although he may be very disappointed that his feelings were not reciprocated.

It could be argued that assertive training has taken the observable manifestations of "poor self-image" and, employing the principles of learning, has directly tried to modify these responses in a manner consistent with a "strong or positive self concept." It is assumed then that if a patient behaves and thinks in a manner indicating a positive self concept, he has, in fact, acquired one.

Assertive training usually is conducted in time-limited groups composed of 8 to 10 adults and frequently two group leaders, a man and a woman. Candidates usually are seen individually before group treatment begins. Assertiveness in general is explained and the individual is assessed through the use of questionnaires and the interview material. The questionnaire offered by Gambrill & Richey (1975) is particularly helpful in that it requires patients to independently rate discomfort and response probability related to certain assertive situations. In addition, individuals who have difficulty asserting themselves often are manipulated by others and find themselves feeling angry, hurt, or otherwise chronically abused without a satisfactory response. These feelings also are assessed. Some patients are found to be generally nonassertive and others are situationally nonassertive, however both types can be treated in the same group.

A patient may wish to change areas of interpersonal assertiveness without changing others. For example, an Orthodox Jewish woman was interested in becoming more assertive with women and children but did not feel it proper to speak freely and equally with men. The therapist accepted this precondition of treatment.

Group sessions usually begin with a discussion of assertive behavior as defined above and as compared with nonassertiveness and aggressiveness. Alberti & Emmons (1974) define nonassertiveness as "the individual denying himself and is inhibited from expressing his or her actual feelings. He often feels hurt or anxious as a result of this inadequate behavior. Allowing others to chose for him, he seldom achieves his own desired goals." They compare this mode of response with the individual who acts aggressively, stating that he "accomplishes his ends usually at the expense of others. Although he frequently finds his behavior self-enhancing and expressive of his feelings in the situation, he usually hurts others in the process by making choices for them and minimizing their worth as persons. . . . Although the aggressive person may achieve his goal, he may also generate hatred and frustration which he will later receive as vengeance."

In essence, assertiveness maximizes the individual's input without violating the rights of others. Assertiveness also reduces self-righteousness, hurt feelings, aggressive fantasies, or explosive outbursts often correlated with nonassertiveness.

At this point in treatment both hypothetical incidents and incidents taken from the patient's lives are discussed to illustrate the difference between these three categories. It is essential for all group members to arrive at a general understanding of the defining characteristics of these three modes of response and to be able to apply these definitions to their own behavior.

The next step involves a discussion of the group members' philosophy in regard to their rights as individuals. Assertive training procedures argue for the right of self-expression in a manner that does not attack or manipulate others. Most often participants have not previously conceived of their nonassertiveness as involving self-denial of rights. This recognition appears to increase motivation to change. A technique for testing a patient's awareness of his right to assert himself consists of posing the question, "Would you feel that another individual was being unfair if you were the recipient of this particular behavior?" If the patient says that he would not see it as unfair, he would be asked to examine whether or not he would feel justified doing or saying the same thing and whether or not he actually has done so without self-recrimination. It is pointed out that nonassertive individuals often appear to believe that all others have rights that they do not have. The irrationality of this kind of thinking is often striking to patients.

A period of self-assessment follows with group members evaluating their behavior and setting individual goals. Patients vary greatly from being nonassertive in specific situations and assertive in most others to performing nonassertively in almost all situations. There are also distinctions between assertive behaviors in commercial relations with strangers and in social and/or intimate interactions. Group members usually set unrealistically high goals in the degree of the changes aimed at, particularly in respect to the initial changes they would like to make. They should be guided toward more realistic goals. When goals are extremely high, patients can easily become discouraged with small successes or may immediately attempt tasks that they are unable to accomplish.

In essence, the goal of assertiveness training involves raising the frequency of assertive responses and lowering the frequency of nonassertive and perhaps aggressive behaviors. Any technique that effectively accomplishes this can be employed. In general, however, assertive training techniques focus on cognitive restructuring, behavior rehearsal, and modeling in the form of role playing and imagery, as well as on special verbal techniques such as "broken record," "fogging," and "negative inquiry" (Smith, 1975). In addition, in vivo desensitization through homework and positive reinforcement from the group and the natural environment always plays an important role.

Cognitive restructuring can be as simple as patient's relabeling certain previously nonacceptable behavior as acceptable. A group discussion of patient behaviors viewed as "rude" or "selfish" often will lead to relabeling some of them as "assertive" with an increase in the probability that the behavior will be performed. Additionally, group members begin to see some of the demands made by others as "unfair" and will be increasingly able to say "no" when these situations arise.

A cognitive behavior modification approach hypothesizes

an inhibiting thought that serves to stifle the assertive response. This inhibition may be based on the assumption that assertiveness will appear hostile, will serve to threaten the relationship, or bring on some type of retaliation. Often, the inhibiting factor involves a fear of being thought to look foolish. With practice, patients can learn to recognize these inhibiting thoughts and to challenge them as representing irrational, exaggerated, and negative thinking. Then, these thoughts can be replaced with more rational, less anxiety-provoking, and, hence, less inhibiting thoughts.

A number of special verbal techniques may be used to aid the beginner who is having a hard time (Smith, 1975). I believe these approaches are analogous to step plans used to teach dancing—they may make one appear stilted and unspontaneous, but they can be helpful at first. "Broken record," for example, consists of continuously repeating a point until the goal is achieved. It is particularly recommended in situations where there is little investment in the personal relationship, for example, in returning defective goods to a store. "Fogging" is used to deal with severe criticism. It requires the "fogger" to continually agree with the possibility that the criticism is accurate without becoming offended or indicating that the criticism will lead to a change in his behavior. "Negative inquiry" is probably the most practical and applicable of the techniques suggested by Smith. It presupposes that criticism can be viewed as the expression of a preference as opposed to aggressively evoking such values as righteousness, intelligence, or common sense to influence another's behavior. The aggressiveness component can be seen by the implication that if the individual being criticized does not choose to change, he is then by implication unrighteous, unintelligent, or lacking in common sense. Negative inquiry relies on questioning the innate righteousness, intelligence, or common sense component of a critical remark and attempts to bring the critic to the point where he can express criticism without an implied condemnation. For example, a husband may ask his wife what is "horrible" about coming home late as opposed to a behavior she would prefer him not to engage in.

Behavioral rehearsal techniques are frequently used to decrease anxiety and improve skills. Group members can be asked to role play specific situations that they expect to confront, or the group can rehearse assertive responses in common situations—saying "no", asking for a favor, or confronting an injustice. Modeling—learning by means of observation—is very important in assertive training. A patient may be having a hard time formulating an assertive response in a particular situation. Another group member may be asked to assertively role play the part while the patient experiencing the difficulty observes. Then, the patient will be asked to role play the behavior directly, adapting the example he has just observed to his own inclinations.

The fact that all members of the group have the same type of problem increases the benefits of modeling. Michenbaum (1971) has demonstrated a greater amount of rewarded behavior being modeled when patients see themselves as similar to the model. In assertive training groups, patients generally see themselves as similar to each other on the factor of nonassertiveness and model their behavior on reports and observations of improvements in assertiveness. This effect is diminished in heterogeneous groups or in individual therapy where the therapist is not self-disclosing.

In vivo desensitization and in vivo positive reinforcement, are crucial to the success of any assertive training program as they most closely approximate the spontaneous performance of desirable behaviors in the environment. The contractual arrangement of specific tasks for participants to attempt on a session by session basis usually is initiated by the second meeting. It is recommended that the group leader offer clear guidelines for such tasks. They should be easy enough to assure a high probability of success. As the patient progresses, the difficulty of the tasks may increase and the therapist's input in their formulation may shrink considerably. Homework contracts always should be seen as an attempt to perform a response. If the patient reports that he was unable to accomplish a task, the fault is viewed as lying with the homework and the task itself can either be practiced or made easier.

Most participants are very gratified when they perform assertive behavior. They have often envied this type of behavior in others. However, they must be reminded that assertiveness will not guarantee that they will always get their way; it only maximizes their input. In cases where assertiveness does not bring the desired results, the alternative response (nonassertiveness) probably would have been ineffective and most likely would have resulted in increased hostility, agitation, and self-depreciation.

Assertive training groups usually are very generous in their support of the progress of members. Sometimes patients report in retrospect that at first tasks were attempted because "I just couldn't let the group down." As most groups are time-limited and assertiveness usually is highly reinforcing both through self-reward and environmental consequences, over-dependence on group reinforcement usually does not occur. In addition, toward the latter part of the series of groups, patients are encouraged to make their own assignments and evaluation in a "thinking out loud" mode before the group has its say. This reduced role of the group tends to prepare the patient for termination. Follow-ups often show not only an almost complete lack of relapse, but a great tendency to continue gains (Mayo, Bloom, & Perlman, 1975).

At the end of a fixed number of sessions, assertive scales are readministered. While most often patients have made measurable progress, many wish to go further. With few exceptions I have required my patients to wait for at least three weeks before they reenroll. I have found that this delay helps demonstrate that gains can be made without treatment. After the waiting period, patients sometimes feel that the group may be unnecessary and that they can continue to train themselves.

REFERENCES

Alberti, R. E., & Emmons, M. L. *Your perfect right: A guide to assertive behavior* (2nd ed.). San Luis Obispo, Ca.: Import Press, 1974.

Fensterheim, H., & Baer, J. *Don't say yes when you want to say no.* New York: David McKay, 1975.

Gambrill, E. D., & Richey, C. A. An assertion inventory for use in assessment and research. *Behavior Therapy,* 1975, **6,** 547–549.

Lange, A. J., & Jakubowski, P., *Responsible assertive behavior, cognitive behavioral procedures for trainers.* Champaign, Illinois, Research Press, 1976.

Mayo, M., Bloom, M., & Pearlman, J. Effectiveness of assertive training for women. Unpublished manuscript. Cited in L. Z. Bloom, K. Colburn, J. Pearlman. *The new assertive woman.* New York: Delacorte Press, 1975.

Michenbaum, D. H. Examination of model characteristics in reducing avoidance behavior. *Journal of Personality and Social Psychology,* 1971, **17,** 298–307.

Rogers, R., The significance of the self-regarding attitudes and perceptions. In M. L. Reymert (Ed.) *Feelings & emotions: The mooseheart symposium.* New York: McGraw-Hill, 1950.

Smith, M. J. *When I say no I feel guilty.* New York: Dial Press, 1975.

Wolpe, J. *Psychotherapy by Reciprocal Inhibition.* Stanford, Ca.: Stanford University Press, 1958.

chapter 11

THEORY AND PRACTICE OF EGO STATE THERAPY: A SHORT-TERM THERAPEUTIC APPROACH*

John G. Watkins, Ph.D.
Helen H. Watkins, Ph.D.

INDIVIDUAL AND GROUP THERAPIES

During the early development of group therapy the question was often raised as to whether individual treatment methods were suitable in dealing with groups. The question has not been finally resolved; however, most therapists who work with groups believe that there is a real difference between individual therapy and group therapy, and they have developed specialized procedures for dealing with the interactions between group members. Groups have been organized around many concepts, such as encounter groups, sensitivity groups, T-groups, family groups, etc. (Kaplan & Sadock, 1971).

*The use of Ego-State Therapy is not restricted to short-term interventions, but may be used equally well for long-term psychotherapy.

However, with the exception of transactional analysis and some variants of Gestalt therapy, very little consideration has been given toward adapting group therapy techniques for the treatment of a single individual. And neither of these intentionally employ hypnotic techniques to accomplish their goals, although hypnosis may occur spontaneously during some of the Gestalt fantasy approaches.

As long as a patient is regarded as a unity, a single individual, group procedures would appear to have little relevance. Transactional analysis (TA) does hypothesize three different "ego states" in a person which Berne (1961) termed Child, Parent, and Adult. Variations of these have also been differentiated such as the "natural child" and the "adaptive child," or the "nurturing parent" versus the "dominating parent." The structure of this group of states and their interaction with each other have been rather precisely delineated by the personality theory on which TA is based (Harris, 1969). Potential ego states other than the child, parent, and adult, plus their variations, are not recognized. In TA theory these three are hypothesized to include all the components of the individual. They are all present, and always present within every person.

In the Gestalt therapies various components of self are often hypothesized (created?) (activated?) and dealt with by projecting their images onto chairs or other spaces within the patient's perceptual environment. His interaction with these components is studied, but it is largely an extension of one-to-one individual therapy, that is, the patient interacts in turn with each of these hypothesized components.

THE EGO PSYCHOLOGY OF PAUL FEDERN

Transactional analysis stems from the work of Paul Federn (1952), a close associate of Freud's, whose ideas have not been well understood or appreciated, either in psychoanalytic or lay circles. This situation was partly because Federn thought and wrote in the German scientific idiom (which is not easy to understand), and partly because his concepts, although quite innovative, conflicted to some extent with Freud's theories. Federn's work was overshadowed by Freud, and it was not until toward the end of his life that Federn realized the extent to which he had moved from traditional psychoanalytic personality theory.

Briefly, Federn hypothesized the existence of *two* forms of mental energy, the "object cathexis" (Freud's "libido") and an "ego cathexis." The first (object cathexis) activated mental processes related to what is experienced as "object," hence, not-self. Without denying the erotic significance, which was so important to Freud, Federn emphasized its "object" aspects. For example, when I perceive the image of a loved person, it stands out as of great importance to me. This is because its perceptual image has been cathected (invested) with a large amount of object energy. An analogy might be given as follows: by focusing a powerful searchlight on an object it becomes the center of perception and attention. The object is then "cathected" with the light.

The real difference between Freud and Federn, however, lay in the concept of "ego cathexis." This cathexis could be conceived as being a kind of living energy, the energy of self, in fact, it is *self,* itself. Federn considered self as being an energy. Any physical or mental item that was invested with this "ego cathexis" (self energy) was experienced by the individual as "subject," hence, being within his own self. An idea invested with ego cathexis is experienced as "my" idea. The perception of another person is normally invested with object cathexis and is experienced as object, as a "not-self" that exists in the real world outside of me.

Similarly, I experience my arm as being "my" arm because it is invested with ego cathexis. If it becomes hysterically (or hypnotically) paralyzed and loses all feeling and self-directed motion, I then feel it as object, as "not me." According to Federn's theory, the ego cathexis has been withdrawn from the arm. The arm is now outside the "boundary" of the ego. The limb has become an "it" instead of a part of me, "my self." When a paralyzed part of the body is restored to normal feeling and voluntary movement, it has now been reinvested with ego cathexis. It becomes "subject" and no longer "object."

An hallucination is an idea that reaches consciousness without having been invested with ego cathexis. Accordingly, it is experienced as a perception, as "not me," as originating outside the self. The person then reports that he is "seeing" his dead father, not that he is "thinking" about him, and we diagnose him as psychotic.

Federn used this theoretical conception to devise a most unusual approach in the treatment of psychotics. Instead of denying that the patient's hallucinations were "real," as is so commonly done, he would tell the patient that he accepted them as real. However, he would call the patient's attention to the fact that the images of the therapist and other people were also real. Federn then asked the patient to consider two kinds of reality: reality A, which consisted of his perceptions of other people; and reality B, which represented the hallucinations. Reality A could be shared with other people, Federn told his patients, "but if you try to share reality B with others, they will think you are crazy. Reality B is a personal and private reality which others cannot appreciate."

Federn then asked his patients to tell him whether any experience came from reality A or reality B. He found that they could always tell the difference. He then told them that if they would keep reality B to themselves and discuss only reality A with others, they could leave the mental hospital and go home. Perhaps he was only teaching them to conceal their psychosis, but apparently by not reinforcing reality B experiences, these hallucinations tended to subside, and the patients actually did recover. Therefore, the first key concept of Federn was the distinction between subject and object as determined by the relative investment of object and ego cathexes into mental or physical processes.

Ego States

Federn's second great contribution was his division of the ego into "states." Federn included within an "ego state" only phenomena that were "self experienced." However, we have found it more convenient to include within an "ego state" all behaviors and experiences that are bound together by some common principle and separated by a boundary from other such states. These behaviors and experiences (including perceptions) may therefore be either object or ego cathected, but they do belong within a common experiential state.

For example, if a patient regresses, say to the age of six, either on the analytic couch or through hypnotic regression, then the behaviors and experiences that were part of his life at that time can be activated and made once more operative. He may remember everybody in the first grade room and where each of his classmates sat. He may be able to speak pieces verbatim learned at that time, which he has forgotten for many years. His six-year-old ego state has been reactivated, or as we term it in ego-state therapy, made "executive."

Since an ego state consists of those behaviors, perceptions, and experiences that are bound together by some common principle and separated by a boundary from other such states, an ego state may be large or small. It may extend over a substantial part of an individual's living, such as his relationships with parent figures, or it may represent a single moment in time, such as a traumatic experience. Ego states exist in different dimensions. A single item might be common to several. For example, a fight with a brother can exist as part of a "relationship-with-brother" ego state; it can also be part of a nine-year-old ego state. When one has been activated, "made executive" (sensed as in the here and now), all items within it are potentially available to present experience. It is therefore possible by concentrating on the one item to "direct cathexis" from one state into the other. If the "nine-year-old" ego state is executive, we may, by concentrating on the fight, move cathexis into the "brother-relationship" state and make the "brother" state exec-utive. Now he has available all items that would be included among the latter. His experienced self in the here and now includes all interactions with his brother.

DISSOCIATION

Multiple or dissociated personalities have been known for many years. The Sally Beauchamp case (Prince, 1906) was one of the first to be described in detail, although stories like Dr. Jekyl and Mr. Hyde had been written earlier. The *Three Faces of Eve* (Thigpen & Cleckley, 1957) created a great sensation when it was first published and a movie was made of it. More recently *Sybil* (Schreiber, 1974) has been published, and a movie also made, describing a young woman with 16 different personalities, who was treated psychoanalytically.

There are some who do not accept the reality of such cases and maintain that they are only faked roles. The well-docu-mented cases that have been studied (and over 100 such have been published) leave little room for doubt by the informed student that personalities can be so divided that one segment is not consciously aware of the other. However, the textbooks describe these cases as extremely rare. We believe that there are many more such individuals than have been diagnosed and studied, partly because mental health professionals, having been taught they are rare, do not recognize them when they appear at clinics.

Pure, classic cases may be infrequent. However, there are probably many borderline and "covert" multiple personality problems in people who appear clinically normal. In many other types of psychopathology it is well recognized that the mentally ill individual is only exhibiting to an extreme degree traits and characteristics that are common to everyone. Thus, the manic-depressive shows in an exaggerated way the mood swings that are quite common to many people. If we apply this concept to multiple personalities, we note that there are many degrees of dissociation. In one case the different personalities do not know that each other exist. Each is aware only that there are blank periods in its existence, time which cannot be accounted for. Here, the boundaries between the two personalities are so rigid and impermeable that there is no penetration. A political analogy is the situation in East and West Berlin. One ego state has no access to behaviors and experiences in the other and may be completely unconscious of the existence of the other.

In some cases of multiple personality there is a kind of one-way awareness. Personality A is aware of the existence of Personality B, but B is not aware of A. Then there are other cases in which the two (or more) states know of each other's existence but treat the other as object, not subject. Eve White talks about how "she," meaning Eve Black, is ruining "her" (Eve White's) life. This condition may also develop after a period of therapy with the first type of case. The various personalities are made conscious of each other's existence, but they still treat each other as foreigners, as ego-alien, and as other people. In time, and with effective treatment, the boundaries between these different personalities may break down, and an integrated person is established.

Since even classic cases of such personalities exhibit relative degrees of dissociation, we are impressed with the possibility that these cases only represent the extreme on a continuum of personality organization. In other words, many people, who are considered within the normal range of functioning, may have comparable divisions within their egos, segments of self, which, however, are not separated by boundaries that are as rigid and impermeable. Maybe they, too, have divisions of ego function, hence, different states, "part persons" or "covert multiple personalities" which alternate and take turns at being "executive."

Conflict Between States

If the various personalities in the clearly dissociated case can clash with each other for hegemony over the individual, anxieties and internal conflict can occur in lesser-disturbed individuals as different states of their ego become cognitively dissonant with each other. In a number of cases of multiple personality, the struggle of an underlying state to "come out" (hence, to become "executive"), with the currently dominant one, which is strong, maintaining its external position, has resulted in a psychosomatic disturbance described by the patient as migraine headache. The two states were battling it out for the rights of territoriality over the body, just as individuals, tribes, and nations do. It is interesting to pose the question as to just what is a "migraine headache" in a "normal" person?

Conflict has been commonly postulated as being at the basis of neurotic symptoms—but conflict between what? The traditional formulation is to consider it as a struggle between two sets of needs, or between socialized and antisocial motivations (super ego versus id). It could equally be considered as a conflict between two different incompatible ego states, each trying to become dominant. And how are conflicts resolved?

Resolution of Conflicts

In the international field Henry Kissinger moved back and forth between Israel and Egypt. During one day he would listen to the needs and claims of the Israelis; the next day he would be paying attention exclusively to the Arab position about the impasse. The point is that at any given moment he was devoting all interest in trying to understand one of the positions and considering ways of meeting the needs of that party. Hopefully he might be able to reconcile these and restore peace to that region of the world.

In the field of scientific research most phenomena are the

result of a number of causing and interacting factors. The researcher, either through experimental design or statistical control, attempts to hold all other variables constant while he studies the effect of one independent factor on the dependent variable. He may then move to the consideration of another related variable with the ultimate hope that all the significance variance found in the dependent one can be accounted for, and each part of it can be allocated in the proper degree to each of the relevant independent variables. Thus analysis of variance or multiple and partial correlation techniques are used to accomplish this purpose.

EGO-STATE THERAPY

Ego-state therapy, as we have been formulating and practicing it, is the application of these same concepts (from the diplomatic field and from the research area) to the understanding and treatment of internal conflicts within a patient. It might be defined as the use of group and family therapy techniques for the resolution of conflicts between the various ego states that make up a "family of self" within a single individual.

Personality Theory

The techniques to be described and illustrated from case examples are based on a theory of personality structure that can be summarized as follows: As the personality develops from birth (and even before), behaviors, experiences, feelings, ideas, memories, attitudes, response potentials, etc., are not stored in some random fashion within the engrams of the brain. Rather they are organized into patterns and cross patterns, large and small, according to the relatedness of their function. We have chosen to call them "ego states," as they were so termed by Paul Federn in his early formulations. A more behavioral name might be "cognitive structural systems" (Hilgard & Hilgard,

1975); however, for therapeutic purposes this seems a bit severe and dehumanizing. These states act in many ways like separate individuals, composed as they are of "part-person" responses. In their pure form they become spontaneously manifest in multiple or dissociated personalities. However, they can be similarly activated within the hypnotic modality.

Hypnosis

One of the characteristics of hypnosis is its reduction of criticality and restriction of the perceptual field (Kline, 1958). This is like zeroing in with a magnifying glass on a small part of an object for the purpose of examining its structure and function most minutely while simultaneously excluding from the field of vision other surrounding and distracting features. In hypnosis the perceptual field of the subject is so narrowed that his experiential world may consist only of himself and the hypnotherapist. The words of the hypnotherapist often become incorporated within the subject, and the suggestions of the hypnotherapist may even become experienced as his own thoughts (Gill & Brenman, 1959). When all energies are concentrated through hypnotic suggestion on a single ego state, the others are suppressed and temporarily deactivated. The single ego state on which all is now focused becomes the "executive state," the self-in-the-now. It experiences its self as "I"; and if aware of the other states, treats them as object, referring to them as "he," "she," "it," or "them." One has now through the hypnotic modality "purified" the functioning of a single state and made its structure and purpose available for intensive diagnostic and therapeutic study. Its origin, purpose for existence, needs, and functioning in the total psychological economy of the patient become much clearer, and it can be dealt with as a separate entity. Through hypnotic control we have replicated within a single individual the situation of a diplomat trying to understand and intermediate between two or more different international states, or that of the scientist who has isolated a single independent variable for the evaluation of its influence on the behavior of an entire organism. As such, many ambiguities in the behavior of an entire person begin to make sense, and more precise control of causative factors becomes possible.

Ego State Therapy as a Strategy

Ego-state therapy is not a system in the sense that psychoanalysis or behavior modification are. Once a significant ego state, which constitutes an important variable in the individual's functioning, has been isolated and activated any of the treatment procedures used by therapists of various persuasions can be employed: suggestion, motivation, desensitization, abreaction, analysis of defenses, interpretations of transference, reflections of feeling, ego strengthening, positive reinforcing, modeling, etc., etc. But these techniques are now being applied to a "part-person," an ego state, and not to the entire organism.

Many therapeutic maneuvers, when applied to a complete individual, are like a shotgun. They mobilize as much resistance as they resolve. Consider the following example: A husband and wife have come to a marriage counselor for marital therapy. The husband, in great distress, discusses his view of their situation. If the therapist offers some encouragement, some positive suggestion, some indication of empathy, or some relief to his mental pain he may antagonize and infuriate the silent but observing and present wife. Likewise, the positive reinforcement, the constructive suggestion offered to the disturbed patient in the hopes of relieving his symptomatic distress may antagonize and mobilize the resistance of an underlying ego state whose goals are quite dissonant to those of the conscious person, hence, objectives of the executive ego state talking to the therapist. As a result, the underlying state sabotages the therapeutic intervention and the patient gets worse. We have seen this happen over and over again. In one case, an underlying ego state, called "Scarlet," said, "I'm the one who is causing her cancer because if I can't come out and enjoy living, she won't either." When Scarlet's "needs" were met there was a retardation of carcinomous deterioration in the patient. A rejection of Scarlet's needs by the therapist might well have exacerbated the progress of the cancer.

Differential Reactions of Ego States

The same event may evoke very different reactions from different ego states. During World War II, one of us (J.G.W.) treated a patient obsessed with a fear of the dark. Under hypnosis he revealed two very separate personalities: Melvin, a weak but high "super-egoed" individual, and George, a strong but sociopathic one. Each of these was studied intensively through interviews, projective tests, and complicated hypnoanalytic maneuvers (Watkins, 1949). An example follows: Card IX M in the *Thematic Apperception Test* depicts a young man sleeping on a couch with an older man bending over him. The Melvin state told the following story about it:

> This is a sickly boy. He has been supporting his father and working very hard. He comes home at night. The old man doesn't like it because he has to work so hard. He is sickly, too. One day the boy flops on a couch. The old man walks over to him and tries to soothe him. He wants to help the boy along. This is an intelligent boy, but he's working at a job that he's not fitted for; so the old man gets dressed and goes to the factory to talk to the foreman. He then gives the boy the right kind of job. The boy is very happy and successful and gets promotions and raises in pay.

When the George state was hypnotically activated, it reacted to the same card as follows:

> This is in a club house. This boy is traveling across the country. He has a few hundred dollars sewed in his shirt, but he doesn't want to spend it. The damn fool ought to know not to keep it there. The old man sees the boy and figures he might keep it on him because he looks good. He goes over and takes the money

out of the shirt. The old man beats it. The boy wakes up and is broke. He goes to the police, but the police don't believe his story. They won't back him up. Instead they throw him for three days in jail as a vagrant. He wants to get back at the police, but he can't do it, and when finally they take him off to the city limits he goes away beaten and broken. He wants to do to others what they did unto him.

Consider the difference in diagnostic evaluation which would follow if Melvin or George happened to be "executive" at the time that the evaluating psychologist administered the tests. How would he represent the patient's attitude toward self? Toward authority figures? Toward parents? What would be the diagnosis and prognosis? And what would be the different therapeutic approaches that would be recommended for this patient? How might a male therapist expect this individual to react to him? What kind of transferences could be anticipated —positive or negative?

This was not a true multiple personality because his Melvin and George states never appeared "pure" and openly called themselves by such names. They could only be overtly activated under hypnosis, but they did alternate in determining the patient's behavior and reactions to others. At that time we had not developed the ego-state conception of personality, nor the techniques of ego-state therapy to be described. Yet, only the activation of these various facets of the patient separately under hypnosis permitted the resolution of his phobia (a latent homosexual reaction) in less than 50 sessions. This case represented one of the earliest ones that cued us into the value of treating various components of the self separately rather than the entire individual at any given session.

Subject-Object

The different alternation of subject and object is most interesting, especially where one state experiences an event from a different locus of self than does another. In one case (which was a true, overt, multiple personality) "Mary" reported a dream in which she was standing beside a friend in a grocery store when a gunman entered. He then shot the friend and Mary woke up screaming. During the next session, Lynne, another personality, reported a dream which she had "the night before last." Lynne was standing on the sidewalk outside a grocery store. A black car drove up and a man with a mask emerged. He went into the store and then Lynne heard a shot and a scream. Lynne stated, "I was outside the store behind a bush. The man was nice looking and in his early fifties. He wore a tan overcoat and brown hat. He didn't see me where I was hiding. I was very frightened and woke up."

Here we see the same experience as viewed from different perspectives. It is obviously the same dream, but the two states experience it differently. The locus of "the I" is different. The scream in this dream was subject for Mary. She reported, "I screamed." For Lynne the scream was experienced as object. ("I heard a scream.") Hence, the experience that one ego state considers as subject and which is infused with ego cathexis becomes object when the ego cathexis is removed to activate the contents of a different state. The content of the experience is the same, only the investment with selfness has changed. At this time both Lynne and Mary might spontaneously emerge, but either could be contacted during any session through hypnosis. This is precisely one of the advantages of hypnosis. Through its modality the locus of the self, "the I" as opposed to "the it" can be changed so that an experience can be viewed subjectively or objectively. And is it not one of the goals of therapy to bring objective understanding to what was subjectively experienced?

Ego States and the "Hidden Observer"

In recent studies the Hilgards (1975) have shown that when a deafness or an analgesia for pain is hypnotically induced, the individual is aware of the sound or pain stimulation at a covert level. Although consciously the subject reports hearing nothing or feeling no pain, there is an underlying entity that senses and records the experience. Hilgard termed this entity "the hidden observer" and described it as a 'cognitive structural system."

We have recently activated "hidden observers" in a number of good hypnotic subjects by inducing deafness, checking to assure that consciously the subjects heard nothing, and then contacting these underlying entities in the same way as Hilgard did by a question as follows: "Although you are hypnotically deaf, perhaps some part of you is hearing my voice and processing the information. If there is, let the index finger on your right hand rise as a sign that this is the case."

In every case the finger lifted. The entity was then asked, "Okay. So there is a part of you that can hear. Part, I want to talk to you. Will you please come out, and when you are here, say 'I'm here'." In each case the entity responded and was then interviewed in depth to determine its area of functioning, its origin, its purpose in the psychological economy of the entire subject, etc.

As we had suspected, these "hidden observers" proved to be ego states who gave themselves specific names such as "Control," "Inner Self," "Me," "Little Part," "Ear," "Lucifer," etc., etc. Each one referred to its self as "I" and to the entire person as "he" or "she." Different states described themselves as follows: "I tell her what to do." "I tell him things that he doesn't want to hear." "I analyze." "I judge and I make the decisions." "I make him outwardly calm, so that others do not see that he is angry." "He doesn't know what he should do; I tell him." "I'm mean." "I was born when she was five years old." They acted in every way like "covert multiple personalities." However, these entities were hypnotically activated in normal subjects. In only one of our subjects was there any evidence of some possible psychopathology. They were all college students whose hypnotizability was known and who had volunteered for the study.

After a "hidden observer" had been evoked and interviewed, the hypnotized subject was now asked, "Is there some other part of you who also could hear and process this information? If there is, let the index finger of the left hand lift." In about half the cases the left finger lifted. A second "hidden observer" was activated and interviewed which proved to be an entirely different ego state, with a different name, different contents, and different functions. This second state was aware of the first, but referred to it as "he" or "she" and distinguished clearly between its own self and the other. In some cases it was obvious that the two states were in conflict with each other, or at least were not fully consonant with each other's purposes and needs.

Finally, the subject was asked, "Are there still other parts of you who can hear and process this information? If there are, let the entire left hand rise." In several of the subjects the hand did rise. No attempt was made to activate these states or interview them further.

Considerable care was taken during the study of these entities to avoid suggesting their content. We tried hard to be very nondirective since we did not want their responses to be merely demand characteristics that were produced by our subjects to please us.

On the basis of these studies we were more than ever convinced that normal personality structure is divided into segments, which have their own identities, and which treat other parts of the ego as object. Hartmann (1958) and other ego psychologists have also hypothesized the existence of such "preconscious automatisms" but have not developed the concept as far as did Federn. The self, thus, resembles a "confederation" of component states. If all of us possess "covert" multiple personalities, "latent dissociation," and "states-rights" ego jurisdictions, as well as a general ego jurisdiction, then it would be quite reasonable that these various components of self might well develop at variance with each other producing inner stress, conflict, and anxiety. The studies on the "hidden observer" phenomena tended to add some experimental verification to this conception of personality that we had already observed so frequently in clinical practice.

Interactions with Ego States

To be optimally effective, psychotherapy must be as precisely focused as possible. For example, if a malevolent-minded ego state A is causing the disturbance in a certain patient, then therapeutic interventions must activate and deal with this specific state and the reactions of the other parts of the personality to it. Well-meaning suggestions, reassurances, reinforcements, etc., presented to the entire individual or to state B may be quite diluted in reaching the specific offending state. They might even have deleterious effects on other states. Furthermore, if an ego state is not executive, hence is inactivated, how do we know that a communication from us is really reaching it at all? We often know very little about how rigid or permeable its boundary is.

It is a truism that one cannot dispatch an enemy in his absence. Yet psychotherapists frequently try to eliminate an offending behavior sequence by applying an intervention to the executive state that is present when the problem may inhere only in a repressed ego state. Johnny is getting the praise or scolding for an action that was really carried out by his brother, Bill. Bill is upstairs asleep. It is not without substance that a criminal may believe, "I am sorry that *it* happened, but *I* didn't do it." The state which performed the crime is not the one now talking. The present executive regards the felonious action as having been carried out by another, an "it," not his own self. Such a conception poses enormous complications for criminal justice and law enforcement. Although such a situation may actually be true in many cases, in others, it could well serve as merely an excuse to avoid responsibility. We have recently discussed this matter in detail in a psychological analysis of the Patty Hearst case (Watkins & Watkins, 1977). Perhaps the question should be asked: If personality dissociation lies on a continuum extending to multiple personalities at the extreme, at what point on this continuum will we hold an individual whose state A is executive responsible for actions by state B? Or how impermeable must a boundary between two states be in order that we conclude it was impossible for one of them to be cognizant of, and control the actions of, another?

If it is true that a single individual is a confederation of ego states that have more or less independence from one another, if generalized control is quite limited, and state-jurisdiction can often prevail, then a Pandora's box has been opened in the behavioral sciences.

For example, in the typical psychological research, a subject is given an initial test. This is followed by an experimental procedure and then a terminal evaluation is administered. Statistical tests are run on a group of such subjects to ascertain whether any changes between the first and last test were significantly greater than chance, or significantly greater than that which occurred between two such tests administered to an equivalent "control" group in which the experimental procedure was omitted. It has naturally been assumed that the person who took the initial test, the one to whom the experimental procedure was administered, and the one who showed up for the final evaluation were the same person, one whose name and experimental number is recorded.

But perhaps this assumption is not true. If ego state A takes the first test and ego state B shows up for the experimental procedure, while a third state C takes the final test, the experiment may be completely invalid. If Henry Jones takes the first test, his brother William comes to the lab for the experimental procedure, and Richard Jones is "executive" on the day of the terminal evaluation, then our experiment is ruined. At the present time it appears that the possibility of such a situation has never been considered or controlled for in psychological research. If our research subjects were all known multiple personalities, the invalidity of the uncontrolled experimental procedure would be immediately recognized. But if the different "states" involved are covert, and part of "normal" personalities, if the boundaries are more permeable, but still present, if the individual is not amnesic to his behavior, then the underlying alteration in identity may not be recognized by the experimenter. We blithely assume we are dealing with a single psychological unit and make no allowance for a possible, partial internal dissociation. But enough of speculation about the implications of ego state theory for the realms of criminal justice and scientific research. Let us consider the clinical evidence, the therapeutic techniques which have been developed and the progress of cases in treatment.

TECHNIQUES OF EGO STATE THERAPY

Nonhypnotic Activation of Ego States

A simple method for activating ego states outside of hypnosis is to use a chair technique developed by one of the authors (H.H.W.). The patient is oriented into the concept that different parts of him may feel differently about a conflict that he has. Several chairs are placed in a circle and the patient is asked to sit in one of them and let some part of himself describe how he feels about the problem. He is to speak in the first person. Thus, "I feel that ———." During this monologue he is not permitted to discuss the matter objectively or to switch to the opposing side of his conflict such as, "I would really like to travel this summer, but I think I should stay here and get a job." In such a case as this, he is asked to stick to *his* (or her) feelings on the "travel" side of his dilemma. When the feelings of that part are fully expressed, then he is asked to move into the next chair for another part to express itself, a part that feels differently from the one who spoke first in the first chair. The patient continues from chair to chair until he cannot find another part that feels differently from the previous ones. Often six or seven chairs may be used. The patient is then asked to stand with the therapist, look at each chair, describe each ego state, its age (if possible), and give each a name or title. Instead of subject, the patient now experiences each ego state as object.

The next step in this procedure is for the patient to act like a cotherapist by understanding the problems of the conflicting ego states and by making appropriate therapeutic interventions. The patient does this by switching chairs, thus his participation in the dialogue as subject is interspersed with looking at the problem as object. Resolution therefore comes from experiencing each ego state as "I" (subject) and as "it" (object).

In the case of ego state therapy the clarification of both sides of an internal controversy can result in a "decision" by a more objective ego state or by the entire person and the initiation of the most constructive behaviors. Ego states, like people, will often be more willing to compromise conflicts when each has had his full "say."

Hypnotic Activation of Ego States

The "chair technique" is most useful during the initial stages of treatment or with unhypnotizable patients. Often activation of states may be significantly accomplished through hypnosis. The patient is hypnotized and suggestions are given aimed at activating various states by directing attention toward them.

To secure the attention of a person, one calls him by his name. This initiates a set in him to receive further stimuli (usually verbal) from the speaker. An ego state, being a part of a person, or a part-person, responds similarly. If it has a name which is known both to itself and the therapist, a request to speak to "Mary," "Survival," or "Dark One" will often serve to bring a response from it, hence, "Yes" or "I'm here." From the standpoint of Federn's theories, the therapist, calling on it, directs "cathexis" into that state and "activates" it, hence, makes it "executive." It becomes the "self-in-the-now."

Often, however, and especially when being contacted for

the first time, it has no such designation. An internal entity has emerged but one does not know what to call it. Our procedure is to ask if it has a name, or what it would like to be called. At other times it will adopt a name, perhaps based on its function within the entire individual, such as, "I'm the one which represents his judgment."

The ascribing of a name to an ego state is not (as some of our critics have insisted) done in order to force a false humanistic artifact upon an abstract psychological process, but simply to make identification possible, just as a research investigator may ask for a test response from Subject #17. Naming certainly may tend to reinforce the humanoid aspects of a state, but we do not assign names ourselves. Rather, we wait until the emerging entity shows "part-person" characteristics and identifies itself.

If we assume that behaviors and experiences are organized into such personality patterns, then the entire pattern can be activated by focusing attention on one of its behavioral or experiential elements such as: "May I speak to whoever or whatever impelled Mary (the entire patient) to go into that bar?" (Mary had previously reported being "drawn" into the bar, although she had intended not to enter. In other words, the impulse to enter the bar came from a part of her that was experienced as object not subject, hence, outside of her control.)

Again, we might make an activation request as follows: "John (the patient's name) reported severe headaches the past few days. I want to talk to whoever can tell me about the cause of the headaches."

We focus especially on those more subtle behaviors manifested by posture, voice, gesture, or feelings that seem to be derived from either some element that is object or from subject elements that are below the threshold of awareness. Focusing of attention, of course, occurs in all normal interpersonal transactions whenever we call another person by his name. However, because of the unique properties of the hypnotic modality, the narrowing of the field of consciousness to an experiential world consisting only of hypnotist and subject facilitates greatly the suppression of attention to other internal or external stimuli, and hence, the activation of only that sector of the individual that is currently desired for study or intervention.

Hypnosis may also be viewed as a modality to facilitate energy change. Through hypnotic intervention we direct ego or object cathexes into or out of various physical and psychological components of the self.

When a hypnoanalytic approach is to be used the patient is first hypnotized and the state is deepened by any of the standard methods (Kroger, 1963; Meares, 1961; Weitzenhoffer, 1957). The therapist then calls upon the part that is responsible for some symptom, function, or behavior. For example, if the patient reports that he was unable to sleep last night, the therapist might say after hypnotizing him, "I want to speak to the one who prevented Joe from getting to sleep last night. Will you come out, and when you are here, just say 'I'm here'."

If states with various names have spontaneously emerged previously, it is an easy matter to say, "I want to speak to the Dark One," or "I want to speak to Control. Control, will you please come out, and when you're here just lift your right hand." Sometimes a new entity will appear and the therapist may say, "Have I talked with you before?" "What's your name?" "Where did you come from?" "What purpose in Marian do you serve?" "How old was Marian when you were born?" "Why were you born?"

Occasionally, a state will become angry at the therapist and refuse to "come out." Frequent requests may be met by silence. It is sometimes possible to ask another state about the matter. "Jane, why won't the Little One come out today?" Jane may then tell the therapist what is bugging Little One, and appropriate strategy can be undertaken to bring Little One back into communication. Theory would hold that a state becomes activated as constant attention is directed toward it by the therapist. At times this requires much perseverance. At other times states emerge and withdraw, spontaneously assuming the executive for only short periods.

We have found that the dismissal or deactivation of a state can be easily accomplished simply by saying, "Thank you, Hideaway. You can go where you need to go. And now I would like to speak to Love."

We make a point of treating each state with the utmost courtesy and respect as a therapist would a member of a group therapy. Ego states, although only part persons, commonly respond like any person. That is, if they are antagonized or belittled by the therapist, they can develop strong animosities and throw up much resistance to the treatment, even to the point of sabotaging it completely. The therapist endeavors to establish as good a relationship as possible with every ego state. Even the destructive ones can be altered better if they are not treated as villains. Through a close and mutually-respecting relationship with the therapist, it becomes much easier to interpret their neurotic defensive maneuvers and to induce change in their attitudes.

We have found that each ego state, even when it is destructive to the welfare of the entire person, considers itself as being motivated by worthy goals. Commonly a state was created at the time of a trauma to the patient. Its objective was to protect that individual, a "protection" that it may have continued to exert long after it was desirable. One such state originated at the age of three when the patient was sexually molested. It stated that its purpose was to "protect" the little girl from men. For the next 20 years it had successfully accomplished its mission by making her overeat, become fat, and maintaining a schizoid personality in her which repelled close relationships. It viewed these actions as necessary to see that "she" suffered no further harm. This state even resorted to frightening hallucinations to scare her away from dates with boys. During the early stages of the treatment when it was first discovered, it was termed "the Evil One." Later, its name was changed to "the Dark One." As the therapist recognized its needs it became less hostile, Finally, a close relationship with it was established by the therapist, and it agreed to cooperate in the treatment of the entire patient. In the course of time the therapist (H.H.W.) turned Dark One into her cotherapist and taught it Wolpe's desensitization techniques (Wolpe, 1961). It carried out successfully the fear desensitization of a phobia suffered by another state (Little One) who had been traumatized at an early age.

At one time, before the Evil One had been changed into the Dark One, the therapist had to protect the patient from Evil One's threats in order to give her some temporary rest from anxiety and panic. A technique was developed called "The Safe Room," in which the patient could escape from the Evil One and rest.

In "The Safe Room" technique the hypnotized patient is led down a fantasied series of carpeted stairs at the bottom of which he visualizes a door. When opened, this leads into a peaceful and comfortably furnished room of the patient's own choosing. This room is insulated from any disturbance so that the patient can remain there for a period of rest and relaxation.

The Evil One kept intruding into this patient's mental privacy in the form of hallucinations, compulsions, and demands upon her. Accordingly, the therapist "accompanied" her patient to the bottom of the stairs, and as she went into the Safe Room, the therapist "grabbed" the Evil One by the arm and kept it out until the patient could go safely within and shut the door. This resulted in a very restful and ego-restoring period for the patient, not to mention the increase in trusting relationship with the therapist who was willing to "go to bat" and protect her against such inner disturbance.

At other times when the therapist was trying to communicate with the patient, the Evil One would set up an internal racket and try to distract the patient from hearing the therapist. During such moments the therapist often broke in quite angrily and shouted, "Evil One! Shut up!" and the Evil One would shut up; the hallucinatory voices temporarily subsided or disappeared. Excerpts of this case have already been published (Watkins, (in press); Watkins & Watkins, 1976).

Perhaps the biggest lesson we learned was that treatment is most rapid when the therapist makes a sincere effort to understand and meet the needs of every significant ego state. This is not always easy, like trying to be a good parent to a large family of children in which there is much sibling rivalry, competition for parental attention, and conflicting wants. The techniques used here represent principles of parent effectiveness training (Gordon, 1970) applied by the therapist in her interaction with the various ego states that constitute the patient's "family of self." The therapist listens intently to ascertain the underlying needs of each state, and attempts to meet them in a new and constructive way. This approach is similar to Gordon's resolution of conflicts between parent and child.

The greatest therapeutic successes seemed to occur when it was possible to negotiate a compromise between two competing ego states. For example, "Father, Little Boy says that he steals hub caps because he is angry since you give him no recognition or praise. You are always criticizing him."

The Father state replies, "But he deserves all the criticism I give him. He is just no good, and will not behave himself."

Therapist: "Father, would you please step aside for a few minutes. I'd like to talk to Little Boy." Little Boy emerges. "Little Boy, if Father would quit riding you, would you be willing to stay out of trouble for awhile and show him that you can be trusted?"

Little Boy: "I don't think he'll leave me alone, but if he would agree to quit bugging me, I'll try to do what he wants."

Therapist: "Thank you, Little Boy. Now, I'd like to talk once again to Father." (Little Boy abdicates the executive and Father returns.) "Father, did you hear Little Boy speaking? What do you think?"

Father: "I heard him, but I don't trust him. I don't think he means it."

Therapist: "How about giving it a try. If I can get him to

agree to stay out of trouble during these next three days would you be willing to lay off of him? Stop criticizing. And if he behaves himself give him a few compliments?"

Father: "Okay. I don't think it'll work, but I'll try."

Father stops the nagging criticisms. The patient does not get into any trouble during the next few days, hence, whenever Little Boy is executive he does not induce the whole patient to act out. The patient, himself, reports that there is a great relief from tension. He has felt better the last few days, and his general work has been more constructive.

Here we see that when one state tries a more integrative behavior and another state stops the punishment, applying instead positive reinforcements, a therapeutic rehabilitation ensues. Inner conflict subsides, and behavior becomes less neurotic. The needs of both states are being better met, and their clash with each other lessens or disappears. Perhaps in time the Father state (introjected from the original father) may so change that it applies continuous positive reinforcements. The patient instead of being constantly depressed from the inner (and unconscious) accusations of a punitive father figure, now derives good "strokes" from this altered introject and begins to act like a son who has developed and flourished through a constructive and rewarding relationship with his parent. A destructive component of self has been changed and replaced by a more benevolent one.

In the practice of medicine the aim of the physician is often to mobilize the resources of the body to fight infections and repair damage. For example, one of the newest approaches to the treatment of cancer (Simonton and Simonton, 1975) attempts to stimulate an individual's "will to resist" and in this way increase the resistance to the host to the ravages of neoplasm. Ego state therapy operates under a similar principle. We mobilize constructive forces within the self to counter malevolent entities such as the introjects of bad parents or other harmful influences internalized by our patient.

In one of our patients a fear state (which described itself

as plural, "We are like tics sitting on the mind.") apparently had developed when the patient was hospitalized at the age of one and a half, isolated from parents, and placed in an oxygen tent. This inner fear no longer served any realistic purpose to the individual but still arose during times that required social interaction. This nonfunctional fear then caused her to retreat from human contact (back into her child oxygen tent).

The Dark One, a state which has been mentioned earlier in this paper, was enlisted by the therapist to "stifle" these "fearsome things." He agreed to do so in three days, and did that precisely. The patient ceased to have these unreasonable fears. This caused us to ponder just how one state can "stifle" another, apparently by removing its energy or by decathecting it? This is a tactic we have used occasionally; namely, enlisting the efforts of a constructive state (or an alliance of such states) to overthrow or hold in line a maladaptive one so that it is not permitted to become executive or exert significant influence on the total behavior of the individual.

The key to the successful practice of ego state therapy lies in the ability of the therapist to conceptualize his patient as a "family of states" rather than a unit. Clinical questions which are ordinarily asked in other therapies may include: "Does the patient really want to get well?" "What is his relationship with his mother?" "His father?" "How does he view the therapist?" "What is his attitude about treatment?"

The ego-state therapist may be thinking: "Is this patient dissociated into many or few states? Are his ego-state boundaries rigid or permeable? What is the relative influence of his 'federal ego jurisdiction' versus 'states rights' in determining his behavior? Which states are constructive? Which destructive? What inner compromises can be made to reduce conflict?"

In approaching our patient from this viewpoint we think of him as being an extremely complex system of equilibrium in which many forces, many parts, many subentities are interacting, cooperating, competing, jockeying for power, and (like governmental committees and programs) once created, struggling to maintain their existence as separate entities even though the original sustaining functions that brought about their inception no longer exist. Some of them behave in ways that are constructive to the general welfare of the entire person; the motivations of others operate to veto legitimate needs of their sibling states and to create maladaptive behavior for the whole individual of which they are a part.

By narrowing the perceptual and experiential field through hypnosis or other psychological techniques, we permit each in turn to express and clarify its role in the total psychic economy and by treating these "part-persons" like separate individuals we find that they react like persons. Hence, they can be cooperative, hostile, affectionate, fearful, and show a great range of feelings, attitudes, and motivations just as entire persons do. But like our diplomatic negotiator between Israel and the Arab states or like our researcher confronted with a multivariate problem, we can better delineate the factors in an internal conflict and make constructive therapeutic interventions more precise—of such is ego state therapy.

To illustrate, a sample of interaction within a treatment session will be presented next by recorded verbatim excerpts. The patient came to treatment complaining of being unable to stay awake at times. He would spontaneously enter an almost trancelike state. He was a very bright student doing an exceptional job in a mathematical field. In fact, when studying, he was able to concentrate so completely that he would not respond to being stuck with a pin. The question was, who or what was initiating this condition that at times even endangered his life by causing him almost to go to sleep while driving a car. Medical and neurological examinations found nothing physically unusual that could account for such a symptom.

During the week preceding this session the patient had been found sitting in a car in a parking lot in a confused condition, suffering from a severe headache, and then was briefly hospitalized. At the beginning of this session the therapist is talking to an underlying ego state, called "Old One," and inquiring as to what happened at that time.

"Old One" was the dominant ego state and executive most

of the time. It was characterized by a driving need to work very hard and be "rational," a sort of demanding super-ego figure. Old One believed in all work and no play and kept the patient, Ed, constantly studying. Emotional feelings were inhibited, and time for recreation was not permitted. As a consequence some of the other ego states, especially the more child states, were rebelling, creating internal conflict, and at times paralyzing Ed's ability to concentrate on his studies.

As will be seen from this verbatim excerpt of the session, the therapist's strategy was, by resonating with Old One's needs and empathizing with his goals for occupational success, to induce him to relax his driving control and permit expression of some of the anger and play needs of Ed's other states. Hopefully, this would bring more balance into the patient's life, resolve the inner conflict that was sabotaging his study goals, and diminish the numerous psychosomatic symptoms he was experiencing as a consequence of this inner battle. During this session a new state spontaneously appeared.

Therapist-Patient Interactions	*Therapist Thoughts and Theoretical Notes*

H: Hello, Old One. Where are you?

E: Sitting in a chair.

H: In what building?

E: Clinical Psychology.

H: Do you know what day it is?

E: Sure.

H: What day is it?

E: 17th of November.

H: Okay, that's fine. Now, what's been happening? I talked to the doctor last Friday and he told me that you had some uncontrolled, he called it a hysterical reaction; he gave you

Although this hour was held on a Thursday, Nov. 20th, "Old One" here has been regressed back to the previous session on Monday, Nov. 17th, to recapture parts of that hour which were not recorded.

some Thorazine and then sent you home. I understand something happened in the parking lot. Why don't you tell me what happened from your point of view?

E: I made a mistake.

H: How do you mean that?

E: It's kind of hard to put in words. I cut the wrong connection. No, the wrong, no, I made the wrong—move. I'm in a severe, complex thing and I didn't understand wholly what I was doing.

Old One very honest, a rigid but uncorruptible, super-ego state. Can admit error.

H: Could you explain that to me a little bit more?

E: I was cutting the subconscious automation mechanism, so it would be okay if I didn't have it for a little while, so I thought that if I cut the automatic things I could make a structure using Shalom to control. I cut the wrong wire.

H: How was it that you cut the wrong wire?

E: Well, I was cutting away anger and I got a pain, and it took over, and I couldn't control it anymore.

"Shalom" another ego state sometimes fronting for Old One.

Old One cannot tolerate anger. It's not "rational." He manages to "cut the wrong wire" so that the patient experiences his frustrated rage as a headache. Pain becomes so severe Old One loses control of the situation. "Ed" is then confused and can't function.

(Later in hour.)

Later during this Thursday session the Old One is reactivated but no longer regressed to Monday. He is now reacting in the actual present.

H: And now I would like to talk to the Old One. Tell me how you are. Hi. What's been going on since Monday?

E: Well, I haven't been doing anything.

The Old One: a very conservative, rational state which directs E always to study; no foolishness.

H: Do you know what else has been going on?

E: Yeah. Ed's getting all worried.

(Ed is name used for the whole patient.)

H: Oh, Ed's getting worried. About what?

E: What's going on. He doesn't know what to do. He's thrashing around, but I can't do anything because if I do then I ruin it.

Old One is wise enough to recognize he has limits in controlling E.

H: Okay. I appreciate your not doing anything as you said you wouldn't. Do you know what happened Monday night when he got sick?

Besides, he agreed he would not interfere and force E and the other ego states always to adhere to his dictatorial philosophy.

E: (Breathes hard.) Not really. There must be something that I'm not sure of going on. It was a bad thing. It was trying to make me be bad, but I wouldn't let it.

H: What was trying to make you be bad? What do you mean?

"It" means object, hence, a "nonself" force not under Old One's control or included within the Old One ego-state.

E: I don't know. Something wanted me to be bad and I didn't have any good reason to be bad.

He labels as "bad" behavior anything of which he disapproves.

H: What do you mean by "be bad"? What does that mean to you?

E: Be irrational.

H: Does that mean "feel"?

E: No.

H: What does that mean then?

"Bad" apparently is anything not logical or rational to Old One.

E: Act irrationally.

H: Like how?

E: Screaming and hollering and jumping up and down. That's not right.

It's hard to get him to be explicit as to what he means by "irrational."

No strong emotional releases; no child behavior allowed!

H: Oh, you don't like yourself when you do that, is that it?

E: No. It's not right.

H: But apparently somebody else is getting ticked off in terms of what was happening.

E: I don't know, but I stopped
it.

H: How did you stop it?

E: I held it up.

H: How did he get sick?

E: I don't know. Getting sick
is a rational thing.

"He" refers to "Ed," the entire patient.

H: Well, it's okay with you if
he gets sick, but it's not okay with
you if he jumps up and down and
screams.

E: No, no way. Uh-uh. Uh-uh.
That's irrational.

Old One will accept psychosomatic symptoms that result from the suppression of emotional release, but will not accept the release behavior. That would be "irrational."

H: I see. I think, Old One,
you're going to have to let him
express a little bit more of his
angry feelings. Now, even though
you have shut out some patternings
of escaping angry feelings; now he
has to learn to deal with them at a
conscious level. You're going to
have to let him do a little bit of
that.

E: I don't want to.

H: Why not? He doesn't have
to yell and scream, but he has to
do something with those feelings.

Old One objects strongly to H's suggestion that he be more permissive.

E: Why?

H: He needs to deal with
them. And you and I made an
agreement, if you remember.

E: You made an agreement
with the Old One. You didn't
make an agreement with me.

H: Oh, I thought I was talking
to the Old One. Who am I talking
to? Is that Ed?

E: No.

H: Is it Omega?

E: No.

H: Is it Freak?

E: Uh-uh.

H: Who is it?

E: I'm not gonna tell you.

At least open to explanation—a foot in the door for the therapist. And on being pushed he leaves (inactivates himself), and a new state becomes executive. Note the defense of an ego state by withdrawal when cornered. It may no longer talk to you. Who is "me"?

H is trying to find out which of several ego states with whom she has previously dealt is now executive.

Oh-oh! A new one.

H: Oh, come on.

E: No . . .

H: Come on . . .

E: That's not fair.

H: I wouldn't hurt you.

E: No? Why not?

H: I don't want to hurt you.

E: I don't believe you.

H: What name would you like me to call you?

E: I don't really have a name.

H: How old do you feel?

E: Well, I'm not very old. I'm older than you!

H: How old are you?

E: Hmm . . . let me think now. I'm three.

H: Oh, I like three-year-old boys. You must be lots of fun. You kind of grinned. Do you like that? Are you stopping him from feeling?

E: No.

H: Hmm . . . You must have snuck in there someplace while I was talking to the Old One, is that what you did?

E: M-hm.

H: You just want to be heard. You want to be heard, don't you?

E: You talk to everybody else, but you never talk to me.

H: I just didn't know you were there.

E: Well . . .

H: Now that I know you're there, I'm gonna talk to you more often.

E: Really?

H: Yeah.

E: Oh, good.

H: We'll have lots of fun.

The manner in speech, pitch, etc., sounds very much like a child. Coaxing gently; H responds to child quality of the ego state.

H reassures apparent fear of new state.

Expects to be hurt from his world. This state continues to distrust therapist. Note how it refuses to respond positively to her demand characteristics.

Like a little boy trying to appear big.

With considerable difficulty she begins to secure its trust and accordingly its cooperation.

How does one build a good relationship with a fearful 3-year-old boy?

Children need to be heard.

"I'm just a little boy, and you don't pay any attention to me." (Implication: "like everybody else")

Therapist meeting need to be heard.

E: Oh, good. I don't have much fun.

Lonely.

H: You don't have anybody to play with?

E: Uh-uh.

H: Well, we'll talk again. And I just want you to keep in mind that I'll talk to you again, and I like talking to you and I enjoy it and I'll look forward to it. And what I want you to imagine now is that I'm kind of walking along with you. Can you imagine that?

Has experienced much ignoring and rejection.

E: With me?

H: What would you like to call me? You can call me anything you like . . . if you have a special name you want to call me.

Big people didn't walk "with me" just for the fun of it. Therapist making friends.

E: No, I don't have a special name.

Can't trust yet with name.

H: Would you like to call me Aunt something?

E: Huh?

H: Would you like to call me Aunt Helen?

E: No. Aunts are no good.

"Aunts" were never very good to him.

H: Oh, I see.

E: (mumbles)

H: Oh, uh . . .

E: All they ever do is knit and stuff. They never do anything fun.

They never played with him.

H: You can just call me Helen, okay? And you and I will play together.

Helen is acceptable, but no "Aunt Helen." Therapist almost cued into an unconstructive transference reaction.

E: Will you be my friend?

H: I will be your friend.

E: Okay.

H: Now, between now and the next time I talk to you again I just want you to imagine that you and I are playing out on a playground, walking down the street hand-in-hand and I'll take good care of you. And we'll have fun.

E: Okay.

H: Okay. Hmm ... You have a name for me, but I don't have a name for you. What shall I call you?

E: You can call me Sandy.

H: Sandy. Okay, Sandy. I'll talk to you again. Alright. Now I want you to step aside and I want to talk to ...

E: I don't want to.

H: Oh, I'll talk to you later, okay? Besides, you can take me with you. You can just take me with you and I will take your hand and you can feel my hand, that's it. And you just run along with Helen playing with you. Now I want to talk to the Old One again.

E: Hello.

H: Hi! I see a little three-year-old, did you see him?

E: What?

H: Do you know that there's a three-year-old by the name of Sandy around there?

E: No.

H: He's kind of fun. You should get to meet him. You didn't know he was there, huh?

E: No. Three-year-old?

H: M-hm. Maybe you don't know all the people around there. I don't know them all either. Maybe you don't know them all.

E: No, I don't think so.

H: Now I want to talk to you again and to remind you, that we had a kind of agreement that I would try to teach him at the

By resonating to a 3-year-old, promising to pay attention to him and "play," H builds enough relationship with this state that he trusts her now with his name.

Sandy wants to stay with therapist.

Conference now required with Old One to get him to accept Sandy, to quit ignoring and suppressing the child.

Old One not aware of Sandy. Ego state boundaries rather impermeable.

Old One begrudgingly admits there are some things he doesn't know about E's "family of self."

Old One obsessed with "rationality." H pins Old One down on his previous "agreement" to let her work with E's emotional waking level to handle his angers and his confrontations in a constructive way. Is that still okay with you?

E: In a constructive, rational way.

H: Well, I don't know what you mean by rational, but he has to express his feelings . . . but they don't have to hurt anyone.

E: No . . . but you're always going to hurt somebody.

H: Oh, people are always saying "You hurt my feelings" and "You do that" and that's just a way of making other people responsible for one's own feelings. Just because he expresses a feeling, that doesn't mean that he's responsible for other people's feelings. He's responsible for his own, and it's important, especially in his marriage relationship, that he tells his wife how he feels.

E: But she never understands how I feel. When I tell her she always gets mad.

H: Well, this is the part that I'm dealing with. Will you let me do that?

E: Sure.

H: And without letting him get sick or something like that.

E: Well he wanted to jump up and down and I said no, absolutely not. So, he got sick.

H: Well, I'm not suggesting that jumping up and down is a good idea, okay? I mean, I'm with you. However, you gotta give him a little out.

E: Okay.

H: You can't punish him with

and "irrational" states rather than simply repressing them, a tactic which has been creating inner turmoil and painful psychosomatic symptoms for E. Old One when confronted "rationally" gives way, but slowly and with much resistance.

Discussion veers to E's difficulties in his marriage because of Old One's intransigence.

Dynamics of somatic symptoms. Angry, frustrated ego states want to "jump up and down." Old One suppresses them. Conflict converts into being "sick."

illness. Give him a little out and
let me deal with that. Alright,
thank you. And now I am going to
arouse you by counting up to five,
and when I count up to five you
will be wide awake, fresh and alert.
Coming up now at the count of
five . . . 1 . . . 2 . . . 3 . . . 4 . . . 5.
Coming up, feeling relaxed and
good and calm, wide awake,
coming up. Okay.

    E: I tried to move my legs;
I'm awake now.

    H: Nice calm, relaxed feeling.
Do you feel relaxed now?

    E: (laughs) You better believe
it, I feel like going to sleep.

    End.

    Time of excerpt: 20 minutes.

Coming out of hypnosis.

Slow in coming up from
hypnosis.

Problem not resolved but
better understood. Therapeutic
strategy: How to persuade Old One
to relax rigid control and permit
other angry and fearful states such
as Sandy (and others) to meet
legitimate needs in a way in which
Old One can accept them as
"rational."

Similar to classical
super-ego–id conflict but
conceptualized and treated in ego
state terms. Very important to
maintain good relationships with
both Old One and the "irrational"
child states if intermediation is to
be successful.

Many surprising interactions occurred between Ed's various ego states that we cannot pursue here except to describe one which seemed especially unusual. Ed had reported that for some time he had been unable to concentrate on his studies in a foreign language course. He felt that he was on the point of failing it. Old One was very upset over the situation. Sandy emerged and said that he was the one who had been disturbing

Ed's study habits. If he, Sandy, was not permitted to play he would not allow Ed to concentrate. Helen asked Sandy not to bother Ed during the day but instead to play in his dreams at night, and Sandy agreed.

In the following session Ed reported that he had been able to concentrate very well, had studied without distraction for the first time in weeks, and in fact had gotten an A on his final exam as a result. However, he was wondering why he had such vivid dreams every night and "in technicolor." When Sandy was activated he told Helen he had let Ed alone to study in the daytime as per his agreement and that, "I've been playing at night instead."

Ego state therapy is filled with many surprises and the various entities show spontaneous behavior and expressions so frequently unusual or contrary to the therapist's expectations. But if persons can be spontaneous and creative, why should not ego states behave similarly? After all, they are "part-persons."

The human condition, either in its entirety or in its segments, is more than a box of machinery and abstract processes. Psychologies and psychotherapies which try to reduce us to simple elements lose the essence of what life is all about.

QUESTIONS REGARDING EGO STATE THERAPY

In presenting our studies to others they often confront us with certain doubts concerning the validity of the therapeutic data we get in this approach. The questions are legitimate and should be raised. While we do not have complete answers to them, the following replies seem to be justified:

1. You describe experiences reported by patients which happened very early in life before they would have acquired language. How can an individual even under hypnosis tell of something that happened before he had learned words?

Many people have been born in another country and did not acquire the English language until they were much older. For example, one of us was born in Bavaria, lived there as a child, and only learned to speak English much later, yet can report in English quite clearly memories of events that happened before any English words had been learned. These were not remembered in German and then translated into English. They were "remembered" in English in which the writer is quite fluent now. We believe that experiences impress themselves on the engrams of the brain from the earliest ages (perhaps prebirth). Meanings are established. Later, when words are attached to such meanings, the individual can describe the early events.

> 2. How do you know that the events described really took place? Maybe they are only fantasies, wishes, or screen memories?

True, one can never be sure. Freud found that many of the trauma reported by his patients were screen memories. However, *for the patient* a reported event has *psychological truth.* Hence, it has meaning and an inner reality that has influenced his behavior and feelings. It must be accepted as a valid piece of communication about his inner self and dealt with accordingly. When a patient remembers that his father hated him, his "memory" and his experience of it that way is more important from the standpoint of therapy than whether or not his father really hated him. For him, his father hated him, and his present adjustment is based on that perception or misperception. It still requires therapeutic intervention. In fact, it is always the psychological reality and not the actual reality which determines experience and behavior.

> 3. How do you know that these so-called ego states are not merely artifacts produced under hypnosis by suggestible patients as a result of the demand characteristics of the situation? They are aware of your belief in "parts" of selves, since

you ask for them, and even if they weren't you could be
transmitting the request to create such "parts" artificially by
unconscious cues,—hence, through the "Rosenthal effect."
(Rosenthal, 1966; Orne, 1969)

This is a good question, and one for which we have no
complete answer. We did try in our research to be as vague and
nondirective as possible. Even when we asked for the activation
of "a part of you" we did not specify its content except in those
cases where we have said, "that part of you which is causing
the headache," etc. In either case "the part" that emerged
described content, identity, and function in far greater detail
than we had ever suggested. Often the "states" emerged spontaneously to our great surprise when they were not expected, and
when we did not anticipate their purpose.

This does not rule out the possible error of suggesting the
activation of a "state" that was nonexistent within the patient
until we created it by the demand characteristics of the situation. However, an equally tenable hypothesis is that these
"states" have not been elicited by many other workers because,
having no reason to suspect a multiple rather than a single
identity in an individual, they have ignored and hence suppressed the entity that was actually there, also by the demand
characteristics of their situations.

In one multiple personality case, an underlying state
"Marge" emerged. Marge claimed to have been in existence for
over two months, and when asked why she had not appeared
before, she replied, "Well, I've been around. You didn't call on
me. I didn't have the opportunity, so that's why I didn't come
out."

Demand characteristics are a two-edged sword in that the
beliefs of the investigator can create a sin of commission or of
omission. We cannot rule out this phenomena; however, we are
very aware of its influence and have consistently tried to mini-
mize it in both our research and our clinical treatment. We also
have some empirical research studies (which will be reported

elsewhere) indicating that simulators would not respond in the same way as genuine "ego states."

4. Aren't you afraid that by the constant artificial dissociation of a patient through hypnotic manipulation you will reinforce dissociating tendencies? Aren't you teaching him to practice and use this defense when he should be learning how *not* to dissociate?

Our experience has been quite the contrary. We find that as our patients become increasingly familiar with their various states, plus the ways these states have been interacting with each other and influencing their total behavior, the boundaries between the states become more flexible and permeable. Communication tends to be established, and the more generalized ego jurisdiction plays a greater role. In fact, dissociation can exist pathologically only to the extent that one state is unaware of the existence or influence of another. As the unconscious cognitive dissonance between states is made conscious and available to all states the possibilities of its resolution or mitigation become greater. In a society of individuals, as the awareness of each for the roles and specializations of function of the others increases, the whole societal organism begins to operate more efficiently, even as understanding and communication between world states promotes a better world society. It is not necessary that all component parts of a "self" lose their individual character and fuse for the person to become adaptive in his behavior. There are times to indulge our child states, and other times when more mature states should be executive. The richness of our existence is not enhanced by the elimination of states, but rather by the balance between ego state functioning and generalized self control.

At another level, we believe that existence equals impact, impact between the subject of our own self and the object of nonself, the impact between "the me" and "the not me." Existence is thus increased as you and I constructively impact each other. We recognize that the fullness of life requires good inter-personal relations with others.

Similarly, *inner* existence is enhanced when the executive state, the present "me," the "self in the now" can constructively impact other personal entities, components of self which are temporarily object to the executive's subject. Thus, inner dialogues take place that make more rich and meaningful the processes within. We are never alone when we can "talk" to ourselves, even if much of this inner impact and conversation occurs at subliminal, hence, unconscious levels. But "talk" to exist requires both a speaker and a listener. Through ego state therapy we seek to make inner confrontations between states cooperative, meaningful, and rewarding to the entire person and to reduce or eliminate the clashes that so frequently make the self a battleground of conflicting forces.

The validation of existence occurs when the "me" and the "not-me" impact and interact. If impacts occurred only between the entire individual and the outer world, if boundaries existed only between his total self and others, an individual might enjoy a rich extravertive life and rewarding *inter*personal relationships with others. But when we add to this meaningful impacts at the boundaries of many different, but constructively interacting components of self, then we are giving equal importance to an individual's *intra*personal relationships. The richness of existence and the "beingness" of the individual in both his outer and inner worlds are enhanced. In ego state therapy we do not seek to create a "world-state" of self, but rather a harmoniously interacting "family of self" for the maximal enjoyment of living by both the whole person and each of his respective parts.

SUMMARY

Ego state therapy represents an application of group and family therapy techniques for the resolution of conflicts between the various ego states which constitute a "family of self" within a single individual. The concept of an ego state was developed by Paul Federn. We define it as a body of behaviors and experiences bound together by some common principle and separated from other such states by a boundary which is more or less permeable. The ego state that represents the individual's behaviors and experiences in the "here and now" is considered to be "executive." Alternation of different ego states appears to be a normal process in personality functioning. However, this distinct difference between states is observed most clearly only when they are isolated and "purified," such as occurs in cases of multiple personality, or when "activated" under hypnosis.

Ego states act like "part-persons" or "covert multiple personalities." When activated they experience their contents as subject, hence, as "I" or "my." They experience the entire individual and other states as object, thus as "it," "he," "she," or "them." As "part-persons" they have a relative autonomy from each other and from the entire individual depending on the rigidity or permeability of the ego boundaries which separate them from each other and from the complete person. They may have developed through normal divisions of function that are economic to the individual, but they are often also created at times of stress to serve defensive or "protective" needs. Unfortunately, once established they may act autonomously, "protecting" the individual in blind, unrealistic ways that are no longer appropriate but are maladaptive and impair present functioning. Since they develop personal needs and goals, which are often narrowly conceived, and since these aims may clash with those of other states, cognitive dissonance, anxiety, and internal conflict may ensue.

Ego state therapy attempts to resolve such conflicts through a kind of internal diplomacy, activating each party to the conflict at a time, determining its purposes and functioning, and working out appropriate compromises so that the various states can function cooperatively together for the realistic and mature adaptation of the entire individual. A consistent general jurisdiction with goals consonant to all parts of the self replaces unrestricted "states rights" and internal conflicts between these "part-person" components. In resolving these conflicts the therapist acts like an international diplomat mediating between antagonistic countries. Like the research scientist who, through experimental design and statistical control, studies the impact on a dependent variable of various independent factors separately, the therapist isolates and "activates" one ego state at a time and determines its effect on the functioning of the entire person.

Individual ego states may be activated by such procedures as the "chair technique," but often more effectively through the modality of hypnosis. Since hypnosis has the effect of narrowing the field of perception and of intensifying the therapist–patient relationship, energies can be concentrated on single states (parts of the person) at a time. This permits a clearer evaluation of their respective roles and a more precise therapeutic intervention to alter their functioning constructively. Ego state therapy is, therefore, a mode of "intrapersonal" involvements between the various parts of a self similar to the "interpersonal" relationships that are dealt with in group and family therapies. The various states are isolated, and their transactions with each other and with the complete self are studied separately. The ultimate goal of this approach is to reduce dissociation, establish inner communication, and resolve intrapersonal conflicts. Hopefully, this will develop an integrated, consonant person whose self-parts function cooperatively with each other and with the whole individual for maximal adaptation in both his inner and outer worlds.

References

Berne, E. *Transactional analysis in psychotherapy.* New York: Grove Press, 1961.

Federn, P. *Ego psychology and the psychoses.* (E. Weiss, Ed.), New York: Basic Books, 1952.

Gill, M. & Brenman, M. *Hypnosis and related states.* New York: International Universities Press, 1959.

Gordon, T. *Parent effectiveness training.* New York: Peter H. Wyden, 1970.

Harris, T. A. *I'm OK—you're OK.* New York: Harper & Row, 1969.

Hartmann, H. *Ego psychology and the problem of adaptation.* New York: International Universities Press, 1958.

Hilgard, E. & Hilgard, J. *Hypnosis in the relief of pain.* Los Altos, Ca.: William Kaufmann, 1975.

Kaplan, H. T. & Sadock, B. J. *Comprehensive group psychotherapy.* Baltimore: Williams & Wilkins, 1971.

Kline, M. V. *Freud and hypnosis.* New York: Julian Press and the Institute for Research in Hypnosis Publication Society, 1958.

Kroger, W. *Clinical and experimental hypnosis.* Philadelphia: Lippincott, 1963.

Meares, A. *A system of medical hypnosis.* Philadelphia: Saunders, 1961.

Orne, M. T. Demand characteristics and the concept of quasi-controls. In R. Rosenthal & R. L. Rosnow (Eds.), *Artifact in behavioral research.* New York: Academic Press, 1969.

Prince, M. *The dissociation of a personality.* New York: Longmans-Green, 1906.

Rosenthal, R. *Experimenter effects in behavioral research.* New York: Appleton, 1966.

Schreiber, F. R. *Sybil.* New York: Warner Paperback Library, 1974.

Simonton, O. C. & Simonton, S. Belief systems and management of the emotional aspects of malignancy. *Journal of Transpersonal Psychology,* 1975, **7,** 29–71.

Thigpen, C. H. & Cleckley, H. M. *Three faces of Eve.* New York: McGraw-Hill, 1957.

Watkins, H. H. Ego-state therapy. In J. G. Watkins (Ed.), *The therapeutic self.* New York: Human Sciences Press, (in press).

Watkins, J. G. *Hypnotherapy of war neuroses.* New York: Ronald Press, 1949.

Watkins, J. G. Ego states and the problem of responsibility: a psychological analysis of the Patty Hearst case. *Journal of Psychiatry and Law,* Winter 1977, 471–489.

Weitzenhoffer, A. M. *General techniques of hypnotism.* New York: Grune & Stratton, 1957.

Wolpe, J. The systematic desensitization treatment of neuroses. *Journal of Nervous and Mental Diseases,* 1961, **132,** 198–203.

Part IV

BRIEF INTERVENTIONS
IN ORGANIZATIONS

Transactional analysis has evolved with a theory and easily applied techniques that can be understood easily by the layman. Its simple, direct approach has been found valuable in teacher training, in organizations, and even in work with children. All the chapters in this section focus on such valuable applications—so that healing is brought not only to individuals, but to organizations as well.

chapter 12

TRANSACTIONAL ANALYSIS AS THERAPEUTIC ORGANIZATIONAL THEORY

Howard J. Douglass, Ph.D.

Although Eric Berne (1963, pp. 211–223) was acquainted with some of the modern literature of group dynamics from sociology, social psychology, and group psychotherapy, he did not incorporate the research findings from this literature into his writings because he believed, ". . . in the whole of the vast 'modern' literature there are few creative ideas as compared to the older writings" (p. 212). In one sense his decision not to use these findings was fortunate because it gave him and his San Francisco colleagues an opportunity to develop, without the constraints which usually hamper more traditional theorists, the unique, original, and extensive theory of transactional analysis (TA) for both individuals and organizations.

Portions of this paper were presented at the 1st Eastern Conference on Transactional Analysis as "TA Communications, Leadership, and the Two Dimensions of Interpersonal Relationships," New York, 1975.

In another sense, however, his decision tended to limit his awareness of the power and potency of the applications of his theory to institutional life, though he did write the book, *The Structure and Dynamics of Organizations and Groups.* And, perhaps, TA theory may have greater potency for bringing about change for large numbers of people in institutional life as a therapeutic organization theory than it will have as a developing theory of individual psychology for treating clients. Writing about this point, Groder (1974) recently noted that he is ". . . convinced that TA is rapidly approaching a peak of integration in the area of individual psychology. There are probably not more than a few years left until the integration is fairly well worked out. These are surprising statements, given the fact that TA theory is only approximately 15 years old.

Regardless of the outcome of the theory for individual psychology, TA theory has power and potency, for a number of reasons, as a basis for therapeutic change in organizational life. First, and perhaps most important, it *does* have close correlations with the modern findings of social psychology, and it may also have correlations with sociology and group psychotherapy, i.e., the areas of group dynamics which Berne eschewed. And these correlations add construct validity to TA theory by demonstrating its similarity to long-established, reasonably well researched and confirmed principles derived from theories in social and industrial psychology. Second, the theory is developing at a time of rapid social change, when organizations are being confronted with a need to change to a different model of organization without knowing which model to adopt to achieve maximum individual-institutional outcomes. With the approaching decline of the authoritarian, pyramid hierarchy, many organizations are considering a variety of new structural designs into which TA theory fits snugly (Oates, 1971). Third, TA theory has not only a formal language, but also a series of vernacularisms which everybody can understand easily. Fourth, it lends itself easily to research studies, the basic unit of social intercourse being the transaction, from which further theory and new applications to organizational life may be made (Berne, 1964). Moreover, the greater precision of this theory as compared with other social psychology theories may be seen in the preciseness with which the number of complementary, crossed, and ulterior transactions are identified (Berne, 1972, pp. 14–21). Fifth, it fits the intellectual air of freedom, the Zeitgeist, extant in people today, providing a way by which both leaders and subordinates, individually or mutually, may analyze their transactions so they may interact from their Adult ego states rather than the Parent-Child ego state transactions characteristic of the authoritarian, hierarchical structure now widespread in institutional life.

These five reasons only minimally suggest the potential that TA theory has for bringing about major therapeutic changes in organizational life. In actuality, the theory applies to any type of organization in which people are assigned to positions having different perceived amounts of rank, status, or power. This prescription includes not only industrial organizations, but also other organizations as diverse as the family, schools, universities, military services, religions, social service agencies (Boy Scouts, Girl Scouts, etc.), unions, and the state and federal governments. Moreover, looked at in a different way, the prescription applies whenever a dyadic relationship exists between two people in institutionalized roles who have unequal amounts of perceived rank, status, or power, i.e., parent-child, foreman-worker, officer-airman, schoolboard-teacher, teacher-student, clergyman-parishioner, master-apprentice, and, in general, the "haves" and the "have nots." Using these dyadic relationships as a basis for discussion, this paper will illustrate some of the similarities between TA theory and knowledge in other social psychology areas. Moreover, from this perspective, some of the ways that TA may be used to bring about therapeutic changes in institutional life will be discussed.

The Two Dimensions of Interpersonal Relationships

Theorists and research scientists who deal with complicated topics in social and organizational psychology frequently
reduce the complexity of their data by a statistical procedure
called factor analysis. This procedure identifies the minimum
number of dimensions (factors) which are needed to account for
most or all of the variation in the data. Mathematicians think
of this process as determining the rank of a matrix; the data in
a matrix of rank one can all be accounted for by a single
dimension or vector; the data in a matrix of rank two require
two dimensions to be accounted for, etc.

These procedures are important for bringing scientific order out of the chaos which may appear to exist in nature or for
bringing together data which, superficially, do not appear to go
together but which, in fact, are related. Fleishman described
this process as it was carried out in one of the Ohio State
University Studies on Leadership. About 1,800 items describing
the behaviors supervisors show in their leadership roles were
written and classified into 10 broad categories of leader behavior, i.e., domination, communication, evaluation, etc. The items
were made into questionnaires and administered in a wide variety of leader-group situations in industry, schools, universities,
and the military services. After the questionnaires were scored,
the 10 categories were factor analyzed and two, more basic,
dimensions of leader behavior resulted; namely, a dimension
that was labeled initiation of structure and a dimension labeled
consideration. These two dimensions are uncorrelated with
each other so that the way a leader is rated on one dimension
does not influence the way he is rated on the other. Further,
these two dimensions together account for approximately 86
percent of the variation which occurs in the way different leaders behave.

Factor analytic studies like this one abound in the social
psychology literature. They may report that two, three, or more
dimensions are needed to summarize data into a conceptual

framework, but the important fact is this: whenever studies are reported on interpersonal relationships in a dyad, they always report at least two dimensions. One dimension relates to how the authority or power in the dyad is assigned, and the other dimension relates to how affection and other socioemotional characteristics are expressed. There may be more dimensions reported than these two, but some variation of these two are always reported. Examples of this manner of conceptualizing behavior exist in such numbers that I am postulating the first axiom of the dynamics of dyadic interpersonal relationships: *There are two necessary but not always sufficient orthogonal dimensions to account for interpersonal relationships in dyads, namely a dimension concerned with authority (rank, status, or power) relationships and a dimension concerned with the social-emotional relationships between the two people.*

Inspection of Table 12–1 shows the variety of areas in social psychology in which the two dimensions are reported. Analogous types of dimensions are found in theoretical and research studies as widely different as the type of family in which a person is reared to the principles of justice by which institutions are organized. Moreover, each dimension displays a unique factor characteristic of widely differing perspectives on the manner in which a person might guide his interpersonal relationships. A person primarily adopting Dimension I as the manner in which he relates to others will tend to be humanistic, considerate, and integrative and will be concerned with the equality of his relationships and their socioemotional characteristics. On Dimension II, a person will tend to relate to others most effectively when the interactions are based on production tasks or work activities and when unequal status, power, equity, or authority relations prevail.

Transactional Analysis Communication Patterns

The widespread differences people show when they relate on either Dimension I or II suggest that communication pat-

Table 12-1 Some Examples of the Two Dimensions of Interpersonal Relationships

Author	Area of interest	Dimension I	Dimension II
Halpin & Winer (1957)	Leader behavior	Consideration	Initiating structure
Freud (1960)	Libidinal ties	To other group members	To the group leader
Fromm (1947)	Ethics	Humanistic	Authoritarian
Brown (1965)	Rules of address	Solidarity	Status
Sampson (1971)	Principles of justice	Equality	Equity
McGregor (1960)	Organization principle	Y-integration	X-authority
Schutz (1955)	Interpersonal	Love	Power
Guetzkow & Gyr (1954)	Conflict	Affective	Substantive
Miller & Swanson (1958)	Family type	Bureaucratic	Entrepreneurial
Parson & Shils (1951)	Loyalty focus	Collectivistic	Individualistic
Bales & Slater (1955)	Leader roles	Socioemotional leader	Task leader
Likert (1961)	Supervisory style	Employee-centered	Production-centered
Blake & Mouton (1964)	Managerial grid	Concern for people	Concern for production

terns on these two dimensions are also different. For instance, the vocabulary used, the nature of the topics discussed, and the control of the conversation appear to be clearly differentiated on the two dimensions, and this is also the situation Berne confirmed in his work on transactions. After he and his associates identified nine complementary transactions that two people could engage in, he singled out two for special consideration due to their frequency of usage in everyday interactions and simplicity, namely, Complementary Transaction Type I, i.e., Adult-Adult ego states and Complementary Transaction Type II, i.e., Parent-Child ego states (Berne 1963, 1964, Niemeier & Douglass, 1975). Later, he wrote that complementary transactions between "psychological equals" include Adult-Adult, Parent-Parent, and Child-Child ego states (Berne, 1964, p. 32). His awareness of the importance of these two transactions is especially significant, for they add to the tradition of ideas concerning the two dimensions of interpersonal relationships, and, more importantly, they identify the communication transactions which people use when they function on one or the other of the two dimensions, i.e., the Complementary Transaction Type I (Adult-Adult ego states) is characteristic of communication acts of people functioning on Dimension I and the Complementary Transaction Type II (Parent-Child ego states) characterizes people functioning on Dimension II.

Noting that these transactions types characterize peoples' behavior on Dimensions I and II does *not* mean that the people communicate only from their Adult ego states or from their Parent and Child ego states. On the contrary, they may communicate from each of their ego states, but the transaction types denote the ego state from which they typically communicate. Moreover, in addition to the quantitative differences in frequency of usage, there is also a qualitative difference in relation to which ego state has control as the executive of the personality (James & Jongeward, 1971). In Type I Transactions, the Adult ego state in each person is the executive of the personality and in Type II Transactions, the Parent ego state in one person and the Child ego state in the other is the executive.

Examples of Leadership Styles

Davis (1967) and Holloman (1968) provide good examples of the leadership styles people use when they interact with subordinates from Type I and Type II transactions (see also Tingey, 1969). In Table 12–2 the Dimension I column is analogous to the Type I (Adult-Adult ego states) superior-subordinate relationship and the Dimension II column is analogous to the Type II (Parent-Child ego states) superior-subordinate relationship. As may be inferred from Table 12–2, the Type II manager, functioning primarily from his Parent ego state believes that he is responsible for the performance of the subordinates and perceives them as functioning primarily in their Child ego state. And the more he accepts this assumption, then the more control, the more authority, and the closer he will supervise them. The Type I manager, on the other hand, believing that he is responsible for the facilitation of the growth of subordinates and, as well, achieving the performance goals of the group, uses the Adult ego state and expects subordinates to use theirs also in achieving both goals.

Coch & French (1948), in their classic study of pajama workers at the Harwood Manufacturing Corporation, show the effectiveness of this latter type of supervisory behavior. They first observed, in a control period, that the production indices for workers were stable at 60 units per hour. Then, they created four experimental treatment work groups. Group 1, the no participation group, was treated the same as it was in the control period, with the foreman instructing (Parent-Child ego states) the workers about the new production job they had. Group 2, the participation-through-representation group, was instructed about the new job by the union steward who had been instructed by the manager (Adult-Adult ego states). Groups 3 and 4, the total participation groups, were identical in that in both cases, the manager and the groups discussed (Adult ego states) how the new job process might be most efficiently handled.

Table 12–2 Type I and Type II Leadership Attitudes and Behavior

Attitudes and behavior	Leadership style		
	Adult-adult dimension type I	Parent-child dimension type II
Manager depends on	Leadership	Power
Managerial behavior orientation	Supportive-democratic	Authoritarian
Relation of manager to subordinates	Personal influence (bidirectional)	Domination (unilateral)
Social gap	Narrow	Wide
Source of authority	From below	From above
Basis of authority	Personal-competence	Legal-contractual
Authority legitimated by	Recognition of contribution to group	Institutionalized values and cultural ideologies
Employee behavioral orientation	Performance	Obedience
Employee needs met	Higher-order	Subsistence
Employee psychological result	Participation	Dependency
Measure of Morale	Motivation	Compliance
Performance result	Awakened drives	Minimum

Sources: This table is an adaptation of two tables, one by Davis and one by Holloman.

When the production records were analyzed a month later, Group 1 was approximately 20 percent below standard; whereas, Group 2 was 13 percent above, and Groups 3 and 4 were 20 percent and 23 percent above standard. Moreover, Group 1 had 17 percent employee terminations and "marked expressions" of aggression; whereas Groups 2, 3, and 4 had no employees leave and Group 2 had only one aggressive act. The crucial value of Type I (Adult-Adult ego states) management is shown in the next part of the study. Group I (no participation) was then given a new job which they discussed with total participation. Within 19 days the group was 25 percent above the production standard, with no aggressive acts occurring and no one leaving the group.

Therapeutic Value

The chief therapeutic value TA has for organizational life, at the present time, is for people to become aware of the *not-OKness* of Type II (Parent-Child) transactions and to realize that their *OKness* can only be achieved if they take control of their lives by using their Adult ego states and by communicating with others on the basis of Type I (Adult-Adult) transactions.

There are numerous justifications for this statement. The chief one is that true autonomy may be achieved only when the individual is aware of and deals with the contamination of the Adult ego state by the Parent and Child ego states (Berne, 1972). Second, the process of concentrating on Adult-Adult ego state transactions leads naturally to the exposure of the symbiotic relationship between the superior and the subordinate, and then to the games, discounts, and passivity, which ensue from the symbiosis (Schiff & Schiff, 1971). Thirdly, the process also leads to an analysis of rituals, pasttimes, and an awareness of organizational scripts. Last, the awareness of transactions is like opening the door to OKness, for it heightens people's awareness of their behavior, the first step toward autonomy.

Moreover, in a general sense, transactional analysis has therapeutic value for organizations because it provides a specific plan of behavior by which people may achieve self-actualization and autonomy.

The next topic to be considered is the part institutionalized existential positions play in maintaining the hierarchical, pyramidal structure which leads to Parent-Child relationships and not-OKness.

Existential Positions

Harris' contribution regarding existential positions in TA theory is ordinarily considered to apply to the posititon a person chooses in order to survive in life (Harris, 1969). But in the context of this paper his contribution also has value in understanding institutional life and the reasons people find difficulty in opting for OKness. The chief reason is that U.S. institutions are structured so as to reinforce and to stroke not-OKness.

The Position of I'm Not OK-You're OK

A short psychological history of a developing child will illustrate the institutional forces acting to keep him in not-OKness.* After the child separates from the symbiotic relationship with his mother, he becomes aware of his dependency on others, particularly mother, though perhaps the father and family as well, and chooses the I'm not OK-You're OK position, "the universal position of early childhood" (Harris, 1969). The parents, having chosen that same position to survive themselves

---

*For an extended discussion of various aspects of this process, see *Trans. An J.* 1975, **5** (1), the social action issue, especially White, Jerome D. & White, Terri. Cultural scripting, 12–23; English, Fanita. Shame and social control, 24–28; Roberts, Denton L. Treatment of cultural scripts, 29–35; and Campos, Leonard P. Institutional discount structures, 60–61.

and having been institutionally stroked for it, believe they are doing the "right" thing by invoking one or more of the five not-OK counterscript slogans (drivers) and by changing the child's ". . . not-OK battery by discounting and stroking negatively," to use Kahler & Capers' (1974) metaphor. The parents may also activate the child's OK battery and invoke one or more of the five OK counterscript messages (allowers). But, given their own existential positions, the chances are greater they will opt for the not-OK messages during the child's early years.

Then, the child goes to school where he faces the same situation: He will be OK if he is promoted to 2nd grade, 3rd grade . . . junior high school . . . high school, and college; in all these grades (years), he is stroked for staying in the I'm not OK-You're OK position by the authoritarian framework of the schools. Shortly after beginning school, he may be taken to church or temple where he becomes aware again of his not-OKness due to the institutional rules; later he may join one of the many rank-oriented, hierarchical social service agencies (Boy Scouts, Girl Scouts, Junior Marine Corps Leagues for 8 to 10-year-old boys) which teach children to develop their potentialities, but which also teach them to stay in their not-OKness. Finally, the child becomes an adult and goes out into the world, only to find, again, that the major institutions: industrial, business, banking, military, and the professions stroke him for not-OKness.

In the U.S. today, that is, OKness stemming from institutional rewards tends to be perceived more as a function of extrinsic rank, status, and power criteria (the rank one wears on his sleeves) than it does on the intrinsic and unique qualities of humanness that each person possesses. Adults frequently are heard to say "Oh, I'm *only* a high school graduate, a housewife, and assistant professor, a secretary, a 1st Lieutenant, a foreman, a junior high teacher," etc., and by these statements they assign validity to institutional, external reward systems, the hierarchy, and they also confirm once again their I'm not OK-You're OKness.

The Position of I'm OK-You're Not OK

The other side of this point of view, the I'm OK-You're not OK position is equally reinforced by institutions in this developmental process. When the child reaches any of the higher goals he strives for, then the children who have not reached them may be considered not-OK. At that point, the child becomes an agent of society (through his Critical Parent ego state and Vengeful Child) to teach not-OKness to younger children. For example, the junior high school student who adopts this viewpoint perceives himself as OK, but his brother or sister who is in a lower grade is not-OK yet. And, given the lock-step nature of education, the younger child cannot catch-up. And this I'm up-You're down hierarchical viewpoint may continue throughout the child's early years and into adolescence, being supported by the institutional rewards and strokes from the family, school, peer group, church, and social service agencies. Finally, as an adult, he is ready to take his place in society, already programmed to function in the hierarchical structure. In the hierarchy, he looks upward, and from the external status system, from an I'm not OK-You're OK position knows that he will be OK when the next step, or some higher status position, on the ladder is reached. At the same time, he looks downward, and from the external status system, recognizes from an I'm OK-You're (They're) not-OK position that they're not-OK, for they are *only* workers, machinists, youngsters, secretaries, laborers, students, parishioners, patients, soldiers, or people in lower-status positions.

The Position of I'm Not OK-You're Not OK

In my organizational experiences, I have not observed any practices that members of institutions have consciously or unconsciously established whose purpose was to stroke or reward people for behavior stemming from this position. Life in an institution (e.g., the family), may be so lacking in strokes that a person (e.g., a child) may choose this position to survive. But, as institutional agents of society, the parents' intention is not to reward I'm not OK-You're not OK behavior. Rather, their intention is to have the child accept their OKness (I'm not OK-You're OK) so that they can exert their authority to mold the child toward the society's behavioral expectations.

Prisons, mental institutions, and welfare agencies, where many people in the I'm not OK-You're not OK position end up, likewise do not have rules to reinforce this position, though the behavior of guards, hospital employees, and welfare agency employees, as *individuals,* may reinforce the position. From the viewpoint of classical bureaucratic theory, the best interests of these institutions are served when the prisoners, patients, and the poor accept the hierarchical authority of the institution and adopt the not-OKness of the I'm not OK-You're OK position. For then, the prisoners can be controlled and rehabilitated, the patients helped, and the poor returned to the job market.

Based on the foregoing discussion, I do not view the position of I'm not OK-You're not OK as relevant to institutional life to any great degree. The chief issues today in U.S. institutions, and perhaps in other countries, are 1) the uses of authority and 2) the social-emotional relationships sanctioned by institutions. These two issues are subsumed within the three other positions, I'm not OK-You're OK, I'm OK-You're not OK, and I'm OK-You're OK. The last of these three positions will be discussed next.

The Position of I'm OK-You're OK

After discussing the I'm not OK-You're OK person's great need for strokes, Harris (1969) made a cogent point about mountain climbing related directly to the substance of this paper, especially if the words, "climbing the institutional success ladder" are taken as the meaning of mountain climbing which is implied in this statement. He wrote, " 'Some of our best people' are where they are because of these efforts to gain approval. However, they are committed to a lifetime of mountain climbing, and when they reach the top of one mountain they are confronted by still another mountain. . . . 'No matter what I do, I'm still not OK'." Later, he wrote, "unfortunately, the most common position, shared by 'successful' and 'unsuccessful' persons alike is the I'm not OK-You're OK position."

These statements made about individuals clearly affirm the substance of this paper which is that the Type II transaction, (Parent-Child ego states), used in institutions to maintain authority, does in fact stroke and reinforce people to remain in the passive-dependent position of I'm not OK-You're OK.

Fortunately, there is a way to change to healthier, more therapeutic, institutional environments. By the words, healthier and therapeutic, I mean institutional environments that are structured so that each person may develop and actualize his potentials to the fullest, where transactions are based on Adult-Adult ego states so that each person may achieve Adult ego state autonomy, and where a person's value is based on intrinsic rather than extrinsic criteria, as is now the case.

Just as an individual may make the decision to live in the I'm OK-You're OK position, so likewise, the people in power in institutions can decide to structure their organizations in this position. Whether they will is another issue. My quarter-century of experience as an organizational consultant suggest the chances are slim, for there appears to be an inverse relationship between the desire to change to institutional OKness and hierarchical position, that is, the higher the person's position, the less he is willing to change the structure. Given the fact that high level executives, teachers, trustees, college and government administrators, clergy, parents, etc., have spent their lives climbing the hierarchical ladder, and often identify their personal OKness in terms of the position they hold, their reluctance to change the structure is understandable.

Yet, their reluctance exists in the face of a tremendous body of research evidence, accumulating over the last 25 years which clearly shows the valuable organizational, productivity, and personal benefits accruing to organizations when they are structured from a participatory (Adult-Adult ego states) management viewpoint rather than a hierarchically-controlled (Parent-Child ego states) viewpoint as they are now. Typical of this evidence are the research results developed in the Leadership Studies of Ohio State University and the University of Michigan's Institute for Social Research. Likert (1958) provided a summary of some of the evidence produced by the latter research program as early as 1958. But, since that time relatively few substantive changes have occurred in the way institutions are structured, despite the fact that the cultural attitudes of humanistic psychology are producing a silent revolution regarding interpersonal relationships.

Therapeutic Value

To adequately discuss the therapeutic benefits that would accrue to institutions, people, and society, if organizations changed their structure to achieve OKness, requires more space than this chapter permits. However, a list of benefits an organization might reasonably expect as a result of changing its structure to an I'm OK-You're OK position, based primarily on research studies (Fleishman, 1967) and partly on some predictions of behavior from TA theory, is included in Table 12–3. The list of benefits is incomplete; its purpose is only to show some of the many desirable therapeutic changes associated with an organizational structure of OKness.

The next consideration is to look at some of the motivational determinants that provide part of the impetus to maintain institutional authoritarian structures.

THE MOTIVATIONAL DETERMINANTS: DRIVERS AND ALLOWERS

In their article on miniscripts, Kahler & Capers (1974) identify five not-OK counterscript slogans or *drivers* and, their

Table 12–3 Some Benefits an Organization May Realize with a Structure of OKness

Employee attitudes	Employee behavior	Within organization	Management attitudes	Management behavior
1. Morale	1. Productivity	1. Trust	1. Consideration	1. Goal setting
2. Motivation	2. Participation	2. Teamwork	2. Concern to improving process	2. Feedback
3. Thoughts of self-actualization	3. Idea generation	3. Humanness	3. Concern for improving product	3. Job enlargement
4. Job satisfaction	*Reduced, loss, or fewer*	4. Face-to-face interaction	4. Concern for improving work conditions	4. Training
5. Need satisfaction	1. Turnover	5. Openness		5. Explanation of decisions
6. Satisfaction with supervision	2. Absenteeism	6. Emphasis on growth		6. Delegation
7. Institutional identification	3. Accidents			7. Opinion-seeking
8. Happiness	4. Grievances			8. Contract-making
9. Responsibility	5. Passivity			9. Deadline-setting
	6. Aggression			10. Stroking employees
	7. Fatigue			*Reduced, loss, or fewer*
	8. Waste			1. Resistance to change
	9. Game playing			2. Productivity pressure
	10. Criticism			3. Evaluation
	11. "Stupid" behavior			4. Game playing
	12. Role playing			5. "Harried" behavior
				6. Discounts
				7. Role playing

239

opposites, five OK counterscript slogans or *allowers*. These drivers fit easily into the theme of this essay, for they are the motivating instigators which, in part, maintain the authoritarian, materialistic, and economic aspects of institutional ideology, both for the people who work in institutions and the institutions themselves. Moreover, drivers are the energizing forces for the Type II (Parent-Child) transactions; allowers are the energizing forces for the Type I (Adult-Adult) transactions.

In Kahler & Capers' formulation of miniscripts, drivers are like doors "leading to a staircase connecting a series of basements." The first basement is based on I'm not OK-You're OK position rackets; the second, I'm OK-You're not OK position rackets; and the third, I'm not OK-You're not OK position rackets. Based on the previous discussion of the I'm not OK-You're not OK position, I will consider only the positions in the first and second basements.

Be Perfect Versus It's OK to Be Yourself

The *Be Perfect* driver relates directly to the various hierarchical structures that become a part of a person's phenomenological view of reality in the I'm not OK-You're OK position. Whether a child thinks of his family, how he relates to the universe, the organization of the school or any of the other major institutions, he becomes aware of the increasing rank, status, and power accorded to people as a function of increasing position on the hierarchy, the equity principle of justice (Sampson, 1971). For example, a child born in a hierarchically-organized family becomes aware (through his Little Professor) that Mother has more power than he has, Father has more power than Mother has (especially when Mother relates in her Child ego state to Father's Parent ego state), the President of the United States or Santa Claus has more power than Father has, and God has more power than anybody.

In this type of family, this view of reality is frequently reinforced by the parents and siblings. Thus, the child comes to view reality in terms of his not-OKness, with OKness being attributed to his achievement of a higher position in life. Unfortunately, he then relinquishes his orientation to OKness and to here-and-now feelings (see *Be Strong* driver below) and adopts a not-OKness along with a futuristic orientation, i.e., I'll be OK when or if. He may go through childhood and adult life in his I'm not OK position, always living in the future and never being satisfied with himself in the present, for there is always another ladder or mountain to climb.

This set of attitudes is further reinforced when the person as an adult and an agent of society achieves a position of authority in a hierarchy as a parent, teacher, manager, etc., for then, he can demand perfection from those "below" him. The *Be Perfect* driver serves to continually reinforce not-OKness.

THE THERAPEUTIC VALUE OF THE ALLOWER. The allower *(It's OK to be Yourself)* from the OK counterscript, permits the individual to be OK, regardless of the position that he may have in the hierarchy. He will still plan to achieve hoped-for goals in order to develop his potentialities, but this behavior is *not* related to his OKness. According to the equality principle of justice (Sampson, 1971), an individual's value is not a function of position on the hierarchy or of achieved rank, status, or power. Rather, it is a function of the respect the person accords himself and the respect others accord him for the humanness the person possesses. The person values himself, not as a *product* of society, but as an individual going through the *process* of life, by living in the here-and-now, by accepting all parts (the positive and the negative) of himself, and by developing his potentialities to the fullest.

Hurry Up Versus It's OK to Take Your Time

The *Hurry Up* driver is a part of the economic ideological system associated with the hierarchy. It has part of its roots in the rational-economic theory of man (Schein, 1965). In this theory, "time is money," and since money cannot be wasted so time cannot be wasted. The *Hurry Up* driver is also based on the "nothing but" view of emotions, one article of which regards "emotions as ... disruptive of orderly behavior," and consequently, it devalues personal feelings and orients people's thoughts outside of themselves toward objective tasks (Krech, Crutchfield, & Livson, 1969). This devaluation also relates to the *Be Strong* driver in the sense that feelings are not important enough to spend time discussing.

The *Hurry Up* driver is a basic component of the I'm not OK-You're OK and the I'm OK-You're not OK positions, and it is very effective in producing not-OKness. In the former case, the subordinate avoids feelings by assuming the boss is too busy with more important activities to have time to talk to him. And when they do talk, they stick to business. In the latter case, the boss avoids his feelings by not having time to talk to employees (he may be playing the game of Harried), and when they do talk, he communicates, often by body language, that the conversation is restricted to business. The payoff here is that the employees' feelings do get expressed through absenteeism, accidents, soldiering on the job,* grievances, strikes, termination, etc.

THE THERAPEUTIC VALUE OF THE ALLOWER.   When people allow themselves to take their time, more productivity results in the sense of better interpersonal relationships, of increased direct productivity on the job, and of reduced indirect negative outcomes. People functioning in the allower regard emotions as primary motives (Krech et al., 1969), and equally as worthy of consideration as thoughts. Consequently, managers and workers (and all the other dyads mentioned above) are not wasting time when they allow each other to express themselves. Each listens for emotional tone and expressed feelings, and they do not deny each others' feelings.

*To make a show of working in order to escape punishment.

Try Hard Versus It's OK to Do It

The *Try Hard* driver is part of the strategy to produce not-OKness because it is quite closely tied in with a losing or a nonwinning script (Berne, 1972). A person with a *Try Hard* driver does not commit himself from the Adult ego state to fulfilling the contracts he makes with himself or with others. Consequently, he does not become a winner. The driver is also related to the desire for perfection and other attitudes associated with the religious idea that though a person does not get his reward here on earth, it will be given in Heaven and to the secular ideas that laziness, shiftlessness, indolence, and sloth are poor human qualities.

Usually, the person who tries hard does so to achieve goals that he finds have status, that others value as desirable. Some examples are going to college, studying to become a professional, learning French verbs, keeping an appointment, and meeting a production quota. These goals are adopted by the person to get positive strokes from other people rather than to achieve the goal for its intrinsic value. Consequently, the goal is only instrumental in achieving the strokes, and the person does not decide that he wants the goal, and commit himself to its achievement. If the strokes are withdrawn by others, then the individual either continues to try harder to acquire the strokes again, or he goes into a period of confusion about the goal until further behavior is decided upon. The sophomore slump for college students illustrates this type of behavior (White, 1964).

THE THERAPEUTIC VALUE OF THE ALLOWER.   In contrast to the not-OKness of the driver, the allower permits the person to choose only those goals to which he is willing to be committed, and it leads to OKness. This means that parents, teachers, and others need to take the time to discuss goals with children and students in order to identify the reasons they are considering striving for the goal. Equally as important, the therapeutic value of the allower ensues from extensive discussions of the feelings the person has about the goal.

In industry, workers often desire to be promoted to foreman in order to gain more status and to earn more money, but they really do not want the foremanship because they, in fact, like the foreman's job. This is the *try hard* driver operating. If management does not identify the worker's motives then they are setting themselves up for a payoff, for the outcome is quite likely to be that after the person is promoted a good worker was lost and a poor foreman was found. The therapeutic value comes from a full discussion of the person's goal aspirations. If the worker will not commit himself to the foremanship, and he is not promoted, then both he and the company benefit. If he will commit himself, and he is promoted, then again both he and the company benefit.

Please Me Versus It's OK to Consider Yourself and Respect Yourself

A person whose behavior is under the influence of his *Please Me* driver feels he is responsible for helping others to feel good. He operates from his Child ego state in Type II Transactions, and he appeals to the Parent ego state of other people to approve his behavior, much like he did when he was a biological child. This driver reinforces and motivates the person to stay in the Child ego state especially when others do stroke him for the behavior. Consequently, this driver is effective in maintaining people in a not-OKness position on the hierarchy.

THE THERAPEUTIC VALUE OF THE ALLOWER. The allower is therapeutic because it grants to the individual on the organizational hierarchy the right to respect himself and others above and below him, the right to confront his passivity in relation to the supervisor's orders, and the right to generate a meaningful dialogue with the superior, i.e., one in which both people are equal, and in which they trust and respect each other.

Hopefully, any issues will be resolved to both people's satisfaction, but even if they are not, the therapeutic value of the allower is still evident, for the subordinate confronts the issue and the supervisor, and that leads to OKness.

Be Strong Versus It's OK to Be Open

Since the major organizations and institutions in the United States, in one way or another, have adopted a set of bureaucratic principles like those of Max Weber (Bendix, 1960), one of the chief developers of bureaucratic ideology, they adhere to a set of rules among which are included the rule of impersonality of interpersonal relations and the rule of a well-defined authority hierarchy. They also have adopted the rational-economic theory of man with its "nothing but" view that expressed feelings disrupt the orderliness of the hierarchy in order to support the impersonality rule.

Moreover, in most institutions, a variety of sanctions are used to insure the not-OK, *Be Strong* driver will be operative so that emotions and honest feelings will *not* be expressed. The paradox of this situation is that despite all the organizational rules and sanctions, people do have feelings, and they do need strokes, the "fundamental unit of social action," so that their "spinal cords will not shrivel up" (Berne, 1964). And people *do* get their strokes, based on the principle of "Love me or hate me," but don't ignore me."*

From childhood, people recognize often that the expression of positive, unconditional or conditional, strokes, in institutional life is frowned upon. Often, this recognition starts first in the family and continues on throughout life. But even if it starts later, the principle is sufficiently pervasive so that it is learned quickly in school and then continues on through life.

Being aware of the negative sanctions on positive strokes,

*This is my principle for the different importance among various kinds of strokes.

but still needing them, the person decides to earn negative, unconditional or conditional strokes. This condition is better than no strokes at all. Also he is aware that the Critical Parent ego state in others is very sensitive to any behavior they do not approve of, and they will give negative strokes for the behavior. Consequently, the person opts to earn negative strokes.

This personal decision is perhaps the chief reason for the multitudinous forms of disruptive, antisocial, aggressive behavior seen in institutional life. Typical examples are the family, sibling rivalry; the school, behavior problems; Boy Scouts-Girl Scouts, horseplay; high school, underachievement; college, dropping-out; marriage, separations and divorces; industry, absenteeism, grievances and strikes, etc.

THE THERAPEUTIC VALUE OF THE ALLOWER. When people allow themselves and others to be open, they create an environment which is conducive to the expression of the full range of thoughts and feelings they and others have. This positive environment emphasizes the recognition of the fine qualities everyone has, and it leads people naturally, to express positive strokes rather than negative ones. Moreover, this allower also permits the free interchange of ideas, and it also leads, naturally, to a consideration of the options which might be decided upon to reach agreement between the people. The result of the *It's OK to be Open* allower is that people receive the positive strokes they need, and thus they do not need to resort to behavior designed to earn negative strokes.

SCRIPTS

As in the other sections of this chapter, the purpose of this section is to describe the therapeutic relationship of TA theory to organizational life. Here, the question is, How do institutions and organizations reinforce the six main classes of scripts? According to Berne (1972), "Scripts are designed to last a lifetime. They are based on childhood decisions and parental programming which is continually reinforced."

This section is based on the premise that subordinates are considered to be in their Child ego states, in an institution operating with Type II (Parent-Child) transactions, and the institution and its agents are considered to be in their Parent ego state. Thus, institutions can script, or at least reinforce existing scripts, in people when they become a part of the institution. Recognizing there are many examples of these script classes, I have written about examples that I have observed to be most numerous in institutions. Moreover, I have given examples from both educational and industrial institutions, though other institutions, the church, the military services, and social services could just as easily have been used.

Never or Tantalus Scripts

This script forbids people from doing what they want to do, and thus they are tantalized by the possibilities of doing it. In schools, for instance, students are often kept from following some of their own intellectual interests in favor of studying required, standard curricula which do not necessarily satisfy their curiosities.

Fleishman (1953) provides a good example of the Never script in industry. Foremen from a large company were sent to a human relations training program for two weeks, where they learned to show less structure (Type II Parent-Child transactions) and to show more consideration (Type I Adult-Adult transactions). From this outcome, I would suppose they would be eager, or at least interested, to use their newly acquired leadership skills. This was not the behavior they showed when they returned to their jobs, for the leadership climate developed by their supervisors had a greater effect on their behavior at the plant than the training course had.

Fleishman computed a conflict index, and found more conflict in foremen who returned to supervisory climates favoring structure (Type II) than those foremen had who returned to supervisors favoring consideration (Type I). Since the plant operated on a hierarchy in which the higher the position a person held, the more structuring (Type II) and the less consideration (Type I) he believed was needed in work groups, it appears the Never script was operating. The foreman clearly read the ulterior message from their supervisors, namely, "You can go to school to learn about leadership, but don't come back here and use it unless I approve."

Always or Arachne Scripts*

This script provides a life of mediocrity or dullness for people who fail to meet or who reject Parent ego state standards of others. The script is illustrated in schools by the teacher-student relationship which ensues when the child comes from a low socioeconomic background and does not meet the middle-class standards of the teacher. If the teacher uses Always scripting, he categorizes the child as not-OK and treats the child from that viewpoint throughout the year, and he may place notes in the child's scholastic folder to insure the child stays in his not-OKness. Or, he may play the game, Student Folder (Ernst, 1972), and once he finds *the* reason to categorize the child for his unacceptable behavior, he disregards any other data that would change his evaluation.

In industry, the Always script behavior arises when management fails to consider for promotion the intelligent, capable high school graduate and, instead, promotes only college graduates because they have earned degrees.

*Arachne, and the other Greek names which follow, are all Greek myths which may help people to understand the related script. In this instance, the theme of the myth Arachne is "always."

Until or Jason Scripts

The theme of this script requires that a person needs to complete tasks established by others (Parent ego state) before he can be rewarded by them or before the person (Child ego state) can obtain a goal he is working for.

School examples of this script are plentiful in the classroom: "You can't learn what you want until you learn what will be on the Regents' Examinations (in New York State)." "You can't take a course you want until you have all the prerequisites." "You can't go to the lavatory until you ask permission." "You can't watch TV (at home) until your homework is done." And with a variation, "You can't enjoy learning in a free, open classroom until I overcome my hang-up about being the authority in this class."

In industrial organizations the theme changes, but the message is the same: "You can't be promoted until you have more grooming" (meaning until your ideas conform to ours). "You can't accept the new job you want until I get a replacement for you." "You can't be promoted to a management position until the attitudes about women are changed in this organization." "You can't have the job you want until you have the most seniority." And, again, with variation, "You can't participate in decisions affecting you until I (the supervisor, company president, board of directors) overcome my hang-up about authority."

After or Damocles Scripts

After scripts are based on not enjoying the pleasure a person is experiencing because dire circumstances will result, i.e., life should not be enjoyed. The teacher who teaches by group discussion methods to gain maximum student understanding, and then tests their understanding by factual multiple-choice tests items illustrates this scripting very well.

A similar illustration in industry is the happiness employees have for a job when it has a good piece-rate or hourly-rate. Management tends to be wary of this behavior, so a time-study engineer is sent to reestablish the job rate, which usually results in lower reimbursement to the workers.

Over and Over or Sisyphus Scripts

These scripts describe behavior of people who strive for and nearly reach the organizations highest goals (from *Try Hard* and *Be Perfect* drivers). When they do not meet the organization's highest expectations, they feel not-OK, even though their performance is above-average and they have every right to feel great and OK. In college, some students illustrate this script behavior by continually earning B+ grades and missing A grades. In industry, salespeople illustrate it also when they continually miss meeting sales quotas, or they always sell enough to be in second rather than in first place on the merit list.

Open Ended or Philemon and Baucis Scripts

In these scripts, people are rewarded positively and/or negatively or both for their good deeds. In schools, students are rewarded positively by learning and acquiring knowledge they need as adults, and this positive reward is symbolized by the diploma they receive. At the same time, they have been rewarded negatively also by being taught not-OK losing, or at least nonwinning, scripts by the authoritarian hierarchy of the school system from the I'm not OK (student)-You're OK (teachers, principals, superintendents, school boards, and communities) position. And this reward does not appear on their diplomas.

Likewise, workers are stroked by the authoritarian hierarchy into not OKness from the I'm not OK (worker)-You're OK (supervisors, company presidents, and boards of directors) position.

The Therapeutic Value of Descripting Institutions

Berne (1970) wrote, ". . . man is tamed from the beginning, and spends his whole life performing stunts for his masters: Mom and Pop first, and then teacher, and after that whoever can grab him and teach him. . . ." My contention is that the function of scripts in institutions is to insure people's behavior will be standardized, predictable, and in agreement with the institution's mores. To insure this standardized behavior, institutions use Type II (Parent-Child) transactions to govern people, by taking over where the biological parents leave off, and establish rules designed to keep employees in the passive, dependent position of the Child ego state. Most of these rules meet the criteria of the six main classes of scripts.

Descripting institutions would allow people to relate to each other using Type I (Adult-Adult) transactions, and this is its primary therapeutic value. It would allow people to use all the potential talent they now have in the service of achieving their own goals, the goals of their organization, and the goals of society. This potentional talent is now held in check by the Parent-Child organizational structure of institutions. One example easily illustrates this point: In this country, women generally are not allowed into *higher-level* institutional positions having status and power due primarily to male scripting and partly to their own female scripting. Yet, women (and others who could have been included in the example, such as blacks, and other minority and ethnic groups, young people, etc.) represent a widespread source of significant potential talent which is now essentially unused. And a reasonable assumption is that they will not be used until institutions begin the process of descripting.

Motivational Need Hierarchies

The purpose of this section is to relate Berne's Type I (Adult-Adult) and Type II (Parent-Child) transactions to Argyris' dimensions of personality development, Maslow's hierarchy of individuals' needs, and Mills' hierarchy of group purposes. This is important to do in order to show the power and potency people have and the needs and purposes for which they are striving when they are using one or the other of the two transactions.

Argyris' (1957) seven characteristics of a multidimensional developmental process for healthy personality growth, in the United States are listed in Table 12–4. These growth trends are continuous, and they depict the usual characteristics a person has when he is a child and when he is an adult.

Only a moment is needed to ascertain that the Childhood column represents the way people in many institutions, (especially industrial organizations) are perceived by management. Moreover, to keep employees at the childhood end of a continuum, management structures relationships in Parent-Child ego state terms.

The Type II (Parent-Child) transaction is a stroking process to reinforce workers so that they remain passive and depend-

Table 12–4   Argyris' Dimensions
of Personality Development

From childhood	To adulthood
A passive state	An increasing activity state
A dependent state	A relative independence state
Few behavioral competencies	Many behavioral competencies
Erratic, casual, shallow interests	Deep interests
Short-time perspective	Long-time perspective
Subordinate position	Equal and/or superordinate position
Lack of self-awareness	Self-awareness and self-control

ent on management, and in a subordinate position. Their jobs are structured in simplified processes which means they need not learn more than a few job skills, leading to shallow interests on the job. Their pay by the piece (i.e., piece-rate) emphasizes a short-time perspective. Because they develop few competencies on the job, they lose their self-awareness of all the potential skills they have to contribute to the company.

Maslow's (1970) two lower-order needs for individuals, the physiological and the safety-level needs, as well as Mills' (1967) two lower-order purposes for groups, the immediate gratification purpose and the sustaining conditions to maintain gratification purpose, also have characteristics similar to the Childhood column, since children and adults treated as children strive to maintain the processes which provide them with gratification of their physiological and safety needs.

Seven characteristics of adult behavior are listed in Argyris' Adulthood column, Table 12–4, which are usually absent from most institutional positions, except at the high managerial and professional levels. Yet, these characteristics are those which every adult person has the right to reasonably expect to be a part of his position. Moreover, Maslow's three higher-order level needs of belonging and love, esteem, and self-actualization, in addition to Mills' three higher-order levels of group purposes, collective goals, self-determination, and group goals also need to be added to the list.

The therapeutic value of TA in institutional life rests, in part, on the fact that a shift from Type II to Type I (Adult-Adult) transactions provides the medium or the bridge by which these adult, higher-order need levels may be attained for people spending their lives in institutions.

SUMMARY

This chapter has shown there are two necessary but not always sufficient dimensions to account for interpersonal relationships in a dyad, and it related these dimensions to Berne's Complementary Type I (Adult-Adult ego states) and Type II (Parent-Child ego states) transactions. These two transactional paradigms are used to relate the existential positions, drivers and allowers, and scripts in TA theory to current practices in institutional life. They are also related to Argyris' personality development trends, Maslow's hierarchy of individual needs, and Mills' level of group purposes.

The therapeutic value of TA in organizational life is also discussed for each of the points cited above. The power and potency of TA theory in bringing about positive, healthy changes in people by changing institutional structures are discussed.

REFERENCES

Argyris, Chris. The individual and organization: Some problems of mutual adjustment. *Administrative Science Quarterly,* 1957, **2**(1), 1–24.

Bales, R. F. & Slater, P. E. Role differentiation in small decision-making groups. In T. Parsons and Robert F. Bales, et al. (Eds.), *Family, socialization, and interaction process.* Glencoe: Free Press, 1955, pp. 259–306.

Bendix, R. *Max Weber: An intellectual portrait.* New York: Doubleday, 1960.

Berne, Eric. *The structure and dynamics of organizations and groups.* New York: Grove Press, 1963.

Berne, Eric. *Games people play.* New York: Grove Press, 1964.

Berne, Eric. *Sex in human loving.* New York: Pocket Books, 1970, p. 135.

Berne, Eric. *What do you say after you say hello?* New York: Grove Press, 1972.

Blake, R. & Mouton, J. *The managerial grid.* Houston: Gulf Pub. Co., 1964.

Brown, Roger. *Social psychology.* New York: Free Press, 1965, pp. 55–59.

Coch, Lester & French, R. P. Jr. Overcoming resistance to change. *Human Relations,* 1948, **1**, 512–532.

Davis, Keith. In the spotlight: The supportive manager. *Arizona Business Bulletin,* 1967, **14**(10), 252–256.

Ernst, Ken. *Games students play.* Millbrae: Celestial Arts, 1972, pp. 98–99.

Fleishman, Edwin A. Leadership climate, human relations training, and supervisory behavior. *Personnel Psychology,* 1953, **6**, 205–222.

Fleishman, Edwin A. (Ed.) *Studies in personnel and industrial psychology.* (Rev. ed.) Homewood: Dorsey, 1967, pp. 361–362.

Freud, Sigmund. *Group psychology and the analysis of the ego.* New York: Bantam Books, 1960, p. 35.

Fromm, Erich. *Man for himself.* Greenwich, Conn.: Fawcett, 1947, p. 18.

Groder, Martin G. Editorial. *Transactional Analysis Journal,* 1974, **4**(4), 6.

Guetzkow, H. & Gyr, J. An analysis of conflict in decision-making groups. *Human Relations,* 1954, **7**, 367–382.

Halpin, Andrew W. & Winer, B. J. A factorial study of the leader behavior descriptions. In Ralph M. Stogdill & Alvin E. Coons (Eds.), *Leader behavior: Its description and measurement.* Columbus: The Ohio State University, 1957. (Research Monograph Number 88), pp. 39–51.

Harris, Thomas A. *I'm OK-You're OK.* New York: Harper & Row, 1969.

Holloman, Charles R. Leadership and headship: There is a difference. *Personnel Administration,* 1968, 31, 38–44.

James, M. & Jongeward, D. *Born to win.* Reading: Addison-Wesley, 1971, pp. 229, 235, Chap. 10.

Kahler, Taibi & Capers, Hedges. The miniscript. *Transactional Analysis Journal,* 1974, **4**(1), 26–42.

Krech, David, Crutchfield, Richard S., & Livson, Norman. *Elements of psychology.* (2nd ed.) New York: Knopf, 1969, p. 556.

Likert, Rensis. Measuring organizational performance. *Harvard Business Review,* 1958, **36**, 41–50.

Likert, R. *New patterns in management.* New York: McGraw-Hill, 1961.

Maslow, Abraham H. *Motivation and personality.* (2nd ed.) New York: Harper & Row, 1970.

McGregor, Douglas. *The human side of enterprise.* New York: McGraw-Hill, 1960, p. 12. For a discussion of this principle in TA terms see Goldhaber, Marylynn & Goldhaber, Gerald M. A transactional analysis of McGregor's theory X-Y. In D. Jongeward et al. *Everybody Wins.* Reading: Addison-Wesley, 1974, Chap. 14.

Miller, D. R. & Swanson, G. E. *The changing American parent: A study in the Detroit area.* New York: Wiley, 1958.

Mills, Theodore M. *The sociology of small groups.* Englewood Cliffs, N.J.: Prentice-Hall, 1967.

Niemeier, David L. & Douglass, Howard J. Transactions and self-actualization. *Transactional Analysis Journal,* 1975, **5**(2), 152–157.

Oates, David. Is the pyramid crumbling? *International Management,* 26:7 1971. 10–13.

Parson, T. & Shils, E. A. (Eds.) *Toward a general theory of action.* Cambridge: Harvard University Press, 1951.

Sampson, Edward E. *Social psychology and contemporary society.* New York: Wiley, 1971, p. 139.

Schein, Edgar. *Organizational psychology.* Englewood Cliffs, N.J.: Prentice-Hall, 1965.

Schiff, Aaron W. & Schiff, Jacqui L. Passivity. *Transactional Analysis J.,* 1971, **1**(1), 71–78.

Schutz, W. C. What makes groups productive? *Human Relations,* 1955, **8**, 429–65.

Tingey, Sherman. Management today. *Hospital Administration,* 1969, 14, 32–41.

White, Robert W. *The abnormal personality.* (3rd ed.) New York: Ronald, 1964, pp. 100–103.

chapter 13

USING TRANSACTIONAL ANALYSIS
IN EDUCATION

Mary K. Otto, M.A.

Transactional analysis (TA) can be of use to a classroom teacher in numerous ways. Understanding ego states and transactions sheds light on many otherwise puzzling situations and leads to new solutions to problems. Learning new ways to use positive strokes and avoid useless negative strokes causes a pleasant change in the general atmosphere of a classroom. Dealing with feelings appropriately rather than collecting stamps* or wallowing in rackets reduces chances for student/teacher games to occur, and on and on.

The tools of TA give teachers a useful framework for talking about classroom behavior, their relationships with students and peers, as well as other specific problem situations in their own classrooms. And these tools provide some useful, immediate options for change. This paper will focus on ways in which teachers can enjoy their teaching and have more effective

---

*"Collecting stamps" is the TA jargon for collecting hurts or grievances.

relationships in the classroom being aware of their ego states and the possibilities for using different ego states in problem situations.

James and Jongeward (1971) refer to Eric Berne's concept of the "bash trap" phenomenon. "When a person is caught in a bash trap he compulsively continues to bash himself against the same situation." I see much of the frustration and "go nowhere" feeling present in some school settings as a reflection of the "bash trap" idea. For example, a teacher tries and tries to get through to a student and cannot reach him, or two students are locked into a competitive struggle for recognition which continues to bring tension and grief to the first one and then the other.

Understanding structural analysis is an important first step to avoid butting a brick wall and to consider options for handling situations differently. In the classroom or elsewhere a person who teaches has three ego states available: He can act out of his Parent drawing on archaic messages about "how to teach" or how to nurture; or he can use his Child—the Free Child to have fun and be sensitive or the Adapted Child to feel bad about himself, maintain his rackets, etc.; and he can use his Adult—the part of him that gives and receives information, makes decisions, and asks questions.

Much traditional teaching is done from the Critical Parent ego state—the part of us that has lots of rules and set ways of doing things, adopted from somewhere outside ourselves. Consider how many classrooms reverberate with such phrases as:

Sit in your seat and get to work. . . .

If you continue to disrupt the class you will be sent to the office.

All papers must be handed in by 4:00 P.M. today or you will fail the course.

Stop acting like a 2-year old and shape up.

A lot of traditional "studenting" is done from the Adapted Child position. Children are taught to sit quietly, to say "yes sir" or "no sir." They also exhibit Adapted Child behavior in being rebellious such as refusing to cooperate and throwing spitballs at the blackboard. Withdrawing into one's own world is a form of Adapted Child behavior.

It is important to note at this point that Critical Parent and Adapted Child ego states definitely have a place in a classroom. Rules, for example, are necessary as an economy measure; they save time that can be put to better use. Being able to adapt is also vital: coming to class, listening, doing assignments are necessary in the learning process just as in other areas of living. However, if teachers and students are locked in to certain ego states—be they Critical Parent and Adapted Child or any others—options for dealing with classroom problems are limited.

By first becoming aware of their own ego states and then those of their students, teachers gain an important tool for change. As an aid to awareness of ego states in the classroom, I have designed an "Ego State Reaction Quiz for Teachers." I generally ask teachers to work on it in small groups, to share their ideas, and to hypothesize variations in tone of voice, gestures, etc. in diagnosing the ego states in the quiz. The following examples can serve as illustrations. Identify each teacher response as P, A, or C.

1. Jean and Katie (grade 5) walk into the classroom arguing about an assignment.
   a. "Cut that out; I've heard enough screaming today." _____
   b. "Do you girls have a question about which pages were assigned?" _____
   c. "Boy, am I exhausted. I wish I could leave now." _____
2. The job of school nurse-teacher is cut from the budget.
   a. "Oh, dear, how will I ever make it?" _____
   b. "I wonder how many other districts are in the same situation." _____
   c. "They'll be sorry for this move." _____

3. The building principal has called a teacher in to talk about
   a particular class.
   a. "Why does he always pick on me?"   ___
   b. "He's a pain in the neck."   ___
   c. "His suggestions will be important in helping me handle
      this group."   ___

Being able to recognize one's own ego states in a given situation takes practice. In addition to encouraging teachers to tape record themselves in the classroom I use a six-chair technique as a way to gain insight into ego states. Teachers create typical problem situations and two people role play the situation as it actually is and two others enact it as it might be. They each occupy three chairs—one for each Parent, Adult, and Child—and move from one to the other as they see themselves switching ego states. The rest of the group serves as observers, directing the participants to move if they are in the wrong chair. It's amazing to see people who swear they are in their Adult ego state, giving what they call "straight information," such as, "I want you to know that nobody who goofs off as much as you do ever gets anywhere!"

As teachers learn to recognize their ego states and to shift consciously from one to another as situations change, they can begin to teach students to do the same thing. This technique can be done directly and deliberately or done indirectly. First-graders respond differently when they receive Adult information to place all wet raincoats in the hall instead of Parent criticisms for dripping all over the floor. Adult communication from a teacher invites the student to use his Adult ego state as well. Older students, too, respond favorably to changes in a teacher's ego states and may become willing to communicate with teachers and peers from all of their ego states, too.

Above I commented on the number of times, Critical Parent/Adapted Child transactions occur in classrooms. Much can be gained by switching some of these transactions to Adult: Adult or Child:Child. Children are willing to hear Adult information and to respond from their own Adult ego states in such situations as contracting for doing a certain amount of work for a certain grade. A great deal of learning—both academic and humanistic (people to people)—can occur on a child to child level. Little children like a teacher who can talk and hear on their level; older students also benefit greatly from the teacher who is willing to share his inner Child, whether through humor, participation in games and activities, or being warm and open at the appropriate time.

So, the next time Jeff cuts class with another "good reason", or the school mimeograph machine breaks down as you are running off an important assignment, consider other options open to you than the ones which produced more difficulty in the past. It is unnecessary to remain caught in the old traps.

REFERENCE

James, Muriel & Jongeward, Dorothy. *Born to win.* Reading, Mass.: Addison-Wesley, 1971, p. 223.

chapter 14

TRANSACTIONAL ANALYSIS: A NEW EDUCATIONAL AND COUNSELING VEHICLE IN A PUBLIC SCHOOL SETTING

Patricia Fitzgerald, Ph.D.

School psychology services traditionally have reached only those youngsters who have been brought to their attention because someone has been concerned about their apparent emotional, behavioral, social problems or learning difficulties noticed by a staff member. We became interested in finding ways of expanding the psychologist function in the school setting so that the development of psychological awareness could become an integrated part of the high school experience, not just a feature of the treatment or management of children with problems.

Transactional analysis (TA) provides a theoretical framework and practical tools with which to teach personality theory, enhance communication skills, raise social-consciousness awareness, and counsel children on all grade levels. A person of any age is capable of some level of psychological understanding—as Jerome Bruner (1960) has said, any subject can be taught at any age level.* In fact, if what is said cannot be expressed in words an eight-year-old can understand it may not be worth saying. With these premises in mind, we undertook the introduction of TA into the life of an upper middle-class suburban high school (grades 9 through 12).

Students had expressed a need for a better understanding of themselves and others. We conceived of the idea of a "Drop-In Center" in order to see if we could meet this need by providing an accessible communications center in which to present problem-solving techniques and teaching models for students and staff. We wanted to provide a place that allowed for the widest possible range of involvement, from full participation to just walking by and maybe seeing something posted on the wall that might stimulate reflection. On the basis of earlier experiences in school psychology work, we believed that:

1. Counseling services are most effective with those who indicate a readiness and willingness to define and work on a problem.
2. The counselor-psychologist has to be openly visible and accessible to the population at large.
3. Diagnosis is a dual process. It is a cooperative task in which something is done *with,* not *to* the student.
4. The counseling process may require individual, group, or peer-led interaction as mutually determined by counselor and counselee.

When these personal premises were placed within a TA theoretical framework, it could be further stated that:

*"Any subject can be taught effectively in some intellectually honest form to any child at any stage of development." p. 33

1. The nonmedical view of "I'm OK, you're OK" tends to dispel implications of "sickness," manipulation, and semantic labeling which frequently contribute to "not-OK feelings." To be "born a winner" confirms the belief that human nature is good. To the person seeking increased understanding and assistance, it more readily opens avenues for such help.
2. Each individual is unique. The counselor respects each person's capability for defining a problem. She aids in the process by "focusing and sharpening" perception. She helps sort out viable options for solutions to problems.
3. The individual is responsible for change and makes a contract with the counselor who then mutually shares her professional competencies in the process. The counselor agrees to do no more than 50 percent of the work.
4. The general population is divided into winners, non-winners, and losers in accordance with goal and time directed activities applied to various fields of endeavor. TA tools help everyone at various stages of development to "get on with" life so as to experience the joys of living.

It was from this thinking that the Drop-In Center evolved as a reality in September, 1974. It started as a bare storefront type, 12 by 19 foot room with four permanently fixed windows facing a corridor wing. The wall opposite the windows became the TA instructional medium. We covered it with rolls of white shelf paper where we introduced new TA concepts and invited people to write or draw their reactions and comments. The windows also provided advertising space as did a "Message Board" on another wall. A bright shag rug, tie-dyed pillows, and plastic chairs in pleasant colors contributed to an effect of warmth and intimacy inside the Center. As time went on and students became involved in the Center, we noticed that they tended to sit on the chairs to discuss a serious problem in their Adult, and reverted to Child when sitting on the floor cushions. The official opening was on Community Night when parents were invited to leave "family symbols" on the graffiti wall. The next day interns began to talk to students, explaining the purposes of the Drop-In Center and inviting them to leave their mark on the "personal identity mural." In our advertising we said that the Drop-In Center was a place to:

1. Meet and get to know new people. It is for the whole school.
2. Talk about things that are important to you. You and your ideas are important.
3. Learn about Transactional Analysis. TA tools help you learn more about yourself and others. You can then figure out where you're coming from and where someone else is at. This is helpful in understanding how to make friends and get along with others.

When the mural was covered with magic marker inscriptions, it was transferred to the cafeteria wall for a school-wide "Who's Who" contest. Students became aware that they did not know many people, particularly in terms of personal symbols. The graffiti mural reflected personal concerns, problems, interests, and values. A TA presentation to a Humanities class and a seminar in "games students play" sparked momentary interest in ego states, transactions, and games in practice, but students were not ready yet to sign up for an advertised weekend minithon. The school library was stocked with basic TA books, and teachers, student-teachers, and interns attended a training minithon.

Informal TA teaching on the Drop-In Center wall initially focused on a definition of personality. Each ego state was introduced in turn, as a symbol on the mural and as an exercise in which students were invited to participate. One youngster symbolized the Parent state by drawing a mammoth double mother-figure in the upper center of the teaching wall. One side, with a smiling face, held an infant in her arms. The other side, with angry features, rigidly held a terrified baby by the heel. The student who drew it had heard only a brief explanation of the meaning of the Parent ego state. Another student suggested that there should be a broken line down the middle since some messages had a double meaning—they might sound good at first but were felt as potently negative. The most intense activity on the wall clustered around this penetrable divider.

It was predicted by many that there would be more negative than positive Parent messages. This proved to be correct. On the nurturing Parent side were quotations drawn from ballad and rock singers, poets, and writers. Teenagers showed how they use ideas from the culture to override critical Parent messages. Their themes were of love, hope, and the freedom to be one's own self. On the critical Parent side real life authority figures heavily discounted the natural worth and goodness of the Child. Examples of conflict-producing "yes-no" directives abounded. The exercise was a stimulus for spontaneous discussions about everyday transactions that go on between Parent and Child. Individual, group, and peer counseling flowed continuously as students chose to come and go according to their own available time. Since the teaching wall was plainly visible to all who passed on the way to classrooms further down the corridor, nobody had to enter the Center in order to learn. Many people stopped, looked in, and discussed what was written. Students were quick to grasp the concepts and to ask questions. An expectancy was built with the unfolding of each concept. The counselor-psychologist came to experience a new flexibility with which to work more effectively with students and staff. There was a release of creative energy and a deeper understanding of adolescent problems.

The Adult ego state was symbolized by a floor-to-ceiling three dimensional "computer," complete with input-output channels, and a "correctional unit" that "reprocessed" prejudicial Parent and "crazy" Child data. Students were invited to add examples of erroneous statements within the realm of their experiences together with corresponding accurate ones on tape rolls that moved in and out of a construction paper garbage pail. This part of the simulated computer generated considerable interest and amusement.

On the wall on either side of the computer were extended scrolls on which to write anonymous contracts for change. Some students associated these with broken resolutions and were unwilling to commit themselves publicly. Although invited to receive computer readouts, many came but only a few were willing to explore and define specific changes. These were people who had frequented the Drop-In Center. Further, it took considerable time for any one individual to decide on a contract, but where this was done, resolutions for changes were completed, within varying time intervals. Most contracts were made in individual counseling sessions. This project stimulated a great deal of thinking that was not immediately measurable. One of the students suggested a wall collage of pictures, photos, drawings, and paraphernalia. It was decided that this was a fun way to get into the Child ego state. Strips of lollipops were hung in the window and exchanged for contributions. Students were found to be heavily invested in this ego state but refused to make any contributions to the Adapted Child section.

Next we initiated a "Stroke-A-Thon." We put up mirrors at different levels across the teaching wall, and invited students to look at themselves and write themselves and each other messages of positive recognition on the wall with magic markers. Students initially expressed feelings of discomfort, awkwardness, and embarrassment. They avoided the mirrors. Many were willing to give only negative or plastic strokes. None were familiar with the notion of a "genuine brag." Again, the project generated considerable discussion and interaction around the topic of stroking and personal needs. Big sheets of newsprint were there for people to use in explorations of the different concepts we brought up.

In good weather TA teaching and counseling was transferred to the outside areas. Students were invited to "Drop-Out" on these days. An understanding of "Little Professor" was encouraged in an outside art gallery of imaginative images of people, drawn and displayed along with the outer windows of the building. Students tended to be puzzled by the concept and response was a mixed reaction of skepticism and incredulity. Clusters of students were willing to draw their personality following a brief description of the three ego states. Some showed immediate insight as to how their needs fitted those of others or why relationships were broken off.

Our end-of-the-year display was the result of a research project on "The Typical HGHS Student Personality": we surveyed a random sample of students on their ideas of what they saw as "typical" of others in the high school and summarized our findings in graphic Parent-Adult-Child (PAC) terms on the teaching wall. Life-sized shadow cut-outs of a boy and girl student flanked a colored circle PAC diagram—Parent, Adult, and Child were each represented by a different-colored circle, and Parent and Adult were each divided into an OK and non-OK side. Data making up the composite picture of the typical HGHS student was color-coded to match the circles, so that at a glance the passerby could see that by student consensus the typical student had a very large Child, a medium-sized Parent, and a small Adult. The Adult and Child were about equally divided into OK and Not-OK characteristics; the Parent was decidedly more critical than nurturing.

Students reacted with lively interest in taking part in the project: another part of the display consisted of circle outlines painted in color and filled with snapshots of students dramatizing PAC postures. In responding to the survey, students immediately separated individual uniqueness from "commonness" and recognized in the composite the problems that existed within themselves, between peer-group members, and in response to those outside influences where they felt a sense of powerlessness, particularly in contest with authority figures in their environment.

The survey gave the counselor-psychologist an opportunity to become an active listener and observer with a wide range of students, all involved in talking to her about important issues. The wall generated heated discussion between "them" and "me." Individuals selected qualities that defined their own personality. These were translated into problems directly related to adolescence and imposed middle-class values as well as those specific to school, community, family, and self.

An overview of the first year history of the Drop-In Center indicated that:

1. There is a need for a place where students can come of their own accord, to discuss problems, and learn about people.
2. Students are quick to grasp TA concepts. These can be taught informally through the use of symbols and graphic models. Symbols act as a stimulus to discussion and interaction.
3. Learning does require a readiness and willingness to work. Human curiosity can be excited by new ideas and youngsters will respond to an invitation to engage in them. Time is need to explore and to understand prior to making a commitment. A controlled, intimate, protected setting is also important to this process.
4. Students who made regular inside contacts with the counselor-psychologist in the Drop-In Center tended to fall into two categories. In one were those students who fell on the fringe or felt isolated from the cliques and specific small peer groups. For them, the Drop-In Center provided a safe refuge from hurting social discrimination. In the other category were those who felt secure in their social image and moved freely from one social group to another.

At the end of the first year, the following proposed changes were discussed with the administrative staff with outcomes as indicated.

1. Two days a week on a modular six-day schedule is insufficient time with which to work with students. The students themselves requested that the Center be open daily. Budget considerations did not permit additional psychologist time and the two-day schedule was to continue.

2. The traditional role of the psychologist was maintained in addition to Drop-In Center commitments. Interns provided valuable extensions in psychological services. The intern program under direct counselor-psychologist supervision would continue.

3. The Drop-In Center benefits from heightened visibility and increased accessibility but also needs the possibility of privacy. It was proposed that the Drop-In Center be moved from the health area to an outer alcove in the social studies department. Emphasis would be placed on the "communication" process. This is an area where every student attends class at some time during the school week. Drapes over floor-to-ceiling windows could be used when privacy was desired. Wide-roll art paper was ordered to take the place of shelf paper which was time-consuming to put up and costly.

4. A Psychology of Personality course could bring TA into the classroom as a legitimate subject, formally taught to a given group of students on a regular basis. Computer course scheduling requires that courses be approved a year in advance of schedule. Such a course could not be given during the 1975–76 school year but would be listed for the following year.

5. Parent education is an important connecting link with work done in school and could reinforce student learn-

ing and change. This course would be offered to ninth grade parents at mid-year.

6. An evening TA Problem-Solving Group for Teens is to meet at the counselor-psychologist's home each week beginning in September and is to be considered an extension of her program. The Guidance Department agreed to make referrals. Students are to agree to make a minimum of six session commitments to come with parent permission and providing their own transportation.

7. Visible administrative support is needed if the service and Drop-In Center are to be recognized as more than an "experiment." The principal announced his support and requested the same from staff in an early faculty meeting. Student government representatives were also informed and their cooperation requested.

In conclusion, the idea of a place to communicate, to explore self, to learn about others became a viable reality. It continues to grow and change in response to student needs. On Parents' Night TA messages from mothers and fathers to their children reflected an expanding understanding of earlier teaching. When the special social issue of women's rights was being debated in social studies classrooms, the concept of life scripts and sex-cultural-family scripting was diagrammed and discussed. The teaching wall was used to summarize group and individual work. The counselor-psychologist drew symbolic representations and wrote out Parent and Adult directives and decisions. Films about Transactions and Life Scripts were projected on the wall and were stimuli for discussion. Contacts with students of the previous year were built upon. The new location attracted students who felt comfortable in academic surroundings. The counselor-psychologist and her interns now started getting in touch with nonacademically oriented students, meeting them in areas outside of the school. As school closed for the mid-year holiday break, students helped build a

Giving Tree with branches of good and positive messages given to one and all. Those who participated confirmed once again the basic premises on which the Drop-In Center was originated: Human nature is good; "I'm OK, You're OK"; and now is the time "to get on with" the joy of living, loving, and learning.

REFERENCE

Bruner, Jerome S., *The Process of Education,* New York: Vintage Books, 1960.

INDEX

CONTRIBUTORS

THOMAS AIELLO, Ph.D., is Assistant Clinical Professor at Albert Einstein College of Medicine Bronx Psychiatric Center, Bronx, N. Y.

NANCI-AMES CURTIS, M.D., is with the Creamery Mental Health Offices, Shelburne, Vermont.

HOWARD J. DOUGLASS, Ph.D., is Associate Professor of Psychology at Rensselaer Polytechnic Institute, Troy, N. Y.

HERBERT FENSTERHEIM, Ph.D., is Clinical Associate Professor at Cornell University Medical College, New York, N. Y.

PATRICIA FITZGERALD, Ph.D., is an educational psychologist (psychotherapist) in private practice at Briarcliff Manor, N. Y.

JOHN GLADFELTER, Ph.D., is Professor of Psychology at the University of Montana, Missoula.

HENRY GRAYSON, Ph.D., is Executive Director of the National Institute for the Psychotherapies, New York, N. Y.

EDWARD GUROWITZ, Ph.D., is co-director of the Vermont Institute for Transactional Analysis in Burlington, Vermont.

NANCY GUROWITZ, B.S., is co-director of the Vermont Institute for Transactional Analysis in Burlington, Vermont.

WILLIAM H. HOLLOWAY, M.D., is Coordinator of Studies in Psychology, the Fielding Institute, Santa Barbara, California, and immediate past President of the International Transactional Analysis Association. He is a psychiatrist in private practice in Garden Grove, California.

MICHAEL KRIEGSFELD, Ph.D., is Director of Residential Training Seminars at the National Institute for the Psychotherapies, New York, N. Y.

WILLIAM C. NORMAND, Ph.D., is Associate Clinical Professor of Psychiatry at Albert Einstein College of Medicine, Bronx, N. Y.

JOHN F. OSTERRITTER, M.D., M.P.H., Ph.D., is a consultant in occupational health and a physician in private practice in New York, N. Y.

MARY OTTO, M.A., is a teacher of English at Briarcliff High School, Briarcliff Manor, New York, and a former member of the International Transactional Analysis Association.

SUSAN SCHRENZEL, M.S.S.W., is Assistant Regional Director, Queens, at the New York City Department of Mental Health, Mental Retardation and Alcoholism Services, New York, N. Y.

ELLIOTT SELIGMAN, Ph.D., is Director of Behavior Therapy, National Institute for the Psychotherapies, and a staff psychologist at Maimonides Mental Health Center, Brooklyn, N. Y.

HELEN H. WATKINS, Ph.D., is a counseling psychologist at the Center for Student Development, University of Montana, Missoula.

JOHN G. WATKINS, Ph.D., is Professor of Psychology at the University of Montana, Missoula.